COOKING WITH

FIRE AND SMOKE

Phillip Stephen Schulz

ILLUSTRATIONS BY
RICHARD PRACHER

A FIRESIDE BOOK
Published by Simon & Schuster
NEW YORK   LONDON   TORONTO   SYDNEY   TOKYO   SINGAPORE

Fireside

Rockefeller Center
1230 Avenue of the Americas
New York, New York 10020

First Fireside Edition 1991

FIRESIDE and colophon are registered trademarks
of Simon & Schuster Inc.

Designed by Irving Perkins Associates, Inc.
Manufactured in the United States of America

3   5   7   9   10   8   6   4   2
9   10   Pbk.

Library of Congress Cataloging in Publication Data

Schulz, Phillip Stephen.
Cooking with fire and smoke.

Includes index.
1. Barbecue cookery.   2. Marinades.   I. Title.
TX840.B3S29   1986   641.7′6   85-30402

ISBN: 0-671-55234-1
ISBN: 0-671-73309-5 Pbk.

Acknowledgments

AS WITH ALL major (and minor) undertakings, one needs to thank those who support and contribute to the project at hand. At the top of the list is Bert Greene, who has guided my career for the past fourteen years—and hasn't given up yet! Thanks also to Judy Blahnik for her endless efforts in this project and life in general.

I am grateful to food consultant Howard Solganik of Great American Foods of Dayton, Ohio, for allowing me to dip into his vast research on the subject of outdoor cooking.

A special note of appreciation to the Barbecue Industry Association and its representatives at Myers CommuniCouncil in New York—and more specifically to Coleman Patio Products in Wichita, Kansas; Ducane Gas Grills in Columbia, South Carolina; and to UNR Home Products in Paris, Illinois, who make The Happy Cooker grill; all of whom generously allowed me to test recipes on their products.

Every successful cookbook is the product of communal nurturing. I was lucky enough to have a wonderfully creative team behind mine. Deep gratitude is tended Carole Lalli, my perceptive editor; Nancy Kalish, her enthusiastic aide; Judy Lee, the talented art director; and Richard Pracher, whose vivid drawings make the pages glow.

FOR MILDRED AND HEROLD SCHULZ

One of my fondest childhood memories is eating outdoors on a clear Colorado summer's night. This book is dedicated to my mother, who lovingly prepared the meals, and to my father, who patiently grew the vegetables in his garden for our table.

Contents

Introduction

by Bert Greene

IN MY OPINION, the volume in hand is the best book ever written on the subject of outdoor cooking.

If that statement seems to glow with enthusiasm, let me tell you it is no exaggeration. For I have observed this book's progress closely—from first spark to smoldering finish—a mere stone's throw from the fire. And only an anesthetized man could inhale the tantalizing aromas or sample the inspired creations that Phillip Schulz managed to coax out of a backyard grill without bandying a few encomiums in the air. Along with the smoke!

Schulz and I are longtime cooking confederates. We met over fifteen years ago when I was at the helm of the flourishing Store in Amagansett, Long Island, and he joined its band of raggle-taggle employees. Fresh from Golden, Colorado (and a less than tonic stint as chef in the U.S. Army) he was, from his very first encounter with an alien stove, a remarkably instinctive cook. But one who took praise reluctantly. When a compliment was pressed upon him (after he had prepared a complicated dish) Schulz either blushed or ambled out of earshot, muttering, "What's the big deal? Anyone who can read a recipe can cook!"

Aside from his acute sensibility, which to my mind is the dead giveaway of a true cook, Schulz's major talent, from the very beginning, was derring-do! Faced with a culinary obstacle course that would cause another, lesser practitioner to quail or demur, this young man would simply rise to his full six feet, two inches of height, narrow his eyes behind his glasses to better focus on the problem—and start working. Furiously! No recipe instruction apparently too complex and no ingredient list ever too intimidating to forestall a Schulz frontal attack on the stove.

And, barring a slight change of venue (from indoor oven to outdoor grill) little has changed in his approach over the passing years.

As I have said, I have known Phillip Schulz long and well. After The Store was sold and I attempted to carve a precarious midlife career change as cookbook writer and cooking teacher, Schulz became my full-time ally at the stove and typewriter. Though, in all truth, adversary better described his function. For it was his constant prodding, pushing and bullying that kept me at the appointed task long after I would have thrown in the kitchen towel. I did not ever, because Schulz would not countenance any such human defection. According to the *Oxford Unabridged Dictionary,* the name *Phillip* means a tamer of wild horses, a lover of hurdles. And never was a cognomen more aptly placed, for this man burns to overcome the wildest impediments life puts in his path.

It was inevitable that Phillip Schulz would write his own cookbook someday. Because, aside from good taste and a real love of well-made food, his nature constantly demands taller hurdles. On the trail of an unusual dish, he will not stop—even after he has produced a brace of perfectly acceptable versions—if he suspects that a more felicitous rendering is lurking somewhere within his grasp. What can I tell you? The man simply wants to do it better than anyone has ever done it before.

Writing a slim (but pithy) tome about vodka a few years ago, he practically turned himself into a full-fledged alcoholic—testing the myriad properties of that potent beverage at the stove, over and over again. This time around, he was more circumspect. No fire eating so far. But enough flame and smoke to keep the neighborhood on constant alert all summer long.

During the copious testing (and retesting) of this book I have watched from a discreet distance as Phillip and our shared factotum, Judy Blahnik, raced about the backyard in Amagansett, scribbling cryptic notes in ballpoint and operating five separate outdoor grills at the same time. Once, in the middle of such a test, the east end of Long Island was inundated by a sudden and torrential rainstorm. Too late to cancel the sizzling fare, they managed to remove two of these not quite portable cookers to the safety of the garage, and never stopping lest the flame subsided, Schulz finished cooking on the remaining three—under an umbrella but soaked to the skin. However, and this is the wholly inexplicable facet of the man's energy, every single dish that was served up for sampling at the dining-room table later was better than the last. Can one argue with such burning illogic—in or out of a kitchen?

I knew Phillip Stephen Schulz's book would be a prodigious wonder long before I cracked open a single page. How could it not be when he was out there, day and night, good weather and bad, talking to the fire? Bending flame and smoke to his will and taking the grill's temperature as often as a gung ho intern, just to make certain that every reader in America would be able to perform the same incendiary (culinary) miracles on his own turf.

What he has written is a serious book for men and women who really want to cook food well outdoors, without scorch and without scourge. I predict that these marvelous recipes, like a phoenix, will rise again, summer after summer, until Schulz thinks of something new to light our fire.

Author's Note

THIS BOOK IS more than a collection of fiery and smoky recipes. It is a manual on how to use the outdoor grill as an alternative stove or oven.

If the terminology seems technical, don't be put off. Learning how and when to utilize direct and indirect heat on a grill is no different from mastering the art of using any untried piece of kitchen equipment. Practice, in this case, always makes perfect—perfect smoke-flavored dishes that is.

In the following pages you will find that I resort to covered-cooking frequently. This technique allows the outdoor cook the maximum degree of control over what is on the fire—whether it be a paella-stuffed striped bass or tandoori-style chicken wings.

Many procedures are new and some of the methods innovative; requiring the person at the grill to rethink or, in some cases, rediscover what "barbecue" really is. *Charred meat,* it definitely is not!

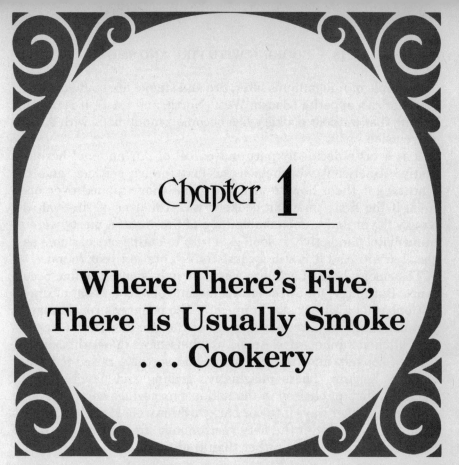

Chapter 1

Where There's Fire, There Is Usually Smoke ... Cookery

COOKING WITH FIRE and smoke—or more precisely—roasting over fire and flavoring with smoke is an ancient art. Cave dwellers did it first, but you'd never know it from a glance at the nation's menus. For cooking with fire and smoke is having such a red-hot culinary renaissance, a newcomer to the grill might easily assume the art of juggling a haunch of ribs over live coals to be a brand-new idea.

Far from it. All historical evidence suggests that earliest man learned about fire before he properly learned to talk. In fact, verbal communication probably developed around a roaring blaze. When tribesmen first shared in the responsibility of hunting for mutual survival, they also learned how to cook the spoils of their quarry.

The initial method used was to hurl meat directly on the conflagration. But as time passed and taste buds flowered, man learned to impale his ingredients on branches instead, so that when held over crackling embers, his dinner burnished rather than burned. And while no archaeologist confirms or denies it, there is a widespread notion that the first spoken sentence was a word of caution (from one caveman to another): "Do not overcook the dinosaur steak!"

A couple of millenniums later, fire and smoke are so much a part of America's appetite (South, West, North, and East), it is not surprising that outdoor cookery has become synonymous with American cuisine.

It is a taste decidedly part and parcel of our national heritage. Native Americans who helped the first foreign settlers tame the land taught them how to grill the game they trapped over open fires. If the first American cookout was a matter of survival, the smoky flavor and unmistakable tang of fire-roasted meats were so immediately addictive, it soon gave rise to eating out of doors as a social event. And it is still a cause for celebration year round.

The smoky haze of grill fire was once only a summertime occurrence. But today, the sweet (and sometime pungent) scent of smoke not only fills a winter sky in much of the country's rural areas, it also perfumes the interiors of some of the trendiest urban restaurant kitchens. Innovative American chefs have taken this ancient form of cookery and (through sauce and sorcery) raised it to new culinary heights. These imaginative grilling and flavoring techniques—much publicized in the nation's magazines and press—are now finding their ways into our backyards as well. However, it must be noted that most of the fiery gastronomic innovations are based on principles of *grilling* rather than traditional barbecuing.

WHAT'S BARBECUE? WHAT'S NOT!

The word *barbecue* itself is a heated handle. Food historians generally agree that it was coined when Spanish explorers in the New World encountered the savvy natives grilling meat and fish on crude wooden racks over open pits of fire. The Spanish called these racks *barbacoa*. The eventual English translation, of course: *barbecue*. Though Webster lists *grilling* (essentially broiling over charcoal) as part of a definition for barbecue, deep-dyed barbecue lovers in the South and Southwest turn livid at the very idea. To them, barbecue is (and always will be) a long, slow process of hot-smoking meats over low-banked coals.

From earliest times, pits were dug in the earth and lined with bricks. Wood was laid and lit, and the meat was placed on metal racks high above the smoldering embers to cook slowly. Very slowly. These covered pits were inevitably tended by "pitmen" who took great pride in their skills. Each had his own carefully guarded secret techniques for producing the moistest results with just the right amount of smoky taste. Sad to say, most commercial barbecue today is produced indoors in various-shaped steel fireboxes. However, old-fashioned, smoke-scented barbecue *is* alive and well in certain parts of the South and Texas where pilgrims by the thousands annually cross the landscape searching for the best bite.

Though the term *barbecue* obviously can mean many things, in my book there are basically four types of outdoor cookery.

THE FOUR WAYS TO COOK SUCCESSFULLY WITH FIRE AND SMOKE

Grilling: It's the simplest and fastest technique. It means broiling meats or foods directly over a high heat source (be it hot coal, gas, or an electric element). Grilling usually takes just minutes. Most smaller cuts of meat and fish (chops, steaks, hamburgers, filets, and even hot dogs) are perfect for grilling.

Covered Cooking: Not dissimilar to cooking in a kitchen oven with one major exception. Out of doors, smoke permeates the food as it cooks. The cover reflects the heat from the coals (or lava rocks in the case of gas grills), creating a controlled environment that substantially cuts cooking times and allows the food to maintain its natural juiciness. It is one of the most versatile methods of grill cookery, and is excellent for whole fish, roasts, and fowl.

Rotisserie Cooking: Basically it's spit roasting. It is the perfect way to cook larger roasts or birds. In rotisserie cooking, the heat source is ultimately placed at the side of the meat, rather than

IN THE BEGINNING WAS THE "B" WORD

Among the myriad "false" etymologies of the term *barbecue,* and one most bruited about and seriously chewed over, is that the word stems from a French duelist's (or butcher's) expression: *barbe-a-queue,* which means "from beard to tail." And is fairly self-explanatory.

Another, offered by *Tar Heel* magazine (North Carolina's favorite monthly), whimsically suggests the word developed out of early (nineteenth-century) advertising. The owner of a Carolinian combination whiskey bar, beer parlor, pool hall, and café, specializing in roast pork, wanted to let folks know what to expect at his establishment. As the fellow couldn't fit all that circumlocution on his storefront, he abbreviated it to "Bar-Beer-Cue-Pig!"

The editor of *Tar Heel* goes on to suggest ways to name your own barbecue enterprise with a beginner's guide that gives one a total of 300 possibilities:

"First, use your nickname, first name, or surname to show you have pride in your product: Bubba's, Harold's, Floyd's, Smith's, or Wilson's for example. Now describe the product: Old-Time, All-American, Hickory-Smoked, Pit-Cooked, Pit, Down-Home ... or Sho'Nuff. Finally, pick your favorite spelling of the product per se: BBQ, Barbecue, Barbeque, Bar-B-Cue, Bar-B-Que, or Bar-B-Q."

Now you're in business!

Or I am. Consider: "Phil's Sho'Nuff, Old-Time, All-American BBQ!" for starters!

directly underneath. This allows for even cooking, and, as the meat turns over and over, self-basting in the bargain.

Smoke Cooking: The slowest process of all, but in my opinion, the only way to create a true down-home "barbecue" flavor. Smoke cooking usually involves the addition of a water vapor to the cooking process. Food cooked this way over low, low tempered heat, with wood chips added for extra (smoky) flavor, is always tender and moist.

Anyone can be a great outdoor cook. You will be surprised how quickly even a neophyte becomes adept at playing with fire. The most important lesson to be learned about the quartet of cooking techniques is to control the heat source and serve the meats *crisp,* but not scorched. All the basics one needs to know are detailed in the chapters that follow.

Chapter 2

Grill Talk

SHORT OF DIGGING a rather unwieldy trench in one's backyard (particularly difficult for city dwellers), true, old-fashioned barbecue is hard to duplicate at home. The homemade barrel smoker made from a surplus steel drum, though long in use among serious Texan barbecue enthusiasts, came to wide public attention only twenty years ago when Lyndon B. Johnson brought his own handcrafted version to Washington. Following the leader, the barbecue industry, in time, introduced commercial smokers for home use. In fact, there is just about everything one could want for fire and smoke cookery on the market these days—from the simplest charcoal grills to complex gas-fed smokers. What is more, the current accessories being sold for outdoor cooking alone could fill half the pages of a Sears, Roebuck spring/summer catalog.

There are four basic types of grills available: *portable* or table-tops, *braziers, covered cookers,* and *smokers.* Prices on grills vary, starting at around $10 and rising upwards to $1000 or more. However, most equipment is often discounted (particularly out of season) well below the manufacturer's suggested retail price, so it pays to shop around. When choosing a grill, no matter how small, always look for one that is solidly constructed of heavy metal for longer life.

CHOOSING THE RIGHT GRILL

Portables (or Tabletops): Beginners tend to start outdoor cooking on low-cost portable grills, hoping to master the art before moving on to bigger and better equipment. It is *not* a good idea. Since simple grilling is all one can ever really muster on a rudimentary unit, the incipient outdoor cook usually becomes frustrated, and ends up buying some larger, pricier model anyway.

A portable grill should be purchased for one reason alone. Because it *is* portable. It makes a wonderful adjunct for tailgate picnics, mountain camping trips, or beachside cookouts. Most portable or tabletop models range from 12 to 18 inches in diameter. Some look like miniature covered cookers (the standard grill in use) and may be purchased in gas and electric versions, as well as the conventional charcoal burners. Hibachis also fall into this category. Prices for portable, tabletop grills run from less than $10 for Hibachi-type grills to around $75 for electric models.

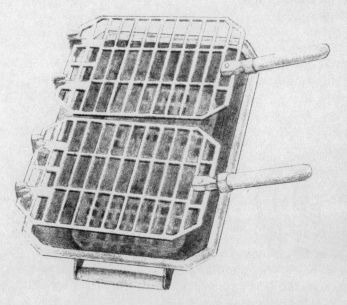

THE COOK'S CAVEAT: *Beware of any merchandise labeled indoor/outdoor electric grills. They claim to be fairly "smoke free," which, needless to say, defeats the whole purpose.*

Braziers: Any uncovered stand-up charcoal grill is called an *open* brazier, the most basic just a pan to hold charcoal fitted with an adjustable rack for grilling. These relatively inexpensive grills are carried in most hardware stores. Braziers come in two shapes: kettle and wagon. The kettle with its rounded underside is the most popular with the consumer. So popular in fact, its rectangular counterpart is slowly being phased out of the market. Braziers also come *hooded,* with only half the grilling surface enclosed. All hooded-type braziers are equipped with rotisseries, which are either electric or battery-powered. The chief advantage of a semicovered grill is ease; a roast may be cooked to perfection without excessive attention on the part of the chef. Prices for braziers range from a low of $10 to a high of about $50. Rotisseries are usually a bit extra.

THE COOK'S CAVEAT: *Cheapest units usually rest on rather shaky legs. As grilling is the main use for any brazier, be advised to opt for the sturdiest model you can find. Using a flimsy brazier can be a hazard for any less than fleet-fingered outdoorsman. Aside from the probability of a "flying entrée" if the griller accidentally knocks against the unit, second- and third-degree burns are also an ever-present danger!*

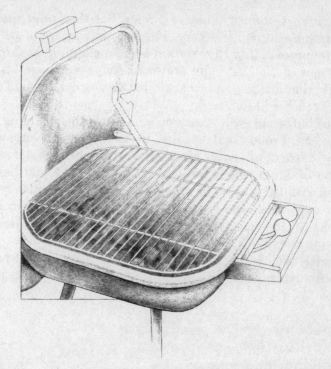

Charcoal Covered Cookers: By consensus, the most popular grill around is the covered cooker (also known as the covered kettle or wagon cooker). Covered cookers come in square, rectangular, or round kettle shapes. Versatility is the key to a covered cooker's performance. With its lid off, this type of grill doubles as a substantial brazier. With the lid securely in place, an ovenlike environment is created, allowing one to roast, smoke, or steam. All covered cookers whether rectangular or circular in design have rounded bottoms to allow for even distribution of heat. An efficient charcoal burning unit should have an adjustable firepan or grid, as well as air vents in the base and lid. Many models can be fitted with rotisserie attachments, which again are usually optional. The average price for a good, sturdy, coal covered cooker is about $50 for the base unit and optional equipment can more than double the price.

THE COOK'S CAVEAT: *Avoid the smaller units as they hold less fuel which makes it difficult to maintain stable heat. And always check for placement of air vents before you buy a covered cooker. In these grills, it is mandatory to have a proper measure of air circulation.*

Gas Covered Cookers: They're pricier, but they offer the easiest form of no-fuss outdoor cookery. The chief advantage of gas models is their failproof ability to maintain even, medium heat throughout long periods of cooking. The grates of gas cookers are lined with lava rocks that are heated by controlled flames. So the food actually cooks by reflected heat.

Serious barbecue enthusiasts dismiss gas grills, claiming the absence of hardwood coal results in lackluster flavor, with no "woodsy" taste at all. After much trial and error, I have found that a handful of damp wood chips added to the rocks just before the point of grilling works flavor wonders. Parenthetically, using stronger marinades and basting sauces when cooking on gas also helps take up the slack. When appropriate, specially starred hints for cooking over gas appear in the recipes that follow.

No matter the degree of prejudice a true outdoor chef may harbor about anything other than fire cookers, the American public is

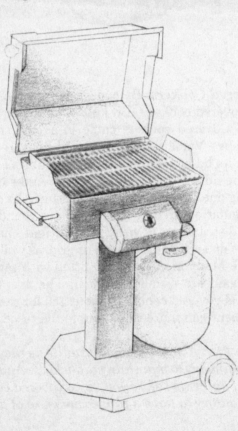

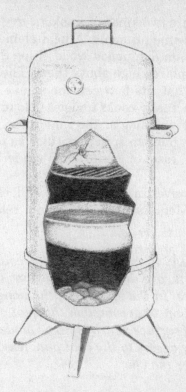

buying gas grills in record numbers. And of a consequence, prices are plummeting. A high-quality gas grill can last a lifetime with proper care—so the initial investment is not truly excessive. From plain to fancy, gas grills run from about $150 to $1000.

THE COOK'S CAVEAT: *The temperature controls on gas grills, and the nature of gas itself, do not permit the low, low heat required for some extended cooking times such as that required for genuine barbecue. If hot smoking is your major goal in outdoor cookery, consider a gas smoker instead, as it has been fine-tuned to surmount this problem.*

Smokers: As noted, genuine barbecue at home (smoke cookery) is a relatively new phenomenon. Smoking in itself is not a way of preserving foods. Though manufacturers promise as much, commercial-style preserving usually requires cold smoke which is almost impossible to duplicate on home turf.

Basically, there are two kinds of smokers: *dry* and *water* (or wet). Both work on the same principle. A heat element (gas, electricity, or charcoal) works on dampened wood chips that cause smoke to swirl around foods placed high above them. The water smoker adds a pan (for liquid) that sits between the smoke and the raw ingredient, so the food actually cooks under a "cloud" of smoky haze, in effect smoking and steaming at the same time. The water smoker has been a boon to huntsmen in particular as the process actually removes the "wild" taste of game, while tenderizing it at the same time.

Many smokers convert into braziers as well, enhancing this product even further. Medium-size smokers are relatively low-tabbed. Plan to spend $50 and up.

THE COOK'S CAVEAT: *If you choose a charcoal unit, rather than gas or electric, be aware that coals will have to be added during the cooking process. In the unit I use, the upper two-thirds of the grill must be lifted off to accomplish this feat. (Make sure there is a clean, stainproof surface nearby.) Some models have a coal door in the side for easy access to the coal pan, which makes life somewhat pleasanter for the chef.*

Chapter 3

Accessories Galore

I USED TO think that an outdoor cook could survive nicely, with any ole spatula and tongs swiped from a kitchen drawer. However, after a series of scorched wrists and fingers, I decided there is, after all, true merit in having special accessories just for the grill.

THE OUTDOOR COOK'S CATALOG OF BASIC EQUIPMENT

The tools one should not be without at the outdoor stove include an extra-long *fork, spatula, tongs,* and *basting brush.* These utensils, equipped with heat-resistant handles made of wood or thermoplastic, can make the difference between a "trial by fire" cookout and a safe-and-sane bout at the grill. Prices vary considerably, wood-handled accessories being the most expensive. A second set of tongs

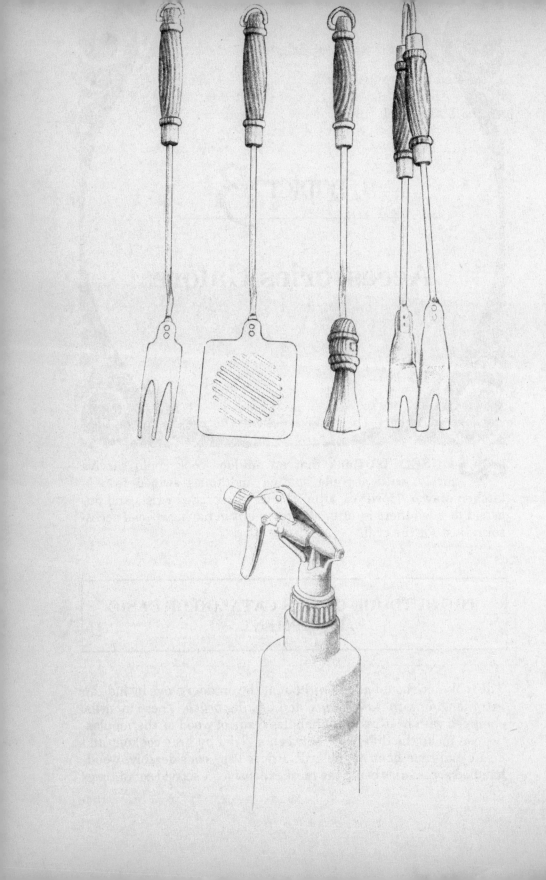

is suggested for charcoal-grill owners, just for the sole purpose of working with the coals. Most grills offer optional *utensil* and *condiment holders* as well which clamp directly onto the fire bowl and come in mighty handy if space is limited.

Supplemental musts for the chef are a pair of *insulated kitchen gloves,* a water *spritzer* (plastic spray bottle) for use in case of flare-up, a healthy supply of *heavy-duty aluminum foil,* plus a batch of aluminum foil *drip pans* to catch meat juices. Recommended as well: a long-stemmed *meat thermometer* for large cuts of meat and a *dome thermometer* for the lid which indicates the internal temperature of the grill. Some units come with built-in thermometers. If yours does, skip this last amenity.

OPTIONAL PARAPHERNALIA

Once you have some basic accessories in hand you may wish to consider the myriad steel-wire racks and baskets available with or for most covered cookers. These racks, designed for use directly on the grilling surface (the grid), offer a variety of functions. There are, for instance, roasting racks for chicken and large cuts of meat, as well as rib racks, potato racks, corn racks, and warming racks (which are actually raised above the grid).

A hinged grill basket that looks like a see-through waffle iron is ideal for cooking delicate fish or any food that might conceivably fall through the bars of a conventional grid. Wire "tumble" baskets that toss foods as they cook are available as rotisserie attachments. Rotisseries, curiously, are considered "accessories" themselves.

LUXE ACCOUTERMENTS

There is a staggering assortment of toys for the grill. Shish kabob sets range from simple six skewered appointments to a complex motor-driven apparatus that automatically rotates the kabobs for the lazy chef. Other playthings for the grill actually include a wok that fits directly into the fire bowl and an old-fashioned griddle for breakfast outdoors.

If you don't have room on your grill for all the accessories, never fear. Side tables made of hardwood can be purchased. These tables (boards would be more accurate) attach to the fire bowl and range in size from the ridiculously small to gargantuan. One dealer has even gone so far as to design a redwood wagon that fits snugly around the grill, complete with cupboards and (for an additional charge) a weatherproof coal chest that will hold up to 10 pounds of briquets.

If that doesn't do the trick, try the "gourmet cart": an entire service unit fitted with a cutting board, a plastic bubble (to keep flies away), and best of all, a special wing for bartenders. Make mine a straight Scotch!

AN EXTRA BARBECUE CUE

Aside from standard grilling equipment (the long-handled tongs, spatula, and fork and insulated gloves), make sure to always keep a small grid-level table, preferably shelved, with a fireproof surface near the grill. You will need it as a receptacle for precooked and finished foods, as well as sauces, pepper, and salt and even on occasion the grid itself—when the fire needs stoking.

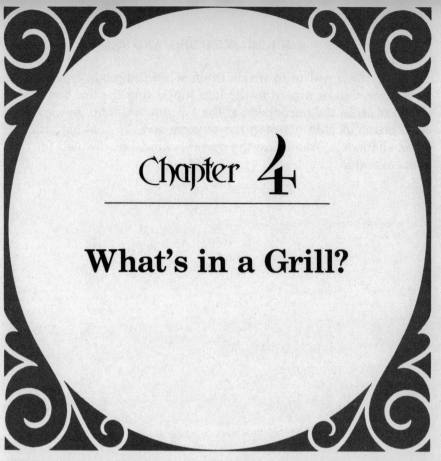

Chapter 4

What's in a Grill?

TO SET THE record straight, a "grill" is the *whole unit* that stands conspicuously outdoors on your patio, and *not* the wire cooking rack, as some handbooks would have you believe.

While no two charcoal grills are alike, all share basic components you should become familiar with. The bottom of a grill, whether it is a rectangular wagon type or a round kettle model, is called a *fire bowl* or *firebox*. I prefer the former as it is the term most often used by manufacturers. The fire bowl generally has some kind of ventilation system, usually a *vent*. (Braziers do not necessarily carry such options.) The *lid* of a covered cooker is almost always equipped with vents and some models even sport built-in temperature gauges as well.

The wire rack on which the actual cooking takes place is known as a *grid*. Water smokers may have as many as three grids, one for the *water pan* and two for holding food. A charcoal water smoker will also have a *coal pan,* just as a charcoal covered cooker will have a *coal grate* that holds the coal.

All but the very cheapest charcoal grills come with *ash catchers*.

Some are designed to fit inside the fire bowl, directly beneath the coal grate. Others attach to the legs supporting the fire bowl.

In gas grills, the burners sit at the bottom of the fire bowl, with a *lava grate,* located between the burners and the cooking grid. Almost all models, other than the portable kind, have wheels for easy maneuverability.

Chapter 5

Care for Your Grill

THE MORE YOU use your grill and become familiar with the ins and outs of the particular model, you will form an attachment (much the way you do to your car) and want to maintain it for smooth performance. A little care is all that is required for a long, happy life at the grill. Following is a set of rules to help achieve that goal.

1. Immediately after removing cooked food from the grid, place a sheet of heavy-duty aluminum foil, shiny side down, on the grid and cover the grill. If you are using a charcoal grill, the briquets will give off heat, and die down naturally if you close all vents. If you are using a gas grill, leave the unit on (with the foil in place) for an additional 20 minutes. The grid, in effect, self-cleans.
2. When the unit has cooled, most steel-wire grids may be scrubbed clean with a wire brush. However, models with porcelain or chrome grids can be damaged (and the warranty voided) if you use a wire brush, so the following technique is advised: When the grid is still warm, rub it with a ball made of crushed aluminum foil, taking care not to burn yourself. After rubbing, wipe the grid clean with wet paper towels. Some manufacturers recommend using oven cleaners;

others forbid it. Be sure to follow the instructions that come with your grill.

3. All grills should be cleaned regularly inside and out with hot, soapy water and a nonmetalic pot brush.

4. Methods for cleaning gas burners are always found in the manufacturer's instruction booklet. A general rule of thumb, though, is never to use a wire brush on these surfaces as you could possibly damage the finish.

5. When the grill is not in use, store it in a fairly dry sheltered area and cover with the all-weather covers that are available for most models.

Chapter 6

The Fire Behind the Smoke

TO MASTER THE art of cooking with fire and smoke, you need merely to become the master of the source of heat that powers your grill, whether it is gas, electricity, or charcoal.

GAS WORKS

Gas grills, though dependent on gas, of course, actually use lava rocks as their direct heat source. These lava rocks (natural volcanic bits of stone) are porous conductors that radiate heat from gas jets situated below them. Lava rocks should last indefinitely. If they become saturated with grease, just turn them over and burn the grease off. The ease of operation, plus the controlled heat on all units (even if it is the basic low, medium, and high settings), have made gas grills extremely popular.

Gas grills work on either *natural gas* or what is known as *LP gas* (liquid petroleum). When buying a grill, specify your needs. All gas grills carry the specific information about the gas to be used on the *grill rating plate*. If you do not live in an area where you can plug directly into existing natural gas lines, a word on handling LP gas is in order.

FILLING IT UP

Since gas grills (and all other type grills for that matter) require some degree of assembly after shipment, nothing is more frustrating than to hook up the gas (albeit tentatively) only to discover there is no liquid fuel in the cylinder. So, be advised that the cylinder will have to be filled by your local gas dealer. Take some paper towels along with you too. Service men are notoriously sloppy about spillage—which you will not want to occur in the trunk of your car.

EQUIPMENT CHECKS

Once your gas grill is connected (again following the instructions), you must make a rudimentary check of the connections for leaks. If the cylinder fits into the cabinet of your grill, do this outside the cabinet.

The test is fairly simple. Brush the connecting points with sudsy water. If small bubbles are detected, shut the gas off and retighten all connections. This test should be repeated every few days, or after any prolonged period of nonuse. Weather can cause expansion or retraction in the rubber connecting hose, so it pays to be careful.

STORAGE TIPS

Always store a gas cylinder, whether attached to the grill or not, in a well-ventilated, cool area. Though manufacturers claim that extremes in temperature will not effect the cylinder, used cylinders can (and do) occasionally suffer from minor leakage. Therefore, never store a cylinder inside your house, garage, or any enclosed area where there is the possibility of a stray spark flying (from the car ignition or even power tools).

THE ELECTRIC CONNECTION

Electric grills, even easier to use than gas grills, surprisingly dominate only 2 percent of the grill market—*and* are losing ground. Part of the reason for the electric grills unpopularity is that units, for the most part, are too small and too expensive. There are two electric grill options for potential buyers at the moment. One works with lava rocks, the other with ceramic tiles. Both are heated by an electric element. An electric grill will take about 10 minutes to preheat.

THE CHARCOAL CHALLENGE

Despite the national preoccupation with no sweat/no time cookery in the kitchen and backyard as well, the most popular outdoor unit is still a charcoal grill. Whatever sort one owns—a portable, brazier, covered cooker, or smoker—the method for building and maintaining even heat in a charcoal-powered unit is absolutely the same.

COAL COUNSEL

Charcoal briquets or pure hardwood coals? This is the controversy of our time. I and most other casual backyard chefs use briquets. The elitest professionals insist on the pure stuff. Charcoal briquets are composites of varying hardwoods with filler added to make them burn longer. Choose the old-fashioned kind rather than the "quick-burning" variety. They have a denser composition and retain heat better.

Pure hardwood coals (like hickory or mesquite) are pricey and not easy to come by, but they have certainly caught the fancy of upscale restaurateurs (as well as the cookout cognoscenti) around the country. These coals, known as lump charcoal, are not new. They are simply the pure coals, left over from burning logs, chopped into small pieces. They burn hot and fast. Great for grilling on professional heavy-duty equipment. Manufacturers of grills meant for home use caution, however, that with constant use, hardwood coal, particularly mesquite, can burn its way right through a metal fire bowl. Also, hardwood coal creates sparks. Sparks that fly. So, if you opt for these coals, remove your grill to the dead center of the backyard—far away from the house! Though lump charcoal imparts more flavor to grilled foods than briquets, one can easily remedy that lack by using actual wood chips or chunks in conjunction with the briquets. These adjunctive flavorings are readily available and will be discussed in a later chapter.

PROPER AIR FLOW

Perhaps the most important thing to know is that a proper measure of air circulation (around the hot coals) is necessary for best results. Therefore, most covered cookers and smokers have grates which hold the coals above the ash catcher or bottom of fire bowl. This elevated placement of the coals, plus the vents in the bottom of the fire bowl, allows air to circulate freely. However, as many portable grills and braziers do not have such features, you will have to help them along.

First of all, it is a good idea to line the bottom of a grateless grill with heavy-duty aluminum foil—shiny side up. Not only does foil help reflect heat, it protects the bottom of the fire bowl from the hot coals. I always use this technique on grills without interior ash catchers as well, making sure to poke holes in the aluminum foil above any vent openings. It makes for easy cleanup later. (Actually, lining any charcoal grill with foil before using will add years to the grill's usefulness and speed up the cooking process in the bargain.) If your grill does not have a grate, line the interior surface of the foil with small pebbles before adding the coals. Do not use sand as a liner, for it is too dense to achieve the proper degree of air circulation desired.

CALCULATING THE COAL

The number of coals required for a charcoal grill depends on the style of cookery you intend to do. Different methods of cookery are discussed in Chapter 7. Basically, however, if you are *grilling,* spread a single layer of coals over the interior grate until they extend about 1 inch beyond the edge of the estimated food area.

For *covered cooking,* more coal will be necessary. For average-sized grills (18 to 22 inches in diameter) it will take 25 to 36 coals merely to start a 3-pound roast. Add 5 extra coals for each additional pound of weight. When longer cooking times are required, be aware that new coals will have to be added to the embers every 30 to 40 minutes to maintain constant heat. Figure on 7 or 8 new added coals as replacements. Be sure to knock some of the gray ash off the smoldering coals before adding fresh. This will intensify the heat, which is vital, since removing the grill cover automatically cools the food down considerably.

To maintain even heat, newly added coals need some prewarming. Some outdoor cooks place extra coals around the edge of the grate (away from the smoldering coals) so they are in a sense preheated by the time they are needed. Another method, and the one I prefer, is to start an auxiliary fire in an aluminum-foil-lined heavy pan (a portable grill is perfect here). The partially lit coals are then added to the original fire as required. When new coals are added to the grill, make sure to replace the coals in the auxiliary unit. Whichever method you choose, never, never add freshly fuel-soaked coals to live embers. It can be extremely dangerous!

FIRE WHEN READY

When you are ready to light your charcoal fire, there are three methods from which to choose: *lighter fluid, electric starter,* and the *chimney starter.*

Lighter Fluids: The use of combustible liquids and wax or jelly starters is the most common method for lighting coals. And while some chefs resist this method because they declare there is a chemical undertaste, lighter fluid makers claim to have eliminated that problem in the eighties.

To prepare coals for lighting with conventional starters, stack the coals in a pyramid shape in the center of the charcoal grate. If you are using lighter fluid, squirt a generous amount over the top of the coals. Allow the fluid to seep into the coals for 1 minute. Light with a match. To use a wax or jelly starter, shake the can well before squeezing the sludgy mass over and between the briquets. Be sure to light before the starter evaporates. Depending on the weather and degree of wind, the coals will be ready for cooking in about 40 minutes.

Electric Starters: An increasingly popular method of lighting coals is the use of electric ignition. But before you run out and buy an electric starter, note that an electrical outlet, not too far away from the grill, is a necessity here. To use an electric starter, nestle the prongs deep in the coals and turn it on. Do not leave an electric starter in the coals longer than 7 or 8 minutes as these devices literally suffer burnout with prolonged overuse. Once the coals around the starter are lit, the remaining coals will take about 30 minutes before they are ready for cooking.

Chimney Starters: Fairly new on the market, these cylindrical-shaped metal canisters are quick and easy to use. Chimney starters have two compartments, a bottom for placing crumbled newspapers

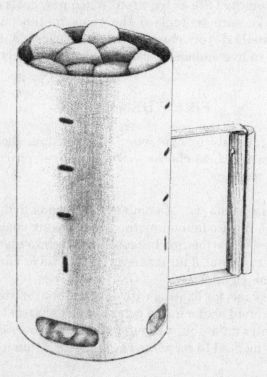

as kindling, and a top with minigrate that holds up to 48 briquets. All one does is light the bottom with a match; 25 coals will be ready for cooking in about 7 minutes. Be sure to look for chimney starters with wooden handles. It makes emptying the coals into a charcoal grate easy and safer later. Actually, this method of starting coals is basically an updated version of the old Boy Scout coffee can trick in which the bottom and top of a large coffee can are removed and holes punched around the bottom for air flow.

TAKING THE GRILL'S TEMPERATURE

Determining when the coals in a charcoal grill are ready for cooking is easier than you think. For one thing, all coals should be a uniform ashy gray color. Do not start cooking if any black areas are showing, as the heat will then be uneven. Grill surface thermometers are available to measure the fire temperature, but the Open Hand Test is always accurate enough for me. Here's how you do it: First, remove the cooking grid, then place your hand (palm side down) over the ashy gray coals at precisely the grid level. If you can hold your fingers steady for only 2 seconds, the coals are adjudged to be hot enough to *sear*. If you can keep your hand there longer—for 3 or 4 seconds—the coals are medium-hot and perfect for *grilling*. If you can manage 5 seconds with your hand in place, the coals are medium and ready for *covered cooking*.

The man or woman at the grill must never forget that *hot* coals are meant for searing only, while the actual cooking takes place over medium (smoldering) coals.

Chapter 7

The Topical Heat Wave

WHEN YOU COOK out of doors, there are two options: cooking with *direct* or *indirect heat*. Direct heat is used for *searing* and *grilling*. Indirect heat is most often used in *covered cooking* and *smoking* where long periods of cooking time are involved. Whichever method you employ, always brush the cooking grid lightly with oil before starting, to keep food from sticking.

SOME DIRECT ADVICE

Gas and electric grills are designed for direct-heat cookery, which is just a matter of cooking foods *directly* over a heat surface. When using these grills, set the controls on high. For fast-cooked foods like fish, the high setting is a prerequisite. However, when grilling hamburgers, steaks, or chops, you may want to reduce the heat to medium if the meat is browning too quickly. Since most of these grills have cool spots, particularly around the edges, learn to use them effectively. Aside from reducing the heat source, if a sudden fiery flare-up occurs, simply move the object you are cooking to a cooler part of the grill—so it continues to cook through without burning.

To prepare charcoal briquets for grilling over direct heat, light the briquets in the manner detailed earlier (see pages 41–43). When coals are the appropriate ashy color, spread the briquets evenly over the coal grate. The grid should rest about 4 to 5 inches above the hot embers. Again, learn to use the cool (temperate) edges of a charcoal grid in case of flare-up. If your grill has an adjustable grid, raise it to maintain temperature control or achieve medium heat. A water spritzer (kept nearby) to douse any unwanted flames is advised as well.

SOME INDIRECT REMARKS

Indirect heat, as the term implies, is a method of cooking *indirectly* over a heat source, rather than directly over it. In charcoal cooking, this can be achieved in two ways. Each requires an inexpensive aluminum-foil *drip pan* which can be purchased at your grill dealer or in any supermarket. One technique (my own) is to place the drip pan under the area where the food will be placed on the grid and to surround the pan with burning coals. Some grills have special briquet racks designed solely for this purpose. *Or* (and this is often an effective technique), you can place the pan at one end of the grate and the burning coals at the other.

In either case, when the food is placed over the pan, the flame never touches it. But the heat and smoke, created in the enclosed environment, cooks it much like an outdoor oven. I always keep a small amount of water in the drip pan. For one thing, the water keeps any fat or grease from the drippings from splashing, and it also keeps the juices from drying up in the pan if you have a mind to save them to use as sauces later.

Remember, during long periods of cooking, you will have to add additional coals as outlined on page 41 to maintain even heat. Also, make a serious effort to learn to use the vents in the fire bowl and lid. Always keep the vents partially closed when coals are at their hottest. As the embers cool down, open all the vents to allow for more air circulation, which in effect increases the internal temperature. Avoid closing vents completely or the coals will be snuffed out.

Gas and electric grill manufacturers do not seem to feel that cooking with indirect heat is essential with their grills (at least one would assume this from the lack of information in their booklets). However, I find that indirect heat *is* a necessity, particularly during long periods of cookery—if only to counteract constant flare-up when the rocks or tiles become over-heat-saturated. Since one can hardly move the rocks or tiles around to suit one's needs, the most effective method, in my opinion, is to place an aluminum-foil pan directly on the lava rocks or tiles. I use two pans, one inside the other, and keep a small amount of water in the bottom to prevent the surface from burning. This trick also introduces moisture into the cooking cycle and effectively prevents foods from drying out.

Chapter 8

The Flavor Behind the Smoke

USING *SMOKE* AS a flavoring is the second-best seasoning prerogative an outdoor cook can exercise. (Marinades are first, but more of them anon.) It is not difficult to add a hint of smoke to what you are cooking. A chart of some suggested options (found on page 50) will give you a general idea of what woods and other natural elements flavor particular foods best. But, remember, experimenting with your own taste buds is half the fun at the grill.

SOME WOODS OF ADVICE

There are some hard-and-fast rules about what woods may and may not be used to add flavor to your fire. For one thing, only hardwoods or fruitwoods, such as hickory, oak, mesquite, pear, or apple, should be used to produce aromatic smoke at the grill. Never, ever use softwoods (like pine and spruce), for these deciduous woods exude noxious resins and pitch which can ruin food's flavor.

The most popular hardwood flavoring in use across the nation is hickory—which has been a standby in the South for generations. And while mesquite is coming on strong (particularly in California and New York), there are still pockets of this country where the guy at a grill thinks it is some kind of insect.

For the record, mesquite is a low-slung hardwood tree that grows like crabgrass throughout the Southwest and Northern Mexico. It was originally used by barbecuers simply because it was there for the taking. In the 1980s, mesquite has become synonymous with mystique at lofty cookouts.

To be fair, mesquite smoke has a delicate, somewhat sweeter savor than such smoke produced by hickory or oak woods. But, discretion must be exercised in the amount of wood used. It is not necessary (or even advisable) to smoke foods indiscriminately. Smoke is meant to add a different dimension to food, rather than mask its original flavor. Other woods compatible for the grill are walnut, maple, pecan, cherry, apple, peach, and alder.

These days many diverse woods are available commercially in the form of wood chips, chunks, and (if you look hard for them) coals. Wood chips and chunks should always be presoaked in water before use. Chips require an hour's soaking time; chunks, two hours. Aside from the smoke released as the wood smolders on the embers, soaking prevents it from burning too rapidly.

I always use wood chips for *grilling* out of cost consciousness. As the cooking process is fast, large, long-burning chunks seem a waste of expensive fuel. A handful of water-soaked chips dispersed on preheated briquets just before cooking give off just the right amount of smoke for normal flavoring processes. With gas grills, scatter the damp chips directly on the lava rocks. A scant handful will not damage the grill, if you follow the procedures outlined in the booklet for your unit. The use of woods as a flavoring agent on gas grills is fairly new. One leading manufacturer recently confided that grill makers themselves were caught off guard by the notion. But flavoring with smoke is obviously here to stay.

To smoke-cook on an electric grill necessitates ingenuity. I suggest that a drip pan with water-soaked chips be positioned at one end of the grill. When the chips begin to smolder and create smoke, place food briefly over the smoke (on the grid) to flavor it first. Then continue to grill over *direct* heat.

When *cover cooking* with charcoal, you can use either chips, chunks, or pure hardwood coals. Two large handfuls of water-soaked chips, or 5 to 6 similarly soaked chunks, or about 8 coals tucked into the regular briquets, should impart enough smoky flavor to satisfy most normal taste buds. If you prefer a deeper, smokier taste, merely go heavier with the wood. But remember, all you need is 30 minutes of smoldering smoke to flavor practically any food. For gas-covered grills, the best method to produce smoke for long periods of cooking is to place water-soaked chips in a drip pan set directly on the lava rocks.

If you are lucky enough to have a grove of hardwood or fruit trees on your property, by all means make your ax count! It is best, however, to create your own chips with a plane or to saw the wood into chunks. But always let it dry thoroughly before using. The taste of burning green wood is just too overpowering.

APROPOS ALTERNATIVES

If you can't find any of the commercial hardwood products available at the marketplace and don't have the heart to mail-order, cheer up. Use nuts instead. Consider, for instance, a package of unshelled walnuts for your next offering. Crack them with a hammer and soak them briefly in water and simply proceed as you would with chips.

Cooking over grapevines, though a long-lived European tradition, is fast catching on here as well. The only problem is one of logistics. Vineyards (with excess grape cuttings) are *hard* to find. American vintners also tend to use the trimmings for mulch, cutting into the cache fancied by outdoor cooks. However, where there is an entrée, there is usually an entrepreneur. Not only are authentic "grape chips" packaged in Northern California, they are also being imported from vineyards in Europe as well. (For sources, see page 322.)

Seasoning fish with seaweed is a natural flavor match. But have a word of warning before you hit the nearest beach. Seaweed must be washed thoroughly, then dried in the sun (or a food dehydrator) before use, as it has a tendency to mold. I discovered this unhappy fact after hours spent collecting flora from the shores of Long Island. Parenthetically, I also thought it was a fairly original notion until I discovered that the practice dates back to seventeenth-century Scotland where haddock (for finnan haddie) was always smoked over kelp. Before using, presoak dried seaweed, of course.

Adding herbs and spices to a wood fire is another Old World flavoring idea. A branch of fennel, a bouquet of bay leaves, a brush of fresh tarragon or rosemary: all can be used to impart uniquely fragrant flavor. Consider using them in conjunction with conventional hardwoods for a broader spectrum of flavor. Likewise, garlic cloves, orange peels, cinnamon sticks, and even whole nutmegs will add new dimensions to smoke. Bear in mind that any flavorings you add must enhance the essential object on the grill. While steak, for instance, is wonderful with heads of garlic stashed in the coals, I'd think twice about cinnamon.

Again remember. No matter what flavoring agent you use, it must always be presoaked prior to the fire. You want the seasoning to smolder and smoke, not burn to a crisp.

BASIC FLAVORING CHART

ALDER WOOD	Perfect with seafood. Mild tasting. Adds a gentle woodsy flavor to salmon, swordfish, and, curiously, pork as well.
FRUIT WOODS (apple, cherry, peach)	Excellent with all golden-tinged meats and poultry (veal, pork, turkey, chicken, goose, or game birds) but too strong for most fish. However, fruit woods work well with shellfish such as lobster or shrimp.
HICKORY AND MAPLE WOODS	Traditionally used to flavor Southern-style ham and pork. A strong, pungent aroma that suits beef and poultry as well. Too strong for fish, however.
MESQUITE WOOD	Best with dark, richly flavored meats such as duck or lamb. Consider thick cuts of beef rather than steak. Fish steaks take on new dimension as well, but go light with the chips.
OAK WOOD	Remarkable with ham, large cuts of beef, and particularly game.
HERBS AND SPICES	Clumps of tarragon, rosemary, or basil branches (first hung to dry) make wonderful alliances with poultry and fish. Fresh herbs can be thrown on the fire as well or added to a drip pan. Use bay leaves and cinnamon sticks with discretion. All herbs and spices, dried or fresh, should be water-soaked before adding to the grill.
NUTS	Walnuts, pecans, or any nuts from hardwood trees can be cracked and water-soaked to take the place of wood chips.
GRAPEVINES	Excellent flavoring for most meats, although too intense for lamb.
SEAWEED	Produces a tangy smoke that enhances lobster, crab, shrimp, mussels, clams, and all mild-flavored fish.

Chapter 9

From Marination to Sen-sauce-ation

ASIDE FROM WOOD and other natural elements that produce smoky flavors, taste is primarily imparted to grilled foods with marinades, dry rubs, bastes, and barbecue sauces.

Marinades tenderize food and flavor it as well before cooking. *Dry rubs* (Southwest specialties) are mixed seasonings that are literally rubbed on the surface of the meat before it hits the grill. Rubs are very often used in conjunction with *bastes* (composed of seasoning sauces brushed onto the surface of meats) during cooking. While bastes add a marginal degree of flavor, they are used mainly to seal in juices, which keep meat moist. *Barbecue sauces,* as the name implies, are flavor adjuncts meant to be served as a condiment to cooked meat, though there are some notable exceptions to that rule.

Marinades: Any combination of herbs, chopped vegetables, and spicy extracts in which meat, poultry, fish, or even vegetables steep prior to cooking is known as a marinade. Some foods, like fish and vegetables, are marinated for flavor only. Long-term marination turns these foods mushy. So use judgment. No more than an hour's time is ever advised.

Other foods improve dramatically (in flavor and tenderness) by long periods of marination. Beef and chicken should be steeped at least half a day or overnight. All marinades contain some acidic liquid (like vinegar, wine, soy sauce, or lemon juice) which act as tenderizers.

Dry Rubs: Combinations of various ground ingredients (like black Malabar or Tellicherry peppercorns, cayenne pepper, paprika, dry mustard, allspice, and even chili powder) all have a tonic flavoring effect when rubbed onto the surface of meat, poultry, and dense-fleshed fish. A bruised clove of garlic lightly pressed over cuts of meat is also considered a dry rub. Salt is not. Salt should never be part of the formula for a dry rub, as it has a tendency to draw out meat's juices.

Bastes: Any liquid that adds moisture to a viand as it is cooking over open fire is known as a baste. A baste may be composed of many salutory ingredients or simply a sluice of melted butter or oil brushed onto food during cooking. Leftover marinades are almost always used as bastes, but should be strained first.

Barbecue Sauces: The various toppings that blanket sides of beef, slabs of pork, and braces of spitted chicken cooked over an open fire usually go by a single sobriquet: barbecue sauce. But, barbecue sauce evokes a different image for different folks all over the gooey geography.

Sweet, tomatoey formulas are synonymous with the deep South. Carolinians, however, wouldn't touch that stuff with a ten-foot pole. Nothing adorns their pork but vinegar and sometimes pepper. In Texas, barbecue sauce is likely to be nothing more than slightly thickened Tabasco, thinned with Lone Star beer. For the vast majority of outdoor cooks, however, barbecue sauce means *ketchup*!

Ketchup plus sugar; ketchup plus mustard; ketchup plus Worcestershire; and sometimes even ketchup plus Coca-Cola! It is these flavorings that innovative Americans add to their barbecue sauce that give it barb.

WHAT'S TO MOP?

In the bespoke state of North Carolina, where to this day, purists decry any other embellishment, fire-cooked meat is traditionally sloshed with a spicy vinegar, literally, and liberally applied during cooking with a clean rag mop!

WHAT'S TO SOP?

In most of what is thought of as barbecue country (from Tennessee to the Texas Panhandle), cooked meat—whether it has been priorly marinated, dry-rubbed, or basted—is served with bowls (or pitchers) of additional hot sauce for sopping. Whatever else is sopped on a plate is dependent upon a diner's decorum.

Chapter 10

All's Fare for the Grill

❧ WHAT YOU PLAN to prepare on the grill, of course, determines your time schedule for outdoor cookery. Needless to say, hamburgers and hot dogs do not require the same preparation as spareribs. A chart of cooking times for various foods appears in Chapter 13, "Grilling and Covered Cooking." Keep in mind, however, that timings are only approximate. Actual cooking times can be altered slightly by fluctuations in temperature, humidity, and degree of wind. There are also some salient points to bear in mind before selecting a menu.

WHAT'S THE BEEF?

Probably the most popular food for grilling in the United States is beef. To most of America, this inevitably translates into hamburger or steak.

When choosing meat for hamburgers, select cuts with a medium amount of fat content. High fat content in ground meat (like 100 percent chuck) causes flare-up. Sirloin is generally the best bet. If using chuck, try to grind it yourself, so you can control the fat content. Ground round, with the least fat (about 15 percent), is perfect for rare hamburgers. For those who like their hamburgers well done, increase the fat content to ensure juicy burgers. And keep a water spritzer nearby.

Best cuts of *steak* are T-bone, porterhouse, sirloin, filet, strip, rib, rib eye, and club. For full flavor, a steak should be at least 1¼ inches thick, but not so dense that the outside chars before the inside warms through. Steaks should be trimmed of excess fat to prevent flare-up. Never use a fork to turn a steak as the juices will be lost when the meat is punctured. Use tongs instead. Less tender cuts of beef, such as chuck, flank, or London broil, while not my first choice, can certainly be successfully grilled. But, make sure to marinate these cuts prior to the grid to tenderize the flesh.

Beef roasts are particularly easy to cook outdoors in a covered cooker. The prime rib roast, whether standing or boned, is the preferred choice, of course, but inexpensive cuts (like eye round) take remarkably well to the grill. Choose a roast with a healthy covering of fat to keep the roast from drying out.

Brisket and chuck roasts require slow, slow cooking and are best (in my opinion) cooked in a water smoker (see pages 272–273).

FINGER LICKIN' CHICKEN

The most economical fare for any grill is chicken. Some adherents insist that the only way to outdoor-cook a chicken is to roast it whole, over indirect heat, on a roasting rack or a rotisserie. Slow cooking, they claim, keeps the moisture in. Other enthusiasts suggest splitting the chicken down the back, removing the backbone, and cooking the bird, flattened on the grill, and covered. However, I grill chicken, cut into pieces, over direct heat (using the cover) and allow 15 minutes for the dark meat to precook, before I add the white meat. This assures that the white meat won't overcook, the common complaint when grilling pieces. And, if one wishes to use a sweet tomatoey barbecue sauce during the cooking, the best method is to cook the pieces over a drip pan until almost tender, before grilling them over direct heat to crispen. For a large crowd (too many drip pans will kill the coals), sear the pieces first, then line the grid with aluminum foil. *Lightly* brush the foil with oil and poke holes in it every 2 to 3 inches apart. Again, add the dark meat first, smother it with sauce, and cook covered. Smother the white meat when you add it as well.

Other types of fowl eminently suited for the grill are game hens, turkey parts, and duckling.

PIG IS FOR PICKIN'

The king of barbecue in the South is pig. Whole roasts are cooked so long the meat literally falls off the bone before it is served. It's no surprise. Pork roasts and ham are perfect for outdoor cookery, as pork takes naturally to smoke. Various woods, as noted, add very special flavors. A few corncobs thrown onto the coals won't hurt either. All pork, including chops, should be cover-cooked, as grilling in the open air dries it out.

Spareribs: Where would a barbecue be without them? Good ribs, however, are hard to find—even on home turf. Too *much* fat is usually the general complaint. One way to get around this is to parboil the ribs before they hit the grill. Another method is to loosely wrap in heavy-duty aluminum foil whole rib sections that have been marinated 2 hours, making sure the edges of the foil are well sealed. Place the packet, or packets if needed, on the grid and cook covered until the fat has been rendered, about 1½ hours. Then carefully remove the ribs from the foil and discard the grease. Finish the ribs over direct heat, basting often with barbecue sauce until crisp, about 5 minutes per side. A third method is to cook the ribs, basting often with sauce, over indirect heat for about 1½ hours before grilling over direct heat to crispen. But care must be taken so as not to let the ribs dry out.

ON THE LAMB

One meat virtually ignored by many outdoor chefs is lamb. Particularly well-suited to fire cookery as it is generally well-marbled and highly flavored, lamb cooks quickly on a grill. The average chop will grill to perfection in 10 minutes. And a butterflied leg of lamb will be *a'point* (as the French describe the desired rosy shade of roasted meat) in about 25 minutes. Ideally, lamb should be consumed when it is rare or medium-rare to best savor the full fresh taste. Marinades are suggested to keep all cuts of lamb (from racks to kabobs) moist and tender.

VEAL REVEALED

Since veal is the most expensive meat one can buy these days, I eschew it entirely on a grill. And while Italian cooks do sear a *lombotine* (veal sirloin) over open fire, most American veal chops dry out irreparably as soon as they hit live coals. Larger cuts of veal, however, may be successfully roasted on a rotisserie. A recipe for a prime one appears on page 267 and cheaper cuts, like the breast, are great in a smoker.

SIZZLIN' SAUSAGE

Of all kinds of forcemeat, sausages take best to the grill. The only maxim to remember is that all fresh links, such as bratwurst, Polish sausage, Italian sausage, or Spanish chorizos, should be steamed or poached first. Then grilled. If you are making your own sausage, beef and lamb sausage should contain about 25 percent fat. Pork or veal, 35 percent. Precooked sausages, like the ubiquitous hot dog, bologna, knockwurst, and kielbasa can be grilled right over direct heat.

NOTHING FISHY HERE

The foods most suited to the average griller's temperament are those that can be prepared most quickly, like fish and shellfish. Firm-fleshed fish varieties, like swordfish, tuna, and salmon, can be cut into steaks and placed directly on the grid. More delicate fish, like trout, flounder, and petrale, should be placed in oiled wire-hinged baskets before grilling. A larger fish, such as sea bass, can be stuffed and foil-wrapped. A fish continues to cook after it is removed from the grill, so be sure *not* to overcook it. Most shellfish can be grilled over direct heat. Lobster or crabs should be killed (or parboiled in salted water for a minute or two), then split and cleaned prior to grilling.

VEGETABLES ADD VITALITY
ON THE GRILL, OR OFF

Searing fresh vegetables on the grill can give them an entirely new taste dimension. Certain root vegetables like onions or winter squash with tough skins (like acorn or Hubbard) can be cooked directly in the coals without interior fire burn. This tonic vegetable roasting is called *ember cooking*. After a long water bath, fresh corn in its husk can be cooked this way too. However, the silk must be removed first. Potatoes are best wrapped in aluminum foil before placing them in the coals. Corn and potatoes may also be cooked on roasting racks. Other vegetables like zucchini, peppers, and eggplant can either be grilled directly au naturel, or seasoned, buttered, and wrapped in foil pouches and placed around the edge of the grid. The smoke from the coals permeates the foil just enough to give a subtle, fiery flavor.

KABOB-B-Q

Combinations of skewered ingredients, or kabobs, are fun food for the griller. All manner of vegetables can be mixed and matched with fish or meat for unusual entrées. If you choose beef for yours, remember that kabobs grill for a short time only and, therefore, require the same tender cuts of beef as a steak dinner. Marinating meat and fish gives kabobs variety. Stainless-steel skewers are the easiest to use and should always be turned with tongs (or an asbestos glove) as the handles become intensely hot. If your skewers are made of wood or bamboo, be sure to soak them in water for at least an hour prior to using to prevent burning. Most kabobs will be done in less than 15 minutes and frequent turning is necessary.

Chapter 11

What to Drink at a Cookout

FOODS PREPARED ON an outdoor grill have a decided smoky tang that translates to unmistakable "richness" on the tongue. Of a necessity, any beverage served as an accompaniment to a *grillade* should be on the light or effervescent side. In my opinion, beer is the perfect matchup because its slightly bitter, assertive taste complements any tinge of scorch. Be cautioned, however, that rich, dark beers tend to be filling.

In the choice of wine, again consider less full-bodied vintages first. Rosé wines seem to pop up at almost every outdoor fete I attend these days—partly because they can be successfully paired with a myriad of entrées: beef, pork, poultry, *and* seafood. Also they are eminently affordable. If you are a white wine fancier, choose a dry rather than a fruity variety. Chardonnays, Muscadets, Chablis, and Soaves are all good bets. Chilled Beaujolais and room temperature Côtes du Rhone, Barbera, Zinfandel, and even some of the less flinty Cabernet Sauvignons make excellent gastronomic partners with grilled beef and chicken, if your personal taste, as mine does, runs to red wine.

In the Deep South where nobody recommends liquor, "not even

corn squeezin's" at a barbecue, tea is invariably offered as the quaff of choice. "Ice tea," that is. And, according to North Carolina's *Tar Heel* magazine, "It is an understood maxim that barbecue restaurants serve tea *one way*—with three-quarters of a cup crushed ice and three parts sugar to one part tea. Even half a lemon cannot cut the sugar-coated edge." However, iced tea (without all that sugar) and iced coffee are both perfectly acceptable potables to have on hand for nonimbibers and children, though the kids will probably opt for pop.

A TIPPLING TIP

Teaching in Florida recently (where outdoor party fare is de rigueur from mid-November to early May), I was accosted by a matron with a fervid problem.

"I hope you are going to impart a few choice words on what to do—when guests won't leave the bar and the fire dies, dead as a door nail . . ." she implored. "Without starting the whole thing from scratch!"

The answer, aside from a clanging dinner bell attached to the grill, is an auxiliary fire. Just before the coals are turning the appropriate ashy gray that signals readiness, cover the grill with the vents wide open and light an additional 12 coals in a foil-lined metal pail. When ready to grill, knock the gray ash off the original coals and add the second batch as an incandescent stand-in!

Chapter 12

Some Safety Tips

REMEMBER, THE OUTCOME of a grilled dinner or (worse yet) a full-fledged outdoor party depends entirely on you. Therefore, keep control of the event. Appoint others to worry about the details of serving, making drinks, and keeping the conversation afloat—your job is only at the fire's side. Most important of all, design the meal so there are no last-minute incendiary hitches. If the barbecue is the centerpiece of your spree—everything else (including the guests) should work around it.

And, bear in mind, the following safety-first maxims basic to all outdoor forms of cooking:

1. Never use the grill indoors, or near any dry grassy areas that might conceivably catch fire.
2. Never *ever* use gasoline, kerosene, or alcohol to light the coals. One may use a commercial starter, but *never* add the lighting fluid directly to a fire.
3. Make sure that all connections to gas cylinders are safely sealed.
4. If using a gas or electric grill, always double the aluminum-foil drip pans used, to prevent the bottoms from unfortuitous burnouts.
5. Never use an extension cord from a kitchen outlet unless it is the

heavy-duty type recommended for outdoor equipment. And make sure any such cord is safely tucked out of the traffic flow—to and from the grill.

6. Always wear asbestos-lined barbecue gloves when you are in attendance at the grill.
7. Be certain there is an adequate light source before you light a fire. Working in the dark can be treacherous.
8. Never wear garments with long-flowing sleeves, loose-flying fringe, or flounces that might possibly catch fire.
9. Make sure you turn off the gas grill after use, or, if you are using a charcoal grill, close all vents—to snuff out the coals.
10. Stay as *sober* as possible. And know that drinking *too much* is the barbecuer's true handicap.

Some Additional Cautions
for Urban Outdoor Chefs

Apartment dwellers who cook in small enclosed gardens, on balconies, rooftops, or even in lofty penthouses should certainly follow the safety tips listed above. But as every metropolis is, by definition, confined, there are supplementary maxims for cooking with fire and smoke within city limits. Here are ten incendiary disciplines.

1. Never use an outdoor grill (including a hibachi) on a fire escape. It's against the law!
2. Do not use a smoker on a terrace unless you are willing to face some very irate neighbors and, in all likelihood, a summons from the fire department.
3. When you select a charcoal grill for use in an urban garden or on a terrace, always choose one with an *interior* ash-catcher.
4. When using an outdoor grill on a terrace or balcony, always use an electric starter rather than flammable liquids or ash-scattering chimney starters.
5. When grilling on an open terrace or rooftop, you would do well to line the area below the grill with heavy-duty aluminum foil to serve as a grease catcher.
6. Use great caution disposing of ashes. Even well-cooled ash may contain residual live coals, which could start a conflagration in the building's incinerator. The safest method for disposal is dampening the ashes thoroughly with water before emptying the grill.

7. When grilling on a terrace, *never* leave *any* barbecue equipment (forks, tongs, and so forth) on a ledge—even as a stopgap measure between bastings. Unidentified flying objects can cause street fatalities.

8. Never store LP (liquid petroleum) gas in the trunk of a passenger vehicle or an apartment closet. Store these cylinders outdoors in well-ventilated areas only.

9. Park the grill far from the beaten path of cocktail guests or over-zealous kitchen aides. Too many cooks not only spoil a barbecue but often tip it over as well!

10. When the grill is not in use, keep it well-secured and off-limits to small children or pets.

Chapter 13

Grilling and Covered Cooking

THE METHODS AND techniques described next range from the most basic skills necessary to turn out a juicy burger to those complex forms of covered cookery that produce the *grillades* found at the country's more innovative restaurants. (See Chapters 14 and 15 for rotisserie and smoker cooking.)

All the recipes below are for use on conventional grills: coal, gas, or electric. If you own only an open brazier, you can still accomplish adroit covered cooking by improvising a cover out of heavy-duty aluminum foil and a few wire coat hangers. Taking a clue from the folks at the Reynolds Wrap Kitchens, clip the hooks off 6 or 7 wire hangers and straighten them. Using 2 or more straightened hangers, by twisting the ends together with a pliers, form a circle that fits just inside your grill. Loop the remaining wires, umbrella fashion, to form half circles. You should have 6 or 7 ribs. Attach the ends of each securely to the bottom circle with pliers and fasten the top together with picture wire. Cover the entire wire frame with heavy-duty foil, leaving a small portion loose at the top to open and close for temperature control.

WHAT'S COOKING?

The recipes that follow give detailed instructions as to the type of heat source to be used: direct or indirect heat as the case may be.

When choosing meat for the grill, it is important that it always be at room temperature. Frozen meats should always be defrosted in the refrigerator slowly, before bringing to room temperature. To prevent the loss of excess juices during the thawing period, wrap the package of meat in several layers of newspaper, then a covering of foil. Allow at least five hours per pound of meat. Overnight defrosting is the best bet, so there is plenty of time for pregrill marination the next day.

All smaller cuts of meat should be trimmed of excess fat. The remaining fat around a steak or chop should be slashed to prevent the meat from curling up. Searing the meat over high heat before finishing the cooking process helps seal the juices inside. This is particularly germane to fast-grilled foods.

TIME AND TIME AGAIN

All cooking times given in the charts of this book are based on the barest minimum required to cook perfect foods under perfect conditions; perfect conditions being a beautiful summer's day, with no breeze, no cloud cover, and a temperature hovering around 80 degrees. Since such halcyon days are rare anywhere under the globe, learn to test meats and poultry with a meat thermometer or by touch, to make sure they are indeed perfectly cooked.

Rare meat will be soft and somewhat yielding to the touch.

Medium-rare meat will give slightly, then bounce back.

Well-done meat will not budge.

Always allow plenty of time for cooking large cuts of meat. Nothing is worse than guests, awash with martinis, waiting well beyond the appointed dinnertime for food to come off the grill. It is far better to cut short the cocktail hour than to shortcut the fare.

Timings for beef and lamb, it must be noted, reflect the author's penchant for rosy cuts. My *medium* may be your *medium-rare*. If it is, don't panic; add a minute or two to the charted cooking times.

Beef

IN THE OPINION of epicures, grilling or barbecuing beef is the only way to bring out its natural, hearty flavor. Methods and techniques vary widely by the cut one chooses. It might be noted that exact timing of beef is a near impossibility. Aside from unpredictable wind and temperature factors, the quality of the meat itself affects any preset timetable. For one thing, higher fat content in a cut of meat makes it cook faster as fat is a heat conductor. Also, aged beef will cook much quicker than fresh meat. Despite these caveats, a very general timing and cooking chart follows.

BEEF CHART ❦

CUT OF BEEF·	TECHNIQUE*·	TIMES AND SUGGESTIONS†·
HAMBURGER (¾ to 1 inch thick)	**Grilling:** Medium-hot with direct heat.	3 minutes 1st side. *Rare:* 4 minutes 2nd side. *Med.:* 6 minutes 2nd side. *Well:* 10 to 12 minutes 2nd side.
TENDER STEAK (Strip, T-bone, filet, rib, rib eye, sirloin, porterhouse, club, 1¼ inches thick)	**Grilling:** Hot for searing. Then medium-hot with direct heat.	Sear 1 minute per side. Sear edges. Then 4 minutes 1st side. *Rare:* 5 to 6 minutes 2nd side. *Med.:* 7 to 8 minutes 2nd side. *Well:* 9 to 10 minutes 2nd side.
LONDON BROIL (2 inches thick)	**Grilling:** Hot for searing. Then medium-hot with direct heat.	*Marinate overnight.* Sear 1 minute per side. Sear edges. Then 8 minutes 1st side. *Rare:* 18 minutes 2nd side. *Med.:* 20 minutes 2nd side. Let stand 10 minutes before serving, sliced on the diagonal
CHUCK STEAK (1¼ inches thick)	**Grilling:** Hot for searing. Then medium-hot with direct heart.	*Marinate overnight.* Sear 1 minute per side. Sear edges. Then 7 minutes 1st side. *Rare:* 8 to 10 minutes 2nd side. *Med.:* 12 minutes 2nd side. *Well:* 15 minutes 2nd side.

Cut	Method	Directions
FLANK STEAK (½ inch thick)	*Grilling:* Hot with direct heat.	Score both sides of the meat; *marinate overnight.* Then 3 to 5 minutes per side.
SHORT RIBS	*Covered Cooking:* Medium-hot with direct heat. Then *Grilling* with medium, direct heat.	Foil-bake ribs (see page 164) 1½ hours. Then grill, uncovered, basting often with barbecue sauce, about 15 minutes.
BEEF KABOBS (use cuts for Tender Steak, cut in 1¼ inch cubes)	*Grilling:* Medium-hot with direct heat.	Grill 2 minutes per side for a total of 8 minutes for rare; 3 minutes per side for medium-rare.
RIB ROAST (4 pounds or less)	*Covered Cooking:* Medium with indirect heat.	Cook on a rack. *Rare:* 14 to 16 minutes per pound (internal temp.: 125°). *Med.:* 18 minutes per pound (internal temp.: 135°).
ROLLED ROAST (4 pounds or less)	*Covered Cooking:* Medium with indirect heat.	Cook on a rack, basting occasionally. *Rare:* 16 to 18 minutes per pound (internal temp.: 125°). *Med.:* 20 minutes per pound (internal temp.: 135°).

* For gas or electric grills, use the high setting for hot, the medium setting for medium-hot. Use the cooler edges of the grid in case of flare-up.

For charcoal grills, hot refers to the 2-second hand test (see page 43). Use the 3- to 4-second test for medium-hot and the 5-second test for medium. To lower the temperature of coal, raise the grid, use the outside edges of the briquets, or cover with cover vents partially closed.

† Times may vary depending on outdoor temperature and velocity of wind.

Hamburger

CHOOSE MEAT FOR a hamburger that is not full of fat. Contrary to my prior injunction about room temperature meats, ground beef is the perfect place to break a rule. Since hamburger meat cooks so quickly, a cold center will help to keep the interior rare. The late, great James Beard in *Barbecue with Beard* (Warner Books, 1975) went so far as to suggest wrapping hamburgers around ice cubes. One cube per hamburger, of course. This technique leaves the center nice and juicy while searing the edges, but as I am highly prejudiced against the texture of absolutely raw meat, it is not a standard practice at my grid. Whether you elect a rare or well-done burger, do not overhandle ground beef. Physical contact causes beef to toughen, so when you add seasonings of any kind, handle the patty gently.

My technique for a hands-off hamburger is somewhat unorthodox but it works like a charm. I merely put the ground meat on a large plate first. Using 2 forks, I separate it over the plate's surface and add whatever adjunctive seasoning pleases my palate. Then, still using the 2 forks, I lift the mixture and fold it over onto itself. I then divide it into individual burgers, gently pressing the sides together to seal. Indiscriminate outdoor cooks throw just about everything but the kitchen sink into their burgers. That is your option. I, however, prefer the only additives to be a jot of melted butter or a splash of heavy cream. Salt and pepper come later. If you like onion, consider chopping and sautéing one in butter before adding it to the meat.

Hamburgers should be grilled over medium-hot coals (or high heat for gas and electric grills). Cooking time: 3 minutes on the first side, then 6 to 7 minutes on the second side for medium-rare. If your coals are not hot enough, the process will take somewhat longer. The important thing to keep in mind is that a hamburger should be well-seared on the first side before turning it over, to prevent it from falling apart. A handful of water-soaked hickory chips added to the coals or rocks before grilling is my favored hamburger flavor.

I generally allow ⅓ pound of beef per burger, but ¼ pound is probably a more typical American size. As a rule of thumb, I serve 2 hamburgers per person. Some trenchermen I know prefer half-pounders, and still serve 2 per person. No matter what your preference as to its weight, however, keep in mind that grilling times are determined by the thickness (not the ounces) of each hamburger.

My way to make a basic burger follows, plus a few variations on the theme. If you plan to serve buns, enhance the flavor by preheating them. Place buns, cut sides down, around the edges of the grid for about 1 minute. Then butter well.

THE BASIC BURGER

The addition of melted butter or heavy cream ensures that the center of the hamburger will not dry out.

    1⅓ pounds ground beef
      1 tablespoon melted unsalted butter, or heavy cream
         Vegetable oil
         Salt and freshly ground pepper

1 · Preheat the grill.

2 · Place the ground beef on a plate and gently spread apart with 2 forks. Sprinkle the meat with butter or cream. Lift the mixture and fold it over on itself. Gently shape into 4 patties, ¾ to 1 inch thick.

3 · If using presoaked wood chips, sprinkle them over the hot coals or lava rocks. Brush the grid lightly with oil.

4 · Grill the burgers over medium-hot heat 3 minutes on the first side, then 4 minutes on the second side for rare, 5 to 6 minutes for medium-rare. Sprinkle with salt and pepper.

Makes 4 hamburgers.

BACON-FLECKED CHEESEBURGER

In the following cheese-cum-bacon burger variation, grated cheese is tucked between layers of bacon-flavored beef to grill and melt simultaneously.

> 1⅓ pounds ground beef
> 2 strips crisp-fried bacon, crumbled
> 5 tablespoons grated cheddar cheese
> Vegetable oil
> Salt and freshly ground pepper

1 · Preheat the grill.

2 · Place the ground beef on a plate and gently spread apart with 2 forks. Sprinkle the bacon over the top of the meat; toss gently to mix. Divide mixture into 8 portions. Gently flatten each portion with a fork. Sprinkle cheese over 4 of them. Place the remaining patties over the cheese and press the edges to seal.

3 · If using presoaked wood chips, sprinkle them over the hot coals or lava rocks. Brush the grid lightly with oil.

4 · Grill the burgers over medium-hot heat 3 minutes on the first side, then 4 minutes on the second side for rare, 5 to 6 minutes for medium-rare. Sprinkle with salt and pepper.

Makes 4 hamburgers.

BBQ BURGER

Consider a sluice of your favorite (red) barbecue sauce for very tonic burgers. But, note that the meat is tossed, rather than folded as above, to ensure even distribution of sauce.

> 1⅓ pounds ground beef
> 3 tablespoons Nathalie Dupree's Coca-Cola Barbecue Sauce or other tomato-based barbecue sauce (see pages 298–307)
> 1 tablespoon finely grated red bell pepper
> Vegetable oil
> Salt and freshly ground pepper

1 · Preheat the grill.

2 · Place the ground beef on a plate and gently spread apart with 2 forks. Spread the barbecue sauce over the meat; sprinkle with grated bell pepper. Toss lightly to mix. Gently shape into 4 patties, ¾ to 1 inch thick.

3 · If using presoaked wood chips, sprinkle them over the hot coals or lava rocks. Brush the grid lightly with oil.

4 · Grill the burgers over medium-hot heat 3 minutes on the first side, then 4 minutes on the second side for rare, 5 to 6 minutes for medium-rare. Sprinkle with salt and pepper.

Makes 4 hamburgers.

TEX-MEXED BURGER

Chile peppers combined with melting Monterey Jack cheese are a solid Southwestern tradition on or off the grill. Hamburgers never had it so good.

    1⅓ pounds ground beef
      4 teaspoons minced canned green chiles
    2½ tablespoons diced Monterey Jack cheese
         Vegetable oil
         Salt and freshly ground pepper

1 · Preheat the grill.

2 · Place the ground beef on a plate and gently spread apart with 2 forks. Sprinkle the chiles over the top; dot with cheese. Lift the mixture and fold it over on itself. Gently shape into 4 patties, ¾ to 1 inch thick, pressing any showing cheese pieces back into the meat.

3 · If using presoaked wood chips, sprinkle them over the hot coals or lava rocks. Brush the grid lightly with oil.

4 · Grill the burgers over medium-hot heat 3 minutes on the first side, then 4 minutes on the second side for rare, 5 to 6 minutes for medium-rare. Sprinkle with salt and pepper.

Makes 4 hamburgers.

LAGER BURGER

Beer is a natural beef tenderizer, adding savor without obtrusive flavor to grilled meat. Again, note that here the meat is tossed, rather than folded.

    1⅓ pounds ground beef
       1 tablespoon Dijon mustard
       2 teaspoons minced scallions
      ¼ teaspoon freshly ground pepper
       2 tablespoons beer or ale
          Vegetable oil
          Salt

1 · Preheat the grill.

2 · Place the ground beef on a plate and gently spread apart with 2 forks. Spread the mustard over the meat. Sprinkle with scallions, pepper, and beer. Toss lightly to mix. Gently shape into 4 patties, ¾ to 1 inch thick.

3 · If using presoaked wood chips, sprinkle them over the hot coals or lava rocks. Brush the grid lightly with oil.

4 · Grill the burgers over medium-hot heat 3 minutes on the first side, then 4 minutes on the second side for rare, 5 to 6 minutes for medium-rare. Sprinkle with salt.

Makes 4 hamburgers.

SAVORY BURGER

A jot of anchovy and a snippet of chives or scallion ends are an unexpected hamburger alliance, and decidedly habit-forming.

    1⅓ pounds ground beef
    1¼ teaspoons anchovy paste
    1¼ teaspoons minced chives or scallion ends
       1 tablespoon vodka
          Vegetable oil
          Freshly ground pepper

1 · Place the ground beef on a plate and gently spread apart with 2 forks. Spread the anchovy paste over the meat. Sprinkle with chives or scallion ends and vodka. Lift the mixture and fold it over on itself. Gently shape into 4 patties, ¾ to 1 inch thick.

2 · If using presoaked wood chips, sprinkle them over the hot coals or lava rocks. Brush the grid lightly with oil.

3 · Grill the burgers over medium-hot heat 3 minutes on the first side, then 4 minutes on the second side for rare, 5 to 6 minutes for medium-rare. Sprinkle with pepper.

Makes 4 hamburgers.

GILDED BURGER

The crowning touch? A delicate coating of mayonnaise on the meat just before the fire. Make sure your fire is hot, *or the mayonnaise will not sufficiently burn off.*

   1⅓ pounds ground beef
    3 tablespoons mayonnaise
    1 tablespoon country-style Dijon mustard (with seeds)
   ¼ teaspoon freshly ground pepper
      Vegetable oil
      Salt

1 · Preheat the grill.

2 · Place the ground beef on a plate and gently spread apart with 2 forks. Spread 2 teaspoons mayonnaise over the meat. Spread with mustard; sprinkle with pepper. Lift the mixture and fold it over on itself. Gently shape into 4 patties, ¾ to 1 inch thick. Spread the top of each burger with slightly less than 1 teaspoon of the remaining mayonnaise.

3 · If using presoaked wood chips, sprinkle them over the hot coals or lava rocks. Brush the grid lightly with oil.

4 · Grill the burgers, mayonnaise side down, 3 minutes. Spread the remaining mayonnaise over the top of each burger and grill 4 minutes on the second side for rare, 5 to 6 minutes for medium-rare. Sprinkle with salt.

Makes 4 hamburgers.

SCANDI BURGER

*Inspired by the Swedish meatball, this hamburger is amended
with ham, sour cream, and fresh dill.*

 1⅓ pounds ground beef
  2 tablespoons sour cream
  ⅛ teaspoon freshly grated nutmeg
 2½ teaspoons chopped fresh dill
  2 ounces (about 2 slices) finely chopped, sliced, boiled
   ham
   Vegetable oil
   Salt and freshly ground pepper

1 · Preheat the grill.

2 · Place the ground beef on a plate and gently spread apart
with 2 forks. Spread the sour cream over the meat. Sprinkle with
nutmeg, dill, and chopped ham. Lift the mixture and fold it over on
itself. Gently shape into 4 patties, ¾ to 1 inch thick.

3 · If using presoaked wood chips, sprinkle them over the hot
coals or lava rocks. Brush the grid lightly with oil.

4 · Grill the burgers over medium-hot heat 3 minutes on the
first side, then 4 minutes on the second side for rare, 5 to 6 minutes
for medium-rare. Sprinkle with salt and pepper.

Makes 4 hamburgers.

Beefsteak

ALL BEEFSTEAK CAN be divided into two categories: tender and less than tender. The tenderest steaks come from the loin and sirloin of the beef and include such familiar cuts as filet, strip, T-bone, porterhouse, sirloin, club, rib, and rib eye. A quick rub with a bruised clove of garlic is all that is needed to anoint a prime cut of steak. However, a sauce accompaniment (such as Guacamole or Tomato Béarnaise) makes a festive adjunct.

Less than tender steaks include chuck, round, or shoulder (London broil), flank, and skirt steaks. It is obligatory to marinate these cuts for several hours prior to the fire, and overnight is the best bet. Furthermore, it is advisable to eat these steaks rare. If your preference runs to well-done meat, I suggest you stick to the "tender" category, as less than tender steaks tend to become tough and stringy as they overcook. However, even lesser grades of meat, imaginatively prepared and properly cooked, can be toothsome and extremely flavorful.

For added flavor, I often use pure hardwood coals such as hickory in conjunction with regular briquets. But packaged hardwood chunks or chips work equally well. Presoak chunks for several hours before using or they will instantly burst into flame. An hour's soak for chips is more than sufficient. Use chips with gas grills. A handful of chips or about 4 large chunks are more than enough.

Always remember to trim all steak of excess fat to prevent continuous flare-up at the grill. Certain cuts of meat, like flank steak

and, sometimes, London broil, have very little fat and need to be dotted with butter to stimulate the flames necessary to cook these cuts quickly.

When serving large steaks, it is traditional to carve the meat on the angle at the table. So keep a sharp knife at the ready.

What follows are some of the tastiest steak recipes I know.

SIMPLY WONDERFUL FILET

To many, the filet of the beef is the ultimate taste treat. But while individual cuts (filet mignon) are easy to grill, the whole filet presents a problem, as one end is inevitably narrower than the other. The way to circumvent this obstacle is to tuck the narrow end far enough under to create a roast of uniform size and tie it in place. Total grilling time (including searing) should be about 10 minutes per inch for rare, 12 minutes per inch for medium-rare. For those who don't wish to bankroll a whole filet, this recipe uses filet mignon. Note that garlic goes in with the coals, rather than on the meat. Serve with one of the suggested sauces.

> 4 filet mignon steaks, each about 1½ inches thick
> Vegetable oil
> 8 cloves unpeeled garlic, soaked in water 30 minutes
> Salt and freshly ground pepper
> Red Pepper Hollandaise, Beurre Rouge, or Tomato Béarnaise (see pages 310, 311, 312)

1 · Preheat the grill.

2 · Brush each filet mignon lightly with oil.

3 · Place the garlic cloves on top of the hot coals or lava rocks in approximately the area where you will be grilling the steaks. Brush the grid lightly with oil.

4 · Sear the steaks over hot or high heat 1 minute per side, including edges. Then place the steaks over medium-hot heat (raise the grid or use the outer edges of the coals to reduce heat) and grill 4 minutes on the first side, then 5 to 6 minutes on the second side for rare, 7 to 8 minutes for medium-rare. Sprinkle with salt and pepper. Serve with one of the suggested sauces.

Serves 4.

BERT GREENE'S SUPER STEAK

A super outdoor recipe from one of America's super indoor cooks, this recipe features a porterhouse steak, seasoned with a savory mix of anchovy paste, oil, garlic, and just plain culinary genius. Serve with Bert Greene's Guacamole Sauce, the Spinach-Herb Sauce, or one of the sauces suggested for the Simply Wonderful Filet above.

> 2½- to 3-pound porterhouse steak, about 2 inches thick
> 1 clove garlic, crushed
> 1 teaspoon anchovy paste
> 2 teaspoons olive oil
> ¼ teaspoon freshly ground pepper
>   Vegetable oil
>   Bert Greene's Guacamole Sauce or Spinach-Herb Sauce
>   (see page 313)

1 · Trim all but ¼ to ½ inch fat from the sides of the steak. Slash remaining fat with a knife at 1-inch intervals.

2 · Using a mortar and pestle, mash the garlic with the anchovy paste, olive oil, and pepper until smooth. Rub this mixture into the steak on both sides. Let stand 1 hour.

3 · Preheat the grill.

4 · Secure the tail section of the steak with water-soaked toothpicks, so that the steak cooks evenly. If using presoaked wood chips or chunks (chips for gas) or other flavorings, sprinkle them over the hot coals or lava rocks. Brush the grid lightly with vegetable oil.

5 · Sear the steak over hot or high heat 1 minute per side, including edges. Then place the steak over medium-hot heat (raise the grid or use the outer edges of the coals to reduce heat) and grill 7 to 8 minutes per side for rare, 8 to 10 minutes per side for medium-rare. (If the coals flare up, quickly remove the steak and spray the fire with a water spritzer or use the cover with all vents closed to smother the flames.)

6 · To serve, transfer the steak to a carving board and let stand 5 minutes. Remove toothpicks and cut off the tail. Cut around the bone to free the meat. Cut across the grain of each piece of meat (including the tail) into slices about ¼ inch thick. Arrange on a platter. Serve with one of the suggested sauces.

Serves 4.

SPICE 'N' PEPPER STEAK

What makes even a tender steak tenderer? A red wine mari-nade—the acidity of the grape does the trick. If you are using choice or prime cuts, dunk for flavor only; cheaper cuts require a longer, even overnight, bath to truly tenderize. Follow the directions for less-than-tender cuts of meat as detailed in the recipes following this one.

    1 tender steak (T-bone, porterhouse, etc.), about 1¼ inches
       thick
    1 clove garlic, bruised
       Vegetable oil
    ¼ cup red wine
    1 teaspoon allspice berries, crushed
    2 teaspoons black peppercorns, crushed

1 · Trim all but ¼ to ½ inch fat from the sides of the steak. Slash remaining fat with a knife at 1-inch intervals. Rub the steak well with garlic. Place in a shallow glass or ceramic dish.

2 · Combine 1 teaspoon oil with the wine, allspice, and peppercorns. Pour over the steak. Marinate covered, turning once, for 1 hour.

3 · Preheat the grill.

4 · If using presoaked wood chips or chunks (chips for gas), sprinkle them over the hot coals or lava rocks. Brush the grid lightly with oil.

5 · Sear the steak over hot or high heat 1 minute per side, including edges. Then place the steak over medium-hot heat (raise the grid or use the outer edges of the coals to reduce the heat) and grill 4 minutes on the first side, then 5 to 6 minutes on the second side for rare, 7 to 8 minutes for medium-rare.

6 · To serve, transfer the steak to a carving board and let stand 5 minutes. Cut around the bone to free the meat. Cut across the grain of each piece of meat into slices about ¼ inch thick. Arrange on a platter.

Serves 2.

LONDON BROIL VINAIGRETTE

I've heard of a famed restaurant chef's secret for flavoring steak; he merely splashes it with a spot of vinaigrette salad dressing before grilling. A lengthier soak will not only add flavor, but also turn even a tough cut like London broil tame. Incidentally, what is labeled London broil at the supermarket is usually either shoulder or round.

> 1 small clove garlic, crushed
> ¼ teaspoon coarse salt
> ½ teaspooon Dijon mustard
> 2 teaspoons lemon juice
> ¼ cup olive oil
> 1 teaspoon red wine vinegar
> ¼ teaspoon freshly ground pepper
> 1 London broil (round or shoulder steak), 2 inches thick
>   Vegetable oil

1 · Mash the garlic and the salt together in a small bowl with the back of a spoon. Stir in the mustard and lemon juice. Whisk in the olive oil, vinegar, and pepper.

2 · Place the steak in a shallow glass or ceramic dish. Pour the vinaigrette dressing over the top. Marinate covered in the refrigerator overnight, turning the steak occasionally. Let stand at room temperature 2 hours before grilling.

3 · Preheat the grill.

4 · If using presoaked wood chips or chunks (chips for gas) or other flavorings, sprinkle them over the hot coals or lava rocks. Brush the grid lightly with vegetable oil.

5 · Sear the steak over hot or high heat 1 minute per side, including edges. Then place the steak over medium-hot heat (raise the grid or use the outer edges of the coals to reduce the heat) and grill 8 minutes on the first side, then 18 minutes on the second side for rare, about 20 minutes for medium-rare.

6 · To serve, transfer the steak to a carving board and let stand 5 minutes. Cut across the grain into slices about ¼ inch thick. Arrange on a platter.

Serves 4 to 6.

BALLPARK CHUCK STEAK

The next recipe is a bequest from one of America's rising food sa-
vants, Howard Solganik of Dayton, Ohio. Howard's formula, de-
vised of ballpark mustard alone, makes a chuck steak choice. The
first three bones of the chuck adjacent to the rib section are the
supplest—so request those cuts from your butcher.

1 chuck steak, about 1¼ inches thick
  Yellow mustard (I use French's)
  Vegetable oil

1 · Trim all but ¼ to ½ inch fat from the sides of the steak.
Slash the remaining fat with a knife at 1-inch intervals. Spread ¼
inch of mustard over both sides of the steak. Do not coat the edges
so they will sear properly. Place the steak in a shallow glass or ceramic dish. Refrigerate covered overnight. Let stand at room temperature 2 hours before grilling.
2 · Preheat the grill.
3 · If using presoaked wood chips or chunks (chips for gas) or
other flavorings, sprinkle them over the hot coals or lava rocks.
Brush the grid lightly with oil.
4 · Sear the steak over hot or high heat 1 minute per side, including edges. Then place the steak over medium-hot heat (raise
the grid or use the outer edges of the coals to reduce the heat) and
grill 7 minutes on the first side, then 8 to 10 minutes on the second
side for rare, about 12 minutes for medium-rare.
5 · To serve, transfer the steak to a carving board and let stand
5 minutes. Cut around the bone to free the meat. Cut across the
grain of each piece of meat into slices about ¼ inch thick. Arrange
on a platter.

Serves 2.

INDONESIAN-STYLE BONELESS CHUCK

Satays are the national dish of Malaysia and no two are alike.
Most often, satays are made of marinated meats cut into strips
prior to grilling. The transplanted Indonesian version below, how-

ever, calls for boneless filets of chuck steak. Another surprise: the marinade is healthily seasoned with peanut butter, a traditional ingredient. Chunk-style is preferred.

> 3 tablespoons peanut oil
> 1 small shallot, minced
> 1 clove garlic, minced
> ½ teaspoon crushed, dried hot red peppers
> ½ teaspoon lemon juice
> 2 tablespoons *nuoc mam* (available in most Oriental groceries; see also note)
> 1 tablespoon soy sauce
> ¼ cup chunk-style peanut butter
> 6 boneless chuck steak filets, about ¾ inch thick and 5 inches long (1½ to 2 pounds)
> Vegetable oil

1 · Heat 1 teaspoon peanut oil in a small skillet over medium-low heat. Add the shallot; cook 1 minute. Add the garlic and hot red peppers; cook until golden, about 5 minutes. Remove from heat and combine with the lemon juice, nu'o'ć mám, soy sauce, peanut butter, and remaining peanut oil in a bowl. Mash all together with the back of a spoon. Spread over the chuck steak filets. Cover and let stand for 3 hours.

2 · Preheat the grill.

3 · If using presoaked wood chips or chunks (chips for gas), or other flavorings, sprinkle them over the hot coals or lava rocks. Brush the grid lightly with vegetable oil.

4 · Grill the steaks over medium-hot coals 3 to 4 minutes per side for rare, 5 to 6 minutes for medium-rare. (If the steaks flare up, use the cover with all vents closed to smother the flames.)

Serves 4 to 6.

Note: To make an approximation of *nuoc mam* (the traditional fish sauce used in Vietnamese cooking), combine the following in a blender container: 2 seeded and chopped ripe red chile peppers, 1 clove garlic, 1 teaspoon sugar, juice of 1 lemon, 1 tablespoon vinegar, 1 tablespoon water, ¼ cup soy sauce, and ¼ cup clam juice. Blend until smooth and strain into a saucepan. Boil 5 minutes and cool. Store in a jar with a tight-fitting lid in the refrigerator. Makes about ½ cup.

TENNESSEE FLANK STEAK

In Tennessee where bourbon is a natural mate to beef, it is also used as a marinade to tenderize flank steak. It is imperative to grill flank steak over hot or high heat to cook it quickly—until just rare. Slice the steak immediately on the angle as flank toughens as it cools.

> 1 flank steak, ½ inch thick (about 1½ pounds)
> 1 clove garlic, crushed
> 2 teaspoons dry English mustard
> ¼ cup bourbon
>   Vegetable oil
> 2 tablespoons unsalted butter
>   Salt and freshly ground pepper

1 · Using a sharp knife, score the flank steak on each side, about ⅛ inch deep, in a diamond pattern. Place in a shallow glass or ceramic dish.

2 · Mash the garlic with the mustard in a small bowl with the back of a spoon. Stir in the bourbon. Pour this mixture over the steak. Refrigerate covered overnight, turning several times. Let stand at room temperature 2 hours before grilling.

3 · Preheat the grill.

4 · If using presoaked wood chips or chunks (chips for gas) or other flavorings, sprinkle them over the hot coals or lava rocks. Brush the grid lightly with oil.

5 · Grill the steak over hot or high heat 3 to 5 minutes per side, dotting the edges of each side with 1 tablespoon butter to ensure the adequate fire action needed to cook the steak quickly. Carve the steak immediately, by cutting across the grain into slices about ¼ inch thick. Sprinkle with salt and pepper.

Serves 4.

EDIE ACSELL'S DENVER STEAK

Edie Acsell is a very talented Colorado cooking teacher with a penchant for no fuss cuisine. Her zesty marinade will turn any refractory cut of chuck, flank, or round steak tranquil. I use flank steak and find that dinner guests can't seem to get enough. Incidentally, the oil in the marinade makes the addition of butter during grilling (as in the previous recipe) unnecessary.

        1 flank steak, ½ inch thick (about 1½ pounds)
        3 cloves garlic, minced
      ½ cup safflower oil
      ½ cup tomato juice
      ½ cup soy sauce (I use Kikkoman)
      ½ cup brown sugar
      ½ teaspoon freshly ground pepper
        Vegetable oil

1 · Using a sharp knife, score the flank steak on each side, about ⅛ inch deep, in a diamond pattern. Place in a shallow glass or ceramic dish.

2 · Combine the garlic, safflower oil, tomato juice, soy sauce, brown sugar, and pepper. Pour this mixture over the steak. Refrigerate covered overnight, turning several times. Let stand at room temperature 2 hours before grilling.

3 · Preheat the grill.

4 · Drain the marinade from the steak and heat to boiling in a small saucepan. Strain this mixture into another saucepan; keep warm.

5 · If using presoaked wood chips or chunks (chips for gas) or other flavorings, sprinkle them over the hot coals or lava rocks. Brush the grid lightly with vegetable oil.

6 · Grill the steak over hot or high heat 3 to 5 minutes per side. Carve the steak immediately, by cutting across the grain into slices about ¼ inch thick. Pass the sauce on the side.

Serves 4.

A RARE MOMENT

Barbecue, historically, is always cooked long enough for the Texan to properly enjoy the piece of meat. According to Texas writer, Caleb Pirtle III, cowboys like the taste, but not the beef, rare.

"One cowboy swaggered into a fancy restaurant," he reported, ". . . sat down at a candle-lit table, and stared down into a plate of rare steak, just singed a little, with blood oozing amidst the sizzling juices.

He jumped. Stood up abruptly. Threw his napkin on the floor and turned to stomp out the door.

"Hell," he said, "I've seen cows get well that were hurt worse than this!"

Beef Ribs

BEEF RIBS, OR rather "short" ribs, are cut from either the bony end of a prime rib roast or the area underneath the rib section of the animal, known as the "plate." If you want to be trendy and serve ribs "pink" as they do in so many of the new hostelries devoted to "California Cuisine" these days, make sure you know precisely from which part of the beef the ribs were cut.

Ribs sliced from the prime section are going to be tender and perfect for "rarefied" ribs. However, the big, meaty (fatty) ribs often found in supermarkets are almost always cut from the plate section. As this cut of beef is also used for "stewing," slow cookery is an absolute requisite.

Meaty ribs are an excellent option for a water smoker if you happen to have one. In my opinion, however, they cook equally well on a covered grill. The trick is to marinate the ribs overnight in some of the sauce that you will serve them with later. Foil-wrap the marinated ribs and cook them covered first. Then remove the foil, slather with more sauce and grill them over medium coals. Fresh, lit coals will have to be added after about 50 minutes or so and should be stirred up, knocking off the gray ash, before the actual *grilling* of the ribs.

Ribs require 1 to 1½ hours in foil (depending on size) to become tender enough for my taste. To foil-wrap the ribs properly, place them in the center of a large oblong piece of heavy-duty aluminum foil large enough to allow for folding at the top and sides. Bring the two sides together over the meat and fold together to seal. Then fold the short ends and crimp to seal. The neatly folded package should have enough air space inside to allow for heat expansion. The smoke generated by hardwood coals, or presoaked wood chunks or chips, will penetrate the foil just enough to give the ribs a mild smoky taste.

I generally allow 1 pound of ribs per person, though smaller appetites may require less. When purchasing ribs, be aware that supermarket meat departments often combine different sizes in the same package, which makes accurate timing somewhat problematic. Order them cut to your specification in advance, or request the butcher to repackage the ribs in uniform sizes. They usually will, as a satisfied cook inevitably becomes a good customer.

"BLUE RIBBON" RIBS

Texans and Oklahomans seem to know more about cooking beef ribs than any other folk around. But the end results of their expertise are totally unrelated. For a real taste of the Lone Star State, use the Texas Soppin' Sauce, which incorporates coriander, cumin, aniseed, and—here's the kicker—as much Tabasco as you can stand. The "north of the panhandle" version comes from Skitch Henderson, masterful conductor of the New York Pops, and maestro of a wondrous brick outdoor barbecue at his home in the Connecticut hills. Based on the foil-wrap technique, both are "blue ribbon" winners in my book.

> Texas Soppin' Sauce or Skitch Henderson's Tulsa Toppin'
>   (see pages 300–301)
> 4 pounds meaty beef ribs
>   Vegetable oil

1 · Make the Texas Soppin' Sauce or Skitch Henderson's Tulsa Toppin'.

2 · Brush the ribs with either of the above sauces. Place in a glass or ceramic dish. Refrigerate covered overnight. Let stand at room temperature 2 hours before cooking.

3 · Preheat the grill.

4 · Place the ribs on two large sheets of heavy-duty aluminum foil. Bring up the edges and seal.

5 · If using presoaked wood chips or chunks (chips for gas), sprinkle over the hot coals or lava rocks. Brush the grid lightly with oil.

6 · Place the foil-wrapped ribs on the grid. Cook covered, with the vents open, until ribs are tender, 1¼ to 1½ hours. (If using a charcoal grill, add more lit coals after about 50 minutes.)

7 · Remove the ribs from the foil and drain. Brush with more sauce. Grill the ribs, basting often with sauce, over medium coals until crisp, 15 to 20 minutes. Serve with the remaining sauce, reheated, on the side.

Serves 4 to 6.

BEER-AND-LIME SHORT RIBS WITH MUSTARD SAUCE

Beer and lime are a longtime Mexican drinking partnership. Together these ingredients provide a perfect match for marinated short ribs. Serve these ribs smoky hot with a cool mustard sauce on the side.

        4 pounds meaty beef ribs
        1 cup beer
        ½ cup lime juice
        3 egg yolks
       2½ tablespoons lemon juice
        ¼ cup Dijon mustard
        ½ cup olive oil
        2 tablespoons chopped fresh parsley
        2 teaspoons finely chopped chives
           Salt and freshly ground pepper
           Vegetable oil

1 · Place the ribs in a large shallow glass or ceramic dish.

2 · Combine the beer and lime juice. Pour this mixture over the ribs. Refrigerate covered overnight, turning several times. Let stand at room temperature 2 hours before cooking.,

3 · Meanwhile, in the large bowl of an electric mixer, beat the egg yolks with the lemon juice and mustard for 4 minutes. On low speed, slowly beat in the oil. The mixture will have the consistency of a thin mayonnaise. Stir in the parlsey, chives, and salt and pepper to taste. Chill thoroughly.

4 · Preheat the grill.

5 · Place the ribs on two large sheets of heavy-duty aluminum foil. Sprinkle each packet with 2 tablespoons marinade. Bring up the edges and seal.

6 · If using presoaked wood chips or chunks (chips for gas), sprinkle over the hot coals or lava rocks. Brush the grid lightly with vegetable oil.

7 · Place the foil-wrapped ribs on the grid. Cook covered with the vents open, until ribs are tender, 1¼ to 1½ hours. (If using a charcoal grill, add more lit coals after about 50 minutes.)

8 · Remove the ribs from the foil and drain. Grill the ribs, basting once with marinade, over medium coals until crisp, 15 to 20 minutes. Serve with the chilled mustard sauce.

Serves 4 to 6.

KOREAN "SEOUL" RIBS

In Korea, and in the trendier grilling establishments of the United States, short ribs are always served rare. It is a very different and untraditional chomp worth trying. Traditionalists, however, may cook them longer—as in the preceding recipes.

    4 pounds ribs, cut from the prime rib section
    4 large cloves garlic, crushed
    2 teaspoons grated fresh ginger root
    2 tablespoons sugar
    2 tablespoons peanut oil
    1 teaspoon dark sesame oil
    2 scallions, finely chopped
    ½ teaspoon crushed, dried hot red peppers
    2 tablespoons toasted white sesame seeds (see note)
    6 tablespoons soy sauce
       Vegetable oil

1 · Place the ribs in a large shallow glass or ceramic dish.

2 · Combine the garlic, ginger, sugar, peanut oil, sesame oil, scallions, hot peppers, sesame seeds, and soy sauce. Coat the ribs with this mixture. Let stand covered 4 hours.

3 · Preheat the grill.

4 · If using presoaked wood chips or chunks (chips for gas), or other flavorings, sprinkle them over the hot coals or lava rocks. Brush the grid lightly with vegetable oil.

5 · Grill the ribs over hot or high heat, turning often, for 8 to 10 minutes. The ribs should be on the "pink" side.

Serves 4 to 6.

Note: To toast sesame seeds, heat a large heavy skillet over medium-high heat. Add the sesame seeds and cook, shaking the pan constantly, until they are lightly browned.

Beef Kabobs

WHEN YOU GRILL beef on a skewer, bear in mind that cubes cut from either the loin or sirloin are the ideal choice. Since a 1¼-inch beef cube will grill in 12 to 14 minutes, it is essential to know the cooking times of any accompanying skewered vegetable. Make sure to check the basic vegetable chart on pages 234–35.

When handling a skewer on a grill, remember it will get *hot*! Use a long-handled tongs or insulated glove for turning. To make ka-bobing painless and to protect wooden skewer handles from burning, I spread coals over two-thirds of the grate, creating a cool spot on the *grid* where the handles may rest. While this practice is not an imperative with all braziers (as the edge of the unit is even with the grid), it comes in mighty handy with covered cookers—for the grid is almost always lower than the sides.

Everyone and his uncle has a favorite recipe for beef kabobs; three of mine follow.

NEW MEXICO CHILI-BOBS

Hot ground chile pepper and paprika team up with bacon and beef chunks for an unalloyed Albuquerque grilling treatment. Blanching the bacon in advance is a must to desalinate it and allow the two meats to cook properly in tandem.

> 4 ounces thick slab bacon, cut into 1¼-inch squares, ½ inch thick
> 1½ pounds sirloin (or other tender beef), trimmed of fat, cut into 1¼-inch cubes
> 3 tablespoons chili powder
> 1 teaspoon paprika
> Pinch of coriander
> Vegetable oil

1 · Cook the bacon squares in boiling water 5 minutes. Drain. Pat dry with paper towels.

2 · Pat the beef cubes dry and place in a medium bowl with the bacon squares.

3 · In a small bowl, combine the chili powder, paprika, coriander, and 3 tablespoons oil. Add to the meat mixture; toss thoroughly. Let stand covered 1 hour.

4 · Preheat the grill.

5 · Arrange the bacon squares alternately with beef cubes on skewers.

6 · If using presoaked wood chips or chunks (chips for gas), or other flavorings, sprinkle them over the hot coals or lava rocks. Brush the grid lightly with oil.

7 · Grill the kabobs over hot or high heat 2 minutes per side for rare, 3 minutes per side for medium-rare.

Serves 4.

CURRIED BEEF KABOBS

This version of a savory Eastern beef madras (usually grilled on a sword end) juxtaposes beef cubes with thick cuts of crisp apple and mushroom caps.

> 1½ pounds sirloin (or other tender beef), trimmed of fat, cut into 1¼-inch cubes
> 1 small clove garlic, crushed
> 2 teaspoons curry powder
> 1 teaspoon turmeric
> ¼ teaspoon ground cumin
> 3 tablespoons beer
> 8 medium mushroom caps, stems removed
> Vegetable oil
> 1 large tart green apple, peeled, cored, and cut into 8 wedges
> Juice of ½ lemon

1 · Pat the beef cubes dry and place in a medium bowl.

2 · In a small bowl, combine the garlic, curry powder, turmeric, cumin, and beer. Add to the meat; toss thoroughly. Let stand covered 1 hour.

3 · Brush the mushroom caps with vegetable oil. Set aside.

4 · Sprinkle the apple wedges with lemon juice. Set aside.

5 · Preheat the grill.

6 · Arrange the ingredients on the skewers in the following order: 1 mushroom cap (stem side up through the center of the cap), 1 beef cube, 1 apple wedge, 2 beef cubes, 1 apple wedge, 1 beef cube, and topped with another mushroom cap (stem side down).

7 · If using presoaked wood chips or chunks (chips for gas), or other flavorings, sprinkle them over the hot coals or lava rocks. Brush the grid lightly with oil.

8 · Grill the kabobs over hot or high heat about 2 minutes per side for rare, 3 minutes per side for medium-rare.

Serves 4.

GRILLED BEEF KABOBS CARIBBEAN STYLE

Coconut milk is another remarkable meat tenderizer, used in tropic climes for years. Try it as a marinade (with ginger, vodka, or light rum) for beef kabobs, interspersing the chunks with onions, cherry tomatoes, and wedges of coconut that toast while the meat grills. The extended marination time allows the beef to cook quickly.

     1½ pounds sirloin (or other tender beef), trimmed of fat, cut
           into 1¼-inch cubes
     ¾ cup fresh coconut milk (see note)
     ½ teaspoon ground ginger
     1 teaspoon crushed, dried hot red peppers
     ¼ cup vodka or light rum
     1 clove garlic
     8 medium white onions
     8 1½-inch pieces fresh coconut (see note)
    12 large cherry tomatoes
       Vegetable oil

1 · Place the beef cubes in a ceramic or glass dish.

2 · Combine the coconut milk, ginger, peppers, and vodka or rum. Pour over the meat. Place the garlic clove in center of meat. Marinate covered, stirring occasionally, 4 hours.

3 · Peel the onions and cut a cross in each root end to keep them from falling apart. Cook in boiling salted water 3 minutes. Rinse under cold running water; drain.

4 · Preheat the grill.

5 · Drain the meat and discard the garlic. Arrange the ingredients on the skewers in the following order: 1 piece coconut, 1 tomato, 1 beef cube, 1 onion, 1 beef cube, 1 tomato, 1 beef cube, 1 tomato, and, finally, 1 piece coconut.

6 · If using presoaked wood chips or chunks (chips for gas), or other flavorings, sprinkle them over the hot coals or lava rocks. Brush the grid lightly with oil.

7 · Grill the kabobs over hot or high heat about 2 minutes per side for rare, 3 minutes per side for medium-rare.

Serves 4.

Note: To prepare a fresh coconut for the above recipe, poke an ice pick through the eye of the coconut. Drain the coconut milk into a glass. Strain the milk through cheesecloth; reserve. Break the coconut shell with a hammer. Pare the coconut. Cut into 1½-inch pieces.

Beef Roast

WHEN YOU CHOOSE beef for outdoor roasting, *tender* is the optimum word to remember. And while no slice tops a prime rib to a prejudiced beef-lover's tongue, many lesser cuts of meat (eye round, for instance) actually improve in flavor and texture when roasted on an outdoor grill.

If you opt for the best (a standing rib roast), ask your butcher for ribs cut from the "small end," which are closest to the tender short loin (as opposed to the "large end" adjacent to the chuck). For even cooking, rib bones should never be more than 7 or 8 inches long. Make sure the chine bone, feather bones, and back strap are removed. It is standard practice to allow 1 large rib for every 2 people.

Rolled roasts are extremely easy to cook outdoors. The most desirable cuts are obviously taken from the rib roast or sirloin. But there are many other tonic (less pricey) options. Consider eye round, bottom round, rump, or arm (the front part of a shoulder roast).

Since beef roasts cook in a relatively short time, lightly grill the meat (to brown it) first over high heat. The roast should then be cover-cooked on a rack over indirect heat until done. Wine may be added to the drip pan—or even water with garlic cloves, for added savor. I use only hickory with roast beef, and just a speck at that. A good roast beef should not be overpowered by the smoke's flavor.

CLASSIC RIB ROAST

Long ago, I learned the quintessential way to prepare a rib roast. I acquired the knowledge when I worked in the kitchen at the legendary Store in Amagansett, on Long Island. The Store was the forerunner of today's myriad gourmet food shops. Rib roast, burnished to a fare-thee-well, but still rare to the fork, was a Store specialty daily. Curiously, my version on the grill, is very little changed.

> 1 3-rib standing rib roast
> Freshly ground pepper
> Vegetable oil
> Salt
> 2 medium white onions, sliced

1 · Preheat the grill.

2 · Rub the roast with freshly ground pepper to taste. Brush lightly with oil.

3 · Brush the grid lightly with oil.

4 · Grill the top and sides of the roast over hot or high heat to brown lightly. Remove from the heat. If using a charcoal grill, spread the hot coals apart and place a drip pan in the center. Add ½ inch water to the drip pan.

5 · If using presoaked wood chips or chunks (chips for gas), or other flavorings, sprinkle them over the hot coals or lava rocks.

6 · Place a roasting rack directly over the drip pan. If using a gas grill, place the drip pan with water directly underneath the rack on the grid. Place the roast on the rack so that the fatty side is up. Sprinkle the beef with salt. Lay the onion slices over the top. Cook covered, with the vents partially open, over medium heat 14 to 16 minutes per pound for rare, about 18 minutes per pound for medium-rare.

7 · To serve, remove the roast to a carving board. Let stand 10 minutes before carving.

Serves 6.

ANNA TERESA CALLEN'S TUSCAN BEEF ROAST

Anna Teresa Callen is one of the best Italian cooks and cookbook writers around. Her recipe for Arrosto di Manzo con la Senape alla Toscana (Beef Roast with Mustard Tuscan Style) was the basis for the following, wholly untraditional cover-cooked outdoor roast of beef.

1 boneless rib roast, about 3 pounds, tied
1 tablespoon Dijon mustard
3 tablespoons unsalted butter
1 tablespoon olive oil
2 tablespoons all-purpose flour
    Vegetable oil
½ cup red wine
    Salt and freshly ground pepper

1 · Pat the roast beef dry with paper towels. Spread the mustard over the meat with a butter knife.

2 · Preheat the grill.

3 · Heat the butter with the olive oil in a large skillet over medium heat just until the butter melts. Pour the mixture onto a cookie sheet or large platter. Sprinkle the flour over the meat, then roll in the butter mixture until well coated.

4 · Brush the grid lightly with vegetable oil.

5 · Grill the roast on all sides over hot or high heat to brown lightly. Remove from the heat. If using a charcoal grill, spread the hot coals apart and place a drip pan in the center. Add ¼ inch water and ¼ cup wine to the drip pan.

6 · If using presoaked wood chips or chunks (chips for gas), or other flavorings, sprinkle them over the hot coals or lava rocks.

7 · Place a roasting rack directly over the drip pan. If using a gas grill, place the drip pan with water and wine directly underneath the rack on the grid. Place the roast on the rack, fattiest side up. Sprinkle the beef with salt and pepper. Cook covered with the vents partially open over medium heat 16 to 18 minutes per pound for rare, about 20 minutes per pound for medium-rare. Pour the remaining ¼ cup wine over the meat after the first 30 minutes.

8 · To serve, remove the roast to a carving board. Let stand 10 minutes before carving.

Serves 6.

ON THE TRAIL OF SMOKE

Barbecue, whether it is advertised as bar-b-que, BBQ, or even bubba-cue, is a taste so inherently printed on America's taste buds that travelers by the thousands annually make pilgrimages to the South and Southwest to sample the genuine "old-fashioned, down-home, pit-smoked," article.

In Kansas City, Missouri, for instance, the trail to uncover the last great barbecue joints is a hegira worthy of the subterranean passages to view the Giotto frescos in Siena. More to the point, each advocate returns with a personally favored hostelry that is championed as the absolute best in the territory. Whether it be the Lexington Barbeque in Lexington, North Carolina, Maurice Bessinger's Piggie Park in West Columbia, South Carolina, Gridley's in Memphis, Arthur Bryant's in Kansas City, Sonny Bryan's in Dallas, or the Kreuz Market and Louie Mueller's, both outside of Austin— the search and the superlatives apparently never end.

One thing everyone seems to know, even without sampling a forkful, is that the best places for "the real stuff" are generally unobtrusive, low on decor if not downright shabby establishments. Many have dirt parking lots and rusting screen doors, not to mention dark, smoke-riddled interiors. Whether they are cafés or cafeterias, one thing is always certain. The food runs out well before nightfall, and the Johnny-come-lately is inevitably out of luck. But that doesn't faze a devotee. True aficionados simply line up earlier the next day, because barbecue is more than a place. It is an event that crosses all social and economic boundaries, just like Mother's Day, Apple Pie, and The Flag!

Poultry

ALL FOWL IS fair game on the grill. Chicken is the nation's top choice, naturally enough, since it broils to golden, crusty perfection in record time. And while whole, large birds (like turkey or oven stuffers) are best relegated to a smoker (see page 268), any small, firm-fleshed bird (like Cornish hen, squab, quail, or partridge, as well as chicken, of course) may be delectably roasted on a rack in a covered cooker, or sizzled to a fare-thee-well on a spit if you have a rotisserie attachment to your grill (see page 254).

Since poultry can dry out during the outdoor cooking process, a precautionary baste should be liberally applied before and during its stint over the fire. Remember, meat continues to cook when removed from the grill, so the internal temperature should be no more than 180 degrees when the poultry is deemed ready for transfer to the table. Roast chicken or hefty turkey breasts intended for carving should rest for about 10 minutes to let the meat firm up.

A prefatory note about flavoring poultry with wood smoke is in order. Fruitwoods, hickory, and mesquite are all highly compatible adjuncts to fowl. Note the chart on page 50 and mix and match at will. A general timing and cooking chart for poultry follows.

POULTRY CHART

TYPE OF POULTRY.	TECHNIQUE*.	TIMES AND SUGGESTIONS†.
CHICKEN		
PARTS	**Covered Cooking:** Hot, then medium-hot with direct heat.	Marinate chicken. Cook dark meat 30 minutes, basting and turning. Cook white meat 15 minutes, basting and turning.
HALVES	**Grilling:** Hot with direct heat for searing skin. Then **Covered Cooking** with indirect heat.	Marinate or stuff under the skin. Grill skin side down, 5 minutes. Cook covered, skin side up, 35 to 40 minutes.
WINGS	**Covered Cooking:** Medium-hot with direct heat.	Marinate wings. Cook 10 minutes per side.
WHOLE (3½ pounds)	**Covered Cooking:** Medium-hot with indirect heat.	Marinate or stuff chicken. Cook on a rack, basting occasionally, about 2 hours, or until internal temp. is 180°.
GAME BIRDS **ROCK CORNISH HENS**		
SPLIT	**Covered Cooking:** Hot with direct heat.	Marinate hens. Cook skin side down 10 minutes. Then skin side up about 15 minutes.
WHOLE	**Covered Cooking:** Medium-hot with direct heat.	Cook on a rack breast down, basting, for 15 minutes. Cook breast up, basting, 25 to 30 minutes, or until internal temp. is 180°.
SQUAB, QUAIL, GROUSE, PARTRIDGE (½ to ¾ pound)		
SPLIT	**Grilling:** Hot with direct heat. Then **Covered Cooking** with medium-hot direct heat.	Grill skin side down for 5 minutes to crisp skin. Cook covered, skin side up, 10 to 15 minutes.

WHOLE	**Covered Cooking:** Medium-hot with direct heat.	Cook on a rack breast down, basting, for 10 minutes. Cook breast up, basting, about 20 minutes.
TURKEY		
BREAST (4 to 5 pounds)	**Covered Cooking:** Medium-hot with indirect heat.	Marinate or season breast. Cook skin side up about 1½ hours.
FILETS	**Grilling:** Hot with direct heat.	Marinate. Grill 1 minute per side.
DRUMSTICK STEAK (pounded)	**Grilling:** Hot with direct heat.	Marinate. Grill about 2 minutes per side.
DUCKLING		
BREAST (boneless, halved, pounded)	**Grilling:** Hot with direct heat.	Marinate. Grill about 2 minutes per side. Serve pink at the center.
HALVES	**Covered Cooking:** Hot with direct heat.	Parboil in seasoned liquid. Cook skin side up 10 minutes. Cook skin side down 12 to 15 minutes.
WHOLE (4 to 5 pounds)	**Covered Cooking:** Medium-hot with indirect heat.	Pull all loose fat from duck. Poke fatty deposits with fork. Cook on a rack 25 minutes per each side, then breast up for about 1 hour.

* For gas or electric grills, use the high setting for hot, the medium setting for medium-hot. Use the cooler edges of the grid in case of flare-up.

For charcoal grills, hot refers to the 2-second hand test (see page 43). Use the 3- to 4-second test for medium-hot and the 5-second test for medium. To lower the temperature of coal, raise the grid, use the outside edges of the briquets, or cover with cover vents partially closed.

† Times may vary depending on outdoor temperature and velocity of wind.

Chicken

CHICKEN IS ONE of the most nourishing (and available) foods on the market today. Point of fact, a 3-ounce serving will provide about 30 percent of the average daily protein requirement for adults. And while the chicken industry has taken some flack recently from food critics who decry the generally pallid taste and high fat content of most commercially raised fowl, the outdoor grill is an amazing restorative for lackluster birds. Marinating supermarket chicken for several hours prior to the fire, as well as constant bastings during the cooking process, will create unexpected savor and succulence. The fat content, moreover, helps to keep the meat moist during cooking. But be advised, the use of a cover is mandatory to keep flames at bay.

As noted earlier, chicken can go dry on the grill, so it is imperative never to overcook it. Whole roasts, halves, and even quarters retain their natural juices better than individual pieces. Since many backyard chefs do serve pieces, however, it is crucial to cook the dark meat for 15 minutes before adding the white meat to the grill to circumvent the breast and wing portions from drying out before the legs and thighs are properly done.

Chicken should be cover-cooked over direct heat with some exceptions. Notably, whole birds that cook best slowly over indirect heat, and sweet-barbecue-sauced chickens that tend to blacken and burn—even with the cover in place. My solution to this problem is to cook sauced chicken over a drip pan until almost tender, and then to place it directly over the hot coals or lava rocks to crispen. (If you own a gas grill, set the drip pan directly on the lava rocks and add water-soaked chips to the pan.)

A lesser-known method that is highly effective when cooking more than one chicken involves the use of heavy-duty aluminum foil. First, sear the chicken pieces over hot or high heat until golden. (Use the cover in case of flare-up.) After removing the chicken from the grid, line the grid with heavy-duty aluminum foil. Brush *lightly* with oil, then poke ventilation holes in the foil every 2 or 3 inches apart. Return the chicken to the grid, slather it with sauce, and cook it covered until done.

Both methods are described in the following recipes, along with some wonderful variations on the theme. My elective here is wood chunks for the fire because they last longer during extended cooking times. However, chips will also do nicely. (A must for gas grills.)

STATE-OF-THE-ART "BARBECUED" CHICKEN
(*Method #1*)

This is it as far as I'm concerned. The use of a drip pan allows sufficient smoke to permeate the chicken before it crisps and darkens over the coals. (Be sure to stir up the coals and knock off the ash to raise the heat before you begin grilling.) There are many tonic moppin' barbecue sauces to choose from beginning on page 298. My preferences for the ultimate chicken feed are Nathalie Dupree's Coca-Cola Barbecue Sauce, All-American BBQ Sauce, Ohio Valley Soothing Syrup, Skitch Henderson's Tulsa Toppin', and Johnny Reb Sauce (see pages 299–302).

> 1 chicken, about 3½ pounds, cut into pieces
> Barbecue sauce (see above)
> Vegetable oil

1 · Place the chicken pieces in a large glass or ceramic dish. Spoon enough barbecue sauce over the pieces to coat (about ½ cup). Toss thoroughly. Let stand covered 4 hours.

2 · Preheat the grill.

3 · If using a charcoal grill, bank the coals on one end of the coal grate; place the drip pan on the other end. If using presoaked wood chips or chunks, sprinkle over the hot coals. If using a gas grill, place the drip pan on one side of the grill and add any presoaked wood chips to the pan. Brush the grid lightly with oil.

4 · Place the dark meat of the chicken on the grid over the drip pan. Cook covered with the vents open over hot or high beat, bast-

ing with extra sauce and turning once, for 15 minutes. Add the white meat to the grill and continue to cook covered, basting and turning once, until both meats are almost done, 10 to 15 minutes. (Juices will run slightly pink when pricked with a fork.)

5 · Remove the grid with the chicken and stir up the coals, knocking off the gray ash. Return the grid with the chicken. Baste the chicken and turn over. Grill until lightly crisped, about 5 minutes. Baste with extra sauce and turn over once more. Continue to grill until lightly crisped and the juices run yellow when pricked with a fork, 5 to 10 minutes longer. Serve with the remaining sauce (reheated) on the side.

Serves 2 to 4.

STATE-OF-THE-ART "BARBECUED" CHICKEN
(*Method #2*)

What follows is the foil technique, the only felicitous method for cooking for a crowd (more than one chicken). Drip pans won't work here because too many aluminum pans will cut off the heat source. Move the chicken around occasionally to prevent it from sticking to the foil.

　2 chickens, about 3 pounds each, cut into pieces
　　Vegetable oil
　　Barbecue sauce, doubled (see preceding recipe)

1 · Preheat the grill.

2 · Brush the chicken pieces lightly with oil.

3 · If using presoaked wood chips or chunks (chips for gas), sprinkle over the hot coals or lava rocks. Brush the grid lightly with oil.

4 · Sear the chicken over hot or high heat until golden, about 3 minutes per side. (Use the cover in case of flare-up.) Remove the chicken from the grid.

5 · Line the grid with heavy-duty aluminum foil and brush *lightly* with oil. Poke ventilation holes in the foil every 2 or 3 inches apart. Place the dark meat of the chicken skin side up on the foil and slather with barbecue sauce (about ½ cup). Cook covered with the vents open over medium-hot heat, basting with extra sauce and turning once, for 15 minutes. Add the white meat to the grill and

slather with sauce (about ½ cup). Cook covered, basting and turning once, until both meats are done and lightly crisped, 10 to 15 minutes. Serve with the remaining sauce (reheated) on the side.

Serves 6 to 8.

TANGY GRILLED CHICKEN

There are bastes ad infinitum for broiling chicken (see pages 287–98 for suggestions), but none pleases my palate more than the following Georgia rendition. It's a pass-along recipe from Pat Fusco, a Georgian in exile in Northern California.

  2 chickens, about 3 pounds each, cut into pieces
  1 teaspoon salt
  1 tablespoon Hungarian sweet paprika
 ¼ teaspoon cayenne pepper
 ¼ teaspoon dry mustard
 ½ teaspoon freshly ground pepper
 ⅓ cup water
  2 tablespoons Worcestershire sauce
 ⅓ cup red wine vinegar
 ¼ cup unsalted butter, cut into bits
   Vegetable oil

1 · Place the chicken pieces in a large shallow glass or ceramic dish.

2 · In a medium saucepan, combine the dry ingredients with the water. Heat to boiling; remove from heat. Add the Worcestershire sauce and vinegar. Stir in the butter. Pour over the chicken. Let stand 1 hour.

3 · Preheat the grill.

4 · If using presoaked wood chips or chunks (chips for gas), or other flavorings, sprinkle over the hot coals or lava rocks. Brush the grid lightly with oil.

5 · Place the dark meat of the chicken on the grid and cover-cook with the vents open over hot or high heat, basting often with extra sauce and turning once, for 15 minutes. Add the white meat to the grid and continue to cover-cook, basting often and turning once, until both meats are crisp and the juices run yellow when pricked with a fork, 15 to 20 minutes longer. (Remove cover and continue to grill if chicken is not adequately crisped.)

Serves 6 to 8.

GALVESTON GRILLED CHICKEN

From the nether end of Texas comes my favorite method of "air-drying, prior to grilling" chicken. The recipe stems from the well-known cooking teacher and chef, Mary Nell Reck. It is a winner in the tongue-sizzling sweepstakes. Bar none!

    2 small chickens, 2½ to 3 pounds each, cut into pieces
    1 lemon, cut in half
    6 cloves garlic, crushed
    1 tablespoon cayenne pepper
    2 tablespoons paprika
      Vegetable oil
      Salt

1 · Rub the chicken pieces with the lemon halves.

2 · In a small bowl, mash the garlic with the cayenne pepper and paprika to form a paste. Rub over the chicken pieces. Place the pieces skin side up on a rack in a shallow pan. Let stand in a cool place (do not refrigerate) uncovered for 24 hours.

3 · Preheat the grill.

4 · If using presoaked wood chips or chunks (chips for gas), or other flavorings, sprinkle over the hot coals or lava rocks. Brush the grid lightly with oil.

5 · Place the dark meat of the chicken on the grid and cover-cook with the vents open over hot or high heat, turning once, for 15 minutes. Add the white meat to the grid and continue to cover-cook, turning once, until both meats are crisp and the juices run yellow when pricked with a fork, 15 to 20 minutes longer. Sprinkle with salt before serving.

Serves 6 to 8.

GRILLED CHICKEN WITH HORSERADISH

Slavic peoples have known the virtue of horseradish as a season-
ing for poultry and fish for centuries. Teamed with lemon and all-
spice, the horseradish will burn off during the cooking, leaving a
zippy flavor that will have everyone guessing.

    1 chicken, about 3½ pounds, cut into pieces
    ½ cup prepared horseradish
    1 teaspoon finely slivered lemon peel
    2 teaspoons freshly ground pepper
    1 teaspoon crushed allspice berries
      Vegetable oil
    ¼ cup unsalted butter, melted

1 · Place the chicken pieces in a shallow glass or ceramic dish.

2 · In a small bowl, combine the horseradish, lemon peel, pepper, and allspice. Spoon this mixture over the chicken pieces. Toss
to coat. Let stand covered 4 hours.

3 · Preheat the grill.

4 · If using presoaked wood chips or chunks (chips for gas), or
other flavorings, sprinkle over the hot coals or lava rocks. Brush the
grid lightly with oil.

5 · Place the dark meat of the chicken on the grid and cover-
cook with the vents open over hot or high heat, basting often with
butter and turning once, for 15 minutes. Add the white meat to the
grid and continue to cover-cook, basting often with butter and
turning once, until both meats are crisp and the juices run yellow
when pricked with a fork, 15 to 20 minutes longer.

Serves 2 to 4.

GREEN CHILE GRILLED CHICKEN

This Southwestern specialty using mild green chiles is tingly rather than tongue burning. Choose the preroasted and peeled canned variety for ease. Hot peppers can be substituted if you must.

> 2 chickens, about 3 pounds each, cut into pieces
> 1 can (4 ounces) mild green chiles
> 2 teaspoons mild ground dried chiles or chili powder
> Vegetable oil
> Salt

1 · Place the chicken pieces in a shallow glass or ceramic dish.

2 · Combine the green chiles, dried chiles or chili powder, and ¼ cup vegetable oil in the container of a blender or food processor. Blend until smooth. Pour this mixture over the chicken. Toss the pieces to coat. Let stand covered 4 hours.

3 · Preheat the grill.

4 · If using presoaked wood chips or chunks (chips for gas), or other flavorings, sprinkle over the hot coals or lava rocks. Brush the grid lightly with oil.

5 · Place the dark meat of the chicken on the grid and cover-cook with the vents open over hot or high heat, turning once, for 15 minutes. Add the white meat to the grid and continue to cover-cook, turning once, until both meats are crisp and the juices run yellow when pricked with a fork, 15 to 20 minutes longer. Sprinkle with salt before serving.

Serves 6 to 8.

Mustard-Seeded Grilled Chicken

Mustard seeds, lime, and sesame oil are the unexpected components of one of the zestiest marinades I know. Allow the bird a good afternoon's soak prior to the fire.

> 1 chicken, about 3½ pounds, cut into pieces
> 1 clove garlic, crushed
> 1 teaspoon mustard seeds
> ½ teaspoon finely slivered lime peel
> ¼ cup lime juice
> ¼ cup sesame oil
>   Vegetable oil

1 · Place the chicken pieces in a shallow glass or ceramic dish.

2 · In a small bowl, combine the garlic, mustard seeds, lime peel, lime juice, and sesame oil. Pour over the chicken pieces. Toss the pieces to coat. Let stand covered 6 hours.

3 · Preheat the grill.

4 · If using presoaked wood chips or chunks (chips for gas), or other flavorings, sprinkle over the hot coals or lava rocks. Brush the grid lightly with oil.

5 · Place the dark meat of the chicken on the grid and cover-cook with the vents open over hot or high heat, basting with extra marinade and turning once, for 15 minutes. Add the white meat to the grid and continue to cover-cook, basting with marinade and turning once, until both meats are crisp and the juices run yellow when pricked with a fork, 15 to 20 minutes longer.

Serves 2 to 4.

GOLD-FLECKED GRILLED CHICKEN

What gilds a grilled fowl better than a dab of cornmeal in context with some fresh herbs and a dash of lemon juice? Nothing as far as I'm concerned. Use the cooler, outer edges of the grid for this one—to prevent the cornmeal from browning too quickly.

    1 chicken, about 3½ pounds, cut into pieces
    1 large clove garlic, crushed
    ¼ teaspoon freshly ground pepper
    ¼ teaspoon cayenne pepper
    ½ teaspoon fresh rosemary leaves minced, or ¼ teaspoon
         dried rosemary leaves, crushed
       Juice of 1 small lemon
    1 tablespoon yellow cornmeal
       Vegetable oil
       Salt

1 · Place the chicken pieces in a shallow glass or ceramic dish.

2 · In a small bowl, mash the garlic with the two peppers until smooth. Stir in the rosemary, lemon juice, cornmeal, and ¼ cup vegetable oil. Pour this mixture over the chicken. Toss the pieces to coat. Let stand uncovered 1 hour.

3 · Preheat the grill.

4 · If using presoaked wood chips or chunks (chips for gas), or other flavorings, sprinkle over the hot coals or lava rocks. Brush the grid lightly with oil.

5 · Place the dark meat of the chicken on the grid and cover-cook over medium-hot heat, basting with extra marinade and turning once, for 15 minutes. Add the white meat to the grid and continue to cover-cook, basting with marinade and turning once, until both meats are crisp and the juices run yellow when pricked with a fork, 15 to 20 minutes longer. Sprinkle with salt before serving.

Serves 2 to 4.

BLOODY-MARY GRILLED CHICKEN

Down South, they warn the guy at the grill to never quaff a drink that can't be used to douse a sudden conflagration. I don't think there is a better libation for the purpose than a properly made Bloody Mary. The chicken seems to like it as well.

    2 chickens, about 3 pounds each, cut into pieces
    ¾ cup V-8 juice
    ¼ cup vodka
    1 teaspoon prepared horseradish
    1 teaspoon lemon juice
    ½ teaspoon soy sauce
       Dash of hot pepper sauce
       Vegetable oil

1 · Place the chicken pieces in a shallow glass or ceramic dish.

2 · In a medium bowl, combine the V-8 juice, vodka, horserad-ish, lemon juice, soy sauce, and hot pepper sauce. Pour this mixture over the chicken pieces. Let stand covered 4 hours.

3 · Preheat the grill.

4 · If using presoaked wood chips or chunks (chips for gas), or other flavorings, sprinkle over the hot coals or lava rocks. Brush the grid lightly with oil.

5 · Place the dark meat of the chicken on the grid and cover-cook over medium-hot heat, basting with extra marinade and turn-ing once, for 15 minutes. Add the white meat to the grid and con-tinue to cover-cook, basting with marinade and turning once, until both meats are crisp and the juices run yellow when pricked with a fork, 15 to 20 minutes longer.

Serves 6 to 8.

GRILLED CHICKEN HALVES WITH GOAT CHEESE

Chicken halves, judiciously stuffed under the skin with goat cheese and snippets of dried tomato, make the most elegant outdoor fare imaginable. Patience is a prime virtue to this dish's assembly. Loosen the skin near the back of each chicken half and gently force your fingers under the remaining skin to loosen. Do not break the natural bond that runs along the front of the breast, or the stuffing will melt out. My favored goat cheese is a mild French Montrachet. My choice of dried tomato? Genovesi, packed in oil and seasonings, from Dayton, Ohio.

    1 chicken, about 3½ pounds
    2 ounces mild goat cheese (about 6 tablespoons)
    4 teaspoons finely chopped dried tomatoes in oil
    2 teaspoons chopped fresh basil
      Vegetable oil

1 · Remove the backbone from the chicken and cut in half through the breast. Gently loosen the skin near the back of each half and force your fingers under the skin to loosen around the breast, thigh, and leg areas. Do not puncture the connective tissue along the front of the breast.

2 · Crumble the goat cheese into a small bowl and add the tomatoes and basil. Mash with the back of a spoon to form a paste. Spread this mixture evenly under the skin of each chicken, forcing it around the leg, thigh, and breast. Let stand covered in a cool place 1 hour.

3 · Preheat the grill.

4 · Brush the grid lightly with oil.

5 · Grill the chicken halves, skin side down over medium-hot heat to brown lightly, 4 to 5 minutes. Remove from the heat. If using a charcoal grill, spread the hot coals apart and place a drip pan in the center. For gas, place the drip pan on the lava rocks.

6 · If using presoaked wood chips or chunks (chips for gas), or other flavorings, sprinkle them over the hot coals or lava rocks.

7 · Return the chicken to the grid, skin side up, directly over the drip pan. Cook covered with the vents half open until the juices run yellow when pricked with a fork, 35 to 40 minutes. Let stand about 5 minutes before serving.

Serves 4.

HUMMUS GRILLED CHICKEN HALVES

Hummus is a remarkably tasty Arabian hors d'oeuvre concocted of sesame seed puree and softened chick-peas. Denizens of the Persian Gulf stuff this creamy stuff into pita bread. But it is also the basis for the most delectable chicken you will ever sample. In this case, the chicken halves are cover-cooked over direct heat, as the hummus coating prevents the meat from burning.

    2 chickens, about 3 pounds each
    4 large cloves garlic
    4 tablespoons white sesame seeds
    6 tablespoons olive oil
    1 cup canned chick-peas
       Juice of 1 large lemon
    1 tablespoon chopped fresh parsley
    ¼ teaspoon salt
    1 teaspoon dark sesame oil
       Freshly ground pepper
       Vegetable oil

1 · Remove the backbones from the chickens and cut in half through the breast. Set aside.

2 · In the container of a food processor or blender, place the garlic cloves, sesame seeds, and 2 tablespoons olive oil. Process until smooth. Add the chick-peas, lemon juice, parsley, and salt. Process once more. Slowly add the remaining 4 tablespoons olive oil and the sesame oil. Spread this mixture over the chicken halves. Sprinkle well with pepper. Let stand covered 4 hours.

3 · Preheat the grill.

4 · If using presoaked wood chips or chunks (chips for gas), or other flavorings, sprinkle them over the hot coals or lava rocks. Brush the grid lightly with oil.

5 · Place the chicken halves on the grid and cook covered over medium-hot heat, turning once until juices run yellow when pricked with a fork, 40 to 50 minutes.

Serves 8.

TWICE-COOKED CHICKEN HALVES

Though some barbecue pundits regularly suggest an indoor oven and outdoor grill in tandem for preparing a meal, I have always scrupulously avoided that stratagem. There is one exception to every rule. And the dish that follows is definitely mine. It's a classic Italian offering from Tuscany. Oven baking prior to the grill gives the chicken a new and totally unusual texture that makes it worth the extra bother.

1 chicken, about 3½ pounds
1 large clove garlic, crushed
1 tablespoon chopped fresh sage leaves
2 tablespoons olive oil
  Salt and freshly ground pepper
  Vegetable oil

1 · Remove the backbone from the chicken and cut in half through the breast. Gently loosen the skin near the back of each half and force your fingers under the skin to loosen around the breast, thigh, and leg areas. Do not puncture the connective tissue along the front of the breast.

2 · In a small bowl, mash the garlic with the sage leaves, and 1 tablespoon olive oil with the back of a spoon to form a paste. Spread this mixture evenly under the skin of each chicken half, forcing it around the leg, thigh, and breast. Let stand covered 1 hour.

3 · Place the chicken halves, skin side up, in a lightly greased shallow baking dish. Brush the tops lightly with olive oil. Sprinkle with salt and pepper to taste. Bake in a preheated 350-degree oven, basting occasionally with pan juices, until barely tender, about 45 minutes.

4 · Meanwhile, preheat the grill.

5 · If using presoaked wood chips or chunks (chips for gas), or other flavorings, sprinkle them over the hot coals or lava rocks. Brush the grid lightly with vegetable oil.

6 · Transfer the chicken halves to a plate and brush lightly with olive oil. Grill uncovered over hot or high heat until golden brown, 3 to 4 minutes per side.

Serves 2 to 4.

BUNNY'S WINGS

My good friend Bunny August is a nutritionist with a taste for off-beat food combinations. One of her inventions for broiled fowl was such a winner I appropriated it after the first bite. It's ideal for cooking up a batch of chicken wings. Serve it as hot as you dare—with a soothing red currant sauce to combat the "fire."

2¼ pounds large chicken wings (about 12)
1 cup fresh bread crumbs
2 tablespoons freshly grated Parmesan cheese
1 tablespoon sesame seeds
½ cup unsalted butter, melted
½ to 1 teaspoon hot pepper sauce (or to taste)
½ cup currant jelly
½ teaspoon Dijon mustard
3 tablespoons orange juice
2 tablespoons dry sherry
⅛ teaspoon Worcestershire sauce
Pinch of ground ginger
Vegetable oil

1 · With a sharp knife, remove the bony tips of the chicken wings. Save the tips for use in stock.

2 · Preheat the grill.

3 · Combine the bread crumbs, cheese, and sesame seeds in a shallow bowl. Mix well. Combine the butter with the hot pepper sauce in another shallow bowl. Dip the chicken wings into the butter mixture and roll in the bread-crumb mixture.

4 · In a medium saucepan combine the currant jelly, mustard, orange juice, sherry, Worcestershire sauce, and ginger. Heat, stirring constantly, to boiling. Reduce heat. Simmer 5 minutes. Keep warm.

5 · Transfer the chicken wings to a lightly oiled, hinged grill basket.

6 · If using presoaked wood chips or chunks (chips for gas), or other flavorings, sprinkle them over the hot coals or lava rocks. Brush the grid lightly with oil.

7 · Place the wing-filled basket on the grid and rest the cover with the vents open on top. Cover-cook, turning once, until wings are crisp and the juices run yellow when pricked with a fork, 25 to 30 minutes. (Close the vents if the wings are browning too quickly.) Serve with the currant sauce as a dip.   *Serves 3 to 4.*

ROSE LEVY BERANBAUM'S TANDOORI CHICKEN "DRUMS"

Master baker Rose Beranbaum (founder of the Cordon Rose Cooking School in New York) developed this recipe for chicken wings masquerading as drumsticks after spending a month in India. Rose uses only the largest joint of the wing for her "drums," but I added the meaty intermediate joint as well and call this version "drums and thumbs." It is so authentic tasting one could believe it came from a true tandoori brick oven, rather than your own grill. Do not be dismayed by the touch of red food coloring. Indians use cochineal. The fiery hue is essential for the proper look of the dish. Serve it with the Raita Sauce.

> 3 pounds chicken wings
> 2 tablespoons lemon juice
> 2 tablespoons lime juice
> 2 teaspoons salt
> ½ cup plain yoghurt
> 2 medium cloves garlic, quartered
> 1 teaspoon minced ginger root
> ½ teaspoon cumin seeds
> ½ teaspoon ground coriander
> ¼ teaspoon turmeric
> ½ teaspoon cayenne pepper
> ¼ teaspoon freshly ground pepper
> ⅛ teaspoon ground cinnamon
>   Pinch of ground cloves
> ½ teaspoon red food coloring
> ¼ teaspoon water
>   Vegetable oil
>   Raita Sauce (see page 318)

1 · Discard the tips from the chicken wings. Cut the remaining chicken wings apart at the joint. Place the middle wing sections in a large shallow glass or ceramic dish. Prepare the remaining wing sections in the following manner. Using a sharp knife, cut through the filaments around the small end of each piece. Then scrape the meat down the bone until it covers the end of the bone. The chicken will have turned inside out and formed a ball. Add to the dish with the middle wing sections. Sprinkle with lemon and lime juice.

2 · Place all ingredients from the 2 teaspoons salt through the

pinch of ground cloves in the container of a blender or food processor. Blend until smooth. Pour over the wings. Refrigerate covered overnight. Let stand at room temperature 1 hour before grilling.

3 · Preheat the grill.

4 · Remove the chicken pieces from the marinade and place on a large ceramic platter. In a small glass bowl, combine the red food coloring with the water. Lightly brush over both sides of each wing piece.

5 · Transfer the chicken pieces to a lightly oiled, hinged grill basket.

6 · If using presoaked wood chips or chunks (chips for gas), sprinkle them over the hot coals or lava rocks. Brush the grid lightly with oil.

7 · Place the wing-filled basket on the grid and rest the cover with the vents open on top. Cover-cook, turning once, until wings are crisp and the juices run yellow when pricked with a fork, 25 to 30 minutes. (Close the vents if the wings are browning too quickly.) Serve with the Raita Sauce as a dip.

Serves 4 to 6.

FIRE-ROASTED BAYOU BIRD

In Louisiana, where jambalaya is consumed prodigiously, left-overs often find their way into the next day's meal—notably as chicken stuffing. In this outdoor translation, wine is added to the drip pan to keep the bird moist. If you use a charcoal grill, additional heated coals will be needed to complete the cooking process—so have them ready to add every 45 minutes or so.

For the stuffing

1 tablespoon unsalted butter
2 teaspoons vegetable oil
1 large shallot, minced
1 tablespoon pine nuts (pignolias)
½ red or yellow bell pepper, cut into thin strips
½ pound small fresh shrimp, shelled and deveined
1 cup cooked rice
1 teaspoon finely slivered lemon peel
Juice of 1 lemon
Salt and freshly ground pepper

1 roasting chicken, about 3½ pounds
1 clove garlic, bruised
Vegetable oil
2 cups white wine
1 cup water

1 · To make the stuffing: Heat the butter with the oil in a medium skillet over medium heat. Add the shallot and pine nuts; cook until golden, about 5 minutes. Add the pepper strips and shrimp; cook, tossing constantly, until the shrimp turn pink, about 3 minutes. Transfer to a medium bowl and add the rice, lemon peel, lemon juice, and salt and pepper to taste.

2 · Preheat the grill.

3 · Wipe the chicken inside and out with paper towels. Rub inside and out with bruised garlic. Spoon the stuffing into the cavity. Sew and truss. Brush the top and sides lightly with oil.

4 · If using a charcoal grill, spread the hot coals apart and place a drip pan in the center. Add the wine and water to the drip pan.

5 · If using presoaked wood chips or chunks (chips for gas), or other flavorings, sprinkle them over the hot coals or lava rocks.

6 · Place a roasting rack directly over the drip pan. If using a gas grill, place the drip pan with wine and water directly underneath the rack on the grid. Place the chicken on the rack, breast side up. Cook covered with vents half open until the juices run yellow when pricked with a fork, 1½ to 2 hours. Let stand 10 minutes before serving.

Serves 2 to 4.

CHICKEN MIXED GRILL

In Argentina, where barbecue bashes are a common form of socializing, a mixed grill usually means chicken, beef, and sausage—in concert. The heady chimichurri (hot chile) marinade used for basting during cooking, and dipping later, is often dubbed "the sauce of life." The sauce here is an adaptation of a recipe for chimichurri that ran in Sphere *magazine way back in 1976.*

For the Argentinian Chimichurri Marinade

  ½ cup vegetable oil
  ½ cup malt vinegar
  ¼ cup water
  2 tablespoons chopped fresh parsley
  3 large cloves garlic, minced
  1 teaspoon cayenne pepper
  1 teaspoon salt
1½ teaspoons chopped fresh oregano leaves
  ½ teaspoon freshly ground pepper

  1 chicken, about 3 pounds cut into pieces
  1 pound sirloin beef, cut into 1¼-inch cubes
  6 sweet Italian sausages
    Vegetable oil

1 · To make the chimichurri marinade: Combine all ingredients in a glass jar with a tight-fitting lid. Let stand at room temperature for 24 hours.
2 · Place the chicken pieces in a shallow glass or ceramic dish; coat lightly with marinade. Let stand covered 3 hours.

3 · Place the beef cubes and sausages in separate shallow glass or ceramic dishes; coat lightly with marinade. Let stand covered 1 hour.

4 · Preheat the grill.

5 · If using a charcoal grill, bank the coals on one end of the coal grate; place the drip pan on the other end. If using presoaked wood chips or chunks, sprinkle over the hot coals. If using a gas grill, place the drip pan on one side of the grill directly on the lava rocks and add any presoaked chips to the pan. Brush the grid lightly with oil.

6 · Place the dark meat over *direct heat* and cover-cook with the vents open, basting with extra sauce and turning once, 15 minutes. Add the white meat and cover-cook 5 minutes. Place the sausages over the drip pan and continue to cover-cook, basting and turning the chicken once, for 10 minutes.

7 · Meanwhile, place the beef cubes on skewers.

8 · Remove the drip pan from the grill and stir up the coals, knocking off the gray ash if using charcoal. Place the beef cubes and sausages over the hottest part of the coals and move the chicken pieces to the cooler edges. Grill the sausages and beef cubes, turning often, until done, about 15 minutes. Serve on a platter with individual bowls of the remaining sauce.

Serves 4 to 6.

Game Birds

To most American palates, game birds are synonymous with widely available Rock Cornish game hens. In fact, that's a misnomer. Called "game hens" by the purveyors, these birds are actually a twentieth-century crossbreed of Cornish game-cocks and Plymouth Rock hens. The Cornish hen is a delectable fowl, all white meat and tender. It generally averages about 1¼ pounds in weight. I invariably serve one whole bird per person, but most hosts will find that half is sufficient if the menu is ample.

True guinea hens, though now commercially raised, were first introduced into Europe from Africa in the sixteenth century and eventually found their way to America. Smaller in size and mostly white fleshed, these fowls have a slightly gamy taste that makes them eminently suitable for the grill. But they are rich. Despite their size, most diners won't eat more than one.

Another, once-wild, now USDA-approved bird, is squab. Squabs weigh anywhere from ¾ pound to 1¼ pounds. The meat is darker and decidedly stronger-flavored. Squab is sometimes called dove or pigeon in fancy meat markets.

Though partridge, quail, and grouse are raised commercially in limited quantities across the United States, most are still shot in the wild and are rather high-flavored for everyday tastebuds. Like my own. But there are aficionados who truly dote on them. Since the average weight of these birds is about half a pound, two per person is the requisite.

The following recipes were designed with Cornish hens in mind—largely because they are the most economical and popular game birds in the marketplace. All are interchangeable with wilder varieties—but note that due to size, cooking times must be abbreviated. Use chunks, chips, or herbs for flavoring.

POLLO STRELLA ALLA DIAVOLO
(Deviled Cornish Hen)

This devilishly easy recipe was invented by Vicénte Funes, the Argentine-born chef/owner of Graziella Restaurant in New York's Greenwich Village. Do not stint on the day-and-a-half marinating period or the hen will suffer for it.

    2 Cornish hens (see note)
    1 cup olive oil
    ½ teaspoon cayenne pepper
    1 teaspoon coarse salt
    1 tablespoon freshly ground pepper
       Vegetable oil

1 · With a sharp knife, split the hens down the breast and flatten. Tuck in the wings.

2 · Pour half the olive oil in the bottom of a shallow glass or ceramic dish. Place the hens in the oil, breast side down. Pour the remaining olive oil over the top, making sure that all the flesh is well coated. Refrigerate covered 36 hours.

3 · Combine the cayenne pepper, salt, and black pepper in a small bowl. Remove the hens from the oil; sprinkle the pepper mixture generously over both sides. Rub in. Let stand 1 hour.

4 · Preheat the grill.

5 · If using presoaked wood chips or chunks (chips for gas), or other flavorings, sprinkle them over the hot coals or lava rocks. Brush the grid lightly with oil.

6 · Place the Cornish hens, skin side down on the grid. Cover-cook over hot or high heat with the vents open, 10 minutes. (If the skin is not crisp enough, briefly remove the cover.) Turn the hens over and continue to cover-cook until the juices run yellow when pricked with a fork, about 15 minutes longer.

Serves 2.

Note: Because of the long marination, Guinea hens, squab, and quail are excellent substitutes. However, grill uncovered to crispen the skin before turning. Cover-cook until done to your liking, 15 to 20 minutes in all.

SMOKED AND SLIGHTLY SIZZLED GAME HENS

A Thai inspiration, the next hen devise is also long marinated (overnight), then basted as it sizzles. What gives the dish its added dimension, however, is a glaze of sesame oil–based sauce applied after the flame. Note that the use of a drip pan increases the cooking time dramatically and that the timing has been increased because game hens are cooked over indirect heat.

    2 Cornish hens (see note)

For the marinade

    Peel of 1 lemon
    Peel of 1 orange
  ½ cup soy sauce
  ½ cup oyster sauce
  ½ teaspoon chopped ginger root
    2 cloves garlic
    1 tablespoon chopped fresh cilantro (Chinese parsley)
  ¼ teaspoon freshly ground pepper
    1 small bay leaf
    2 tablespoons honey

For the sauce

    2 teaspoons vegetable oil
    1 large clove garlic, minced
    1 teaspoon minced ginger root
  ¼ teaspoon crushed, dried hot red peppers
    2 shallots, minced
    1 green onion, minced
    1 tablespoon soy sauce
    1 teaspoon red wine vinegar
    2 tablespoons brown sugar
 1½ tablespoons water
    2 tablespoons sesame oil

    Vegetable oil

   1 · Cut away the backbones from the hens and press the hens flat.
   2 · Combine the ingredients for the marinade in a blender container. Blend until smooth. Pour half the mixture over the bottom

of a shallow glass or ceramic dish. Place the hens, skin side down, in the marinade. Pour remaining marinade over the top. Refrigerate covered overnight. Remove from refrigerator 1 hour before cooking.

3 · Preheat the grill.

4 · Meanwhile to make the sauce: Combine all sauce ingredients through the water in a small saucepan. Heat to boiling; reduce heat. Simmer over medium-low heat 4 minutes. Strain into a heatproof bowl. Stir in the oil. Let stand in a warm place to prevent the sauce from congealing.

5 · If using a charcoal grill, bank the coals on one end of the coal grate; place the drip pan on the other end. If using presoaked wood chips or chunks, sprinkle over the hot coals. If using a gas grill, place the drip pan on one side of the grill directly on the lava rocks and add any presoaked wood chips to the pan. Brush the grid lightly with oil.

6 · Place the hens, skin side up, directly over the drip pan and cover-cook over medium-hot heat, basting every 15 minutes with marinade, until almost done, 1 to 1¼ hours. (Add more heated coals after 45 minutes if using a charcoal grill.)

7 · Remove the grid with the hens and stir up the coals, knocking off the gray ash. Return the grid and grill the hens until almost blackened, about 5 minutes per side. Transfer to a serving platter; brush with the sauce.

Serves 2.

Note: This recipe is excellent with all game birds. Reduce cooking time to about 45 minutes.

THE SILO GAME BIRDS

The following apricot-sauced bird is a culinary collaboration between Ruth and Skitch Henderson. While Skitch conducts (and not just the cookouts), Ruth runs a fabulous cooking school/gourmet cookware shop in a renovated barn, named The Silo, in New Milford, Connecticut. Together, they have orchestrated a winner. (Note that the foil method is used here to prevent the sauce from burning.)

   4 small Cornish hens (see note)
     Half a lemon
1½ tablespoons coarse salt
   1 teaspoon finely minced fresh sage
   ½ teaspoon minced chives
   ¼ teaspoon ground mild paprika or mild ground chiles
   ⅛ teaspoon cayenne pepper
   1 jar (12 ounces) apricot preserves
   ½ cup chicken stock
   1 tablespoon soy sauce
   1 tablespoon Dijon mustard
   ½ teaspoon chopped fresh thyme
   1 teaspoon finely grated lemon peel
   ½ teaspoon freshly ground pepper
     Vegetable oil

1 · Cut away the backbones from the hens and press the hens flat.

2 · Rub the hens with half a lemon; sprinkle with the salt, sage, chives, paprika or mild ground chiles, and cayenne pepper. Rub in. Place in a shallow glass or ceramic dish and refrigerate covered overnight. Let stand at room temperature 1 hour before cooking.

3 · Combine the apricot preserves, chicken stock, soy sauce, mustard, thyme, lemon peel, and pepper in a medium saucepan. Heat to boiling; reduce heat. Simmer 5 minutes. Set aside.

4 · Preheat the grill.

5 · If using presoaked wood chips or chunks (chips for gas), or other flavorings, sprinkle them over the hot coals or lava rocks. Lightly brush the grid with oil.

6 · Sear the hens over hot or high heat until well browned on both sides, about 4 minutes per side. Remove the hens from the grid.

7 · Line the grid with heavy-duty aluminum foil and brush *lightly* with oil. Poke ventilation holes in the foil every 2 or 3 inches apart. Return the hens, skin side up, to the grid and slather with the apricot mixture. Cover-cook, basting often with apricot mixture until the juices run yellow when pricked with a fork, 30 to 40 minutes.

Serves 4.

Note: Squab or pheasant are compatible with the fruit sauce in this recipe. Reduce the covered-cooking time to about 20 minutes.

ROASTED WALLBANGER HENS

If you ever had a Harvey Wallbanger (a serious screwdriver with a head of Galliano), you know the drink sneaks up on you. Though all alcohol burns off during the covered-cooking process a Wallbanger marinade will turn even the gamiest bird tame.

2 Cornish hens (see note)
¾ cup orange juice
3 ounces vodka
2 tablespoons Galliano
2 large curls orange peel

1 · Wipe the Cornish hens inside and out with paper towls. Place breast side down in a large glass or ceramic bowl.

2 · Combine the orange juice, vodka, and Galliano. Pour over the hens. Let stand covered 1 hour.

3 · Preheat the grill.

4 · Remove the hens from the marinade and place an orange curl in each cavity.

5 · If using presoaked wood chips or chunks (chips for gas), or other flavorings, sprinkle them over the hot coals or lava rocks.

6 · Place a large roasting rack on the grid. Place the hens on the rack, breast side down, and cover-cook over medium-hot heat with the vents half open, 15 minutes. Baste with extra marinade and turn breast side up. Continue to cover-cook, basting occasionally, until the juices run yellow when pricked with a fork, 25 to 30 minutes.

Serves 2.

Note: Perfect for any game hen. Reduce cooking time to a total of 30 minutes.

SOPHIE'S HENS AND PORK

The next recipe is a bequest from a lady named Sophie. A friend of a friend's deceased mother, she was obviously a heck of a cook. Her recipe, by way of Cincinnati, is a tantalizing combination of pork and fowl.

    2 Cornish hens
    4 boneless pork loin chops, about ¾ inch thick
    3 cloves garlic, crushed
    6 tablespoons soy sauce
 1½ teaspoons Hungarian paprika
    2 teaspoons seasoned salt
    6 tablespoons unsalted butter, melted
      Vegetable oil

1 · Cut away the backbones from the hens and press the hens flat. Place skin side up in a large shallow dish with the pork chops.

2 · Combine the garlic, soy sauce, paprika, salt, and butter in a medium bowl. Mix well. Pour over hens and chops. Let stand covered 2 hours.

3 · Preheat the grill.

4 · If using presoaked wood chips or chunks (chips for gas), or other flavorings, sprinkle them over the hot coals or lava rocks. Lightly brush the grid with oil.

5 · Sear the chops over hot or high heat 1 minute per side. Set aside.

6 · Place the hens on the grill skin side down. Cover-cook over medium-hot heat with the vents open, 10 minutes. Baste the hens and turn over. Add the pork chops and baste both meats. Continue to cover-cook, basting and turning the pork chops once, until both meats are done, 15 to 16 minutes. Serve half a hen and 1 chop to each person.

Serves 4.

Turkey

    UP UNTIL A few short years ago, no American ever thought of eating turkey before Thanksgiving, and particularly not in warm weather. Though why, I have no idea, since that succulent staple of the holidays was actually domesticated by the Aztec, Maya, and Inca Indians during the summer and invariably fire-roasted at first harvest in July. Nowadays we do not even have to wait *that* long for a drumstick. Fresh or frozen commercially raised turkey is available at supermarkets year round—and outdoor cookery makes its preparation a virtual breeze. More to the point, it's good for us.

Turkey is extremely rich in vitamin B, higher in protein than chicken, and lower in serum cholesterol than any other fowl. It is also low in fat content. Which is a plus for dieters, but necessitates a watchful eye on the grill to keep the tender meat from drying out.

A whole turkey, even a small bird (8 to 10 pounds), cannot be successfully roasted in most conventional covered cookers because the elevation from grid to inside cover rarely exceeds 8 inches. Although small turkeys can be effectively grill-roasted on some gas grills and rotisseries, in my mind preparing a turkey in a water smoker provides the ultimate taste sensation in terms of color, texture, and downright juiciness (see page 275).

These days, fresh turkey cuts (breasts, whole and fileted, and drumsticks, whole or pounded into steaks) may be found at meat counters everywhere. They are all perfect foils for a grill: elegant but inexpensive dinner options all summer long.

I use wood chunks with a whole breast, chips with the faster-cooking filets and drumstick steaks.

GRILLED TURKEY BREAST WITH GINGERED RHUBARB SAUCE

My classic way to prepare a turkey breast (whole) is to marinate it in oil and spices for at least 6 hours prior to the grill. If you opt for skinned, boned halves to save time, marinate for 1 hour and grill for a scant 9 minutes per side. The accompanying Gingered Rhu-

130

barb Sauce complements either version perfectly. A five-pound turkey breast, bone in, will take 1½ to 2 hours to cook, so charcoal users should have partially lit coals on hand to add to the fire after the first 45 minutes.

    Vegetable oil
½ teaspoon ground mace
½ teaspoon crushed allspice berries
1 whole turkey breast, bone in (about 5 pounds)

Gingered Rhubarb Sauce

1½ cups chopped rhubarb (fresh or frozen)
¼ cup orange juice
¾ cup sugar
1 teaspoon freshly grated ginger root

½ cup unsalted butter, melted

1 · In a small bowl, combine 2 tablespoons vegetable oil with the mace and allspice. Rub this mixture over the turkey breast. Let stand covered in a cool place 6 hours.

2 · Meanwhile, to make the Gingered Rhubarb Sauce: Combine all ingredients for the sauce in a medium saucepan. Heat to boiling; reduce heat. Simmer over medium-low heat, stirring occasionally, until tender and thickened, but not too thick, about 20 minutes. Set aside to cool.

3 · Preheat the grill.

4 · If using a charcoal grill, spread the hot coals apart and place a drip pan in the center. Sprinkle any presoaked wood chips or chunks, or other flavorings, over the coals. For gas grills, place the drip pan on the lava rocks and add any presoaked flavorings directly to the pan. Brush the grid lightly with oil.

5 · Place the turkey breast on the grid over the drip pan. Cover-cook, basting occasionally with melted butter, with the vents halfway open until the juices run yellow when pricked with a fork, about 1½ hours.

6 · To serve, transfer the breast to a carving board. Let stand 10 minutes. Carve the breast into thin slices and serve with the Gingered Rhubarb Sauce (at room temperature or slightly chilled).

Serves 4 to 6.

TURKEY SCALLOPS IN BALSAMIC VINEGAR

Fresh turkey filet is one "fast food" the whole family can enjoy without any guilt. The next dish grills quicker than you can say "Big Mac." It's easy to prepare too, merely sprinkled with oil and vinegar. Best if it's rich balsamic vinegar from the Emilia-Romagna region of Italy. As the filets sear in minutes, they must be thin. Pound them if necessary.

   6 turkey filets, pounded thin
  ¾ teaspoon olive oil
1½ tablespoons balsamic vinegar
    Salt and freshly ground pepper
    Vegetable oil

1 · Lay the turkey breasts on a large sheet of wax paper.

2 · Combine the olive oil and the vinegar in a small bowl. Brush over the top side of the filets. Sprinkle with salt and pepper. Turn the filets over and brush with oil and vinegar; sprinkle with salt and pepper. Cover with another sheet of wax paper. Let stand 1 hour.

3 · Preheat the grill.

4 · If using presoaked wood chips or chunks (chips for gas), or other flavorings, sprinkle them over the hot coals or lava rocks. Brush the grid lightly with oil.

5 · Grill the turkey filets over hot or high heat 1 minute per side.

Serves 4 to 6.

GRILLED TURKEY FILETS OR STEAKS
IN CRANBERRY MUSTARD

Cranberry is, of course, a perfect taste matchup to turkey. Combined with country-style Dijon mustard (with seeds), it seems like Thanksgiving in July. Use either fresh filets or pounded drumstick steaks.

6 turkey filets, or drumstick steaks, pounded thin
4 teaspoons country-style Dijon mustard (with seeds)
2 tablespoons cranberry juice
Salt and freshly ground pepper
Vegetable oil

1 · Lay the filets or steaks on a large sheet of wax paper.

2 · Combine the mustard and the cranberry juice. Brush over the top side of the turkey. Sprinkle with salt and pepper. Turn the turkey pieces over and brush with remaining mustard mixture. Sprinkle with salt and pepper. Cover with another sheet of wax paper. Let stand 1 hour.

3 · Preheat the grill.

4 · If using presoaked wood chips or chunks (chips for gas), or other flavorings, sprinkle them over the hot coals or lava rocks. Brush the grid lightly with oil.

5 · Grill the turkey pieces over hot or high heat 1 minute per side for filets, about 2 minutes per side for steaks.

Serves 4 to 6.

SUPERCRUNCHY TURKEY FILETS

If turkey is the most nutritious of fowls, quick cookery plus the addition of a wheat germ coating makes it a super health food. Best of all, no one needs suspect what gives this dish its crunch. For an alternate version, see note.

6 turkey filets, unpounded
2 teaspoons chopped chives or scallion ends
¼ cup lightly toasted wheat germ
½ teaspoon seasoned salt
¼ cup unsalted butter, melted
  Vegetable oil

1 · Pat the turkey filets dry with paper towels.

2 · Combine the chives or scallion ends, wheat germ, and salt in a shallow bowl. Mix well. Place the butter in a shallow bowl. Dip the turkey filets in butter, then coat with the wheat germ mixture. Place the filets on a large sheet of wax paper.

3 · Preheat the grill.

4 · If using presoaked wood chips or chunks (chips for gas), or other flavorings, sprinkle them over the hot coals or lava rocks. Brush the grid lightly with oil.

5 · Grill the filets over hot or high heat 1½ minutes per side to ensure crispness.

Serves 4 to 6.

Note: For a very noteworthy variation on this theme, lay a thin slice of Monterey Jack cheese over the top of each filet after turning them. Cook the second side covered, with the vents open, for 1½ minutes or until the cheese melts.

Duckling

THE DUCKLING FOUND in your supermarket's freezer is very likely from Long Island, the greatest duck-producing area in the United States. Flash-frozen at 60 degrees *below* zero, these birds come rock-hard and must be thoroughly thawed in your refrigerator before any preparation for the grill can begin. Good butchers carry fresh birds from time to time but be forewarned: they are likely to be more expensive.

As nothing is less palatable than greasy fowl, grill-roasted duckling is most often put through a serious exercise of basting and fork poking, to release excess fat, or worse yet, just plain overcooked, which, in my opinion, turns the flesh stringy and flavorless. One slightly unorthodox way to degrease duckling is to parboil it halved (in seasoned liquid) before grilling. Another method, borrowed from the Chinese, is to "hang" the duck in a coolish place overnight—until the excess fat dries out.

Since duckling is virtually *all* dark meat and fairly rich at that, some hosts allow 1 duck for 4 diners. Not I. I never find duckling meaty enough for large appetites and invariably serve a half per person.

I advise a combination of pure hardwood coals and regular briquets as the heat source for duckling, as it allows an extended period of hot or high heat during the covered-cooking process. Presoaked wood chunks or flavoring chips should be added to the fire as well; duck takes naturally to smoke.

APPLE-SEARED DUCKLING

The flavoring of the following recipe for (first parboiled, then grilled) duckling is dependent on two important steps: First, the breast must be thoroughly pricked with a fork and the lower thighs lightly slashed with a knife before the meat is placed in the pot. Second, the fire must be absolutely grill-ready by the time the meat is precooked. The glaze is brushed on during the grilling.

135

2 ducklings, 4½ to 5 pounds each
2 cups apple cider
¼ cup brown sugar
6 cups water
1 whole lemon, sliced
1 whole orange, sliced
1 apple, cored and quartered
2 cloves
1 cinnamon stick
Vegetable oil

1 · Cut away the backbones from the ducks. Cut in half through the breast. Remove the wings as well. Poke the breast at 1-inch intervals with a sharp fork. Slash the fatty thigh portion around the leg with a sharp knife. Set aside.

2 · Combine the apple cider with the brown sugar in a medium saucepan. Heat to boiling; reduce heat. Simmer until the mixture has reduced to 1 cup. Remove from heat.

3 · Preheat the grill.

4 · About 20 minutes before the coals are ready, combine the water, lemon, orange, apple, cloves, and cinnamon stick in a large pot. Heat to boiling. Add the duck halves and simmer covered 15 minutes. Remove ducklings from the pot and pat dry with paper towels. Brush with reserved apple glaze.

5 · If using presoaked wood chips or chunks (chips for gas), sprinkle them over the hot coals or lava rocks. Brush the grid lightly with oil.

6 · Place the duck halves skin side up on the grid and prick all over with a fork. Spoon more glaze over the top and cover-cook over hot or high heat with the vents *completely closed* 10 minutes. Remove cover and prick the skin once more. Spoon more glaze over the top and turn skin side down. Grill, basting occasionally with glaze until crisp and done, 12 to 15 minutes.

Serves 4.

TEA-SOAKED, TEA-SMOKED DUCKLING

For centuries the Chinese have literally "tea-smoked" duckling over a fire scented with damp tea leaves and raw rice. My parboiled version economically uses the tea (in bags, please) as a flavoring first. Note that the hot duckling is also rubbed with seasonings prior to the flame—do this with a spoon to spare your fingers.

> 2 ducklings, 4½ to 5 pounds each
> 1 teaspoon salt
> 2 teaspoons peppercorns
> 4 scallions, minced
> 1 teaspoon minced fresh ginger root
> 3 tablespoons dry sherry
> 8 cups water
> 5 Chinese black tea, tea bags
> 1 whole lemon sliced
> ½ cup raw rice
>   Vegetable oil

1 · Cut away the backbones from the ducks. Cut in half through the breast. Remove the wings as well. Poke the breast at 1-inch intervals with a sharp fork. Slash the fatty thigh portion around the leg with a sharp knife. Set aside.

2 · In a small skillet, place the salt and the peppercorns. Cook over high heat, stirring constantly, 4 minutes. Transfer to a mortar or heavy bowl. Add the scallions, ginger, and sherry. Mash with a pestle or the back of a spoon until smooth. Reserve.

3 · Preheat the grill.

4 · Bring the water to a boil in a large pot. Turn off the heat and add the tea bags. Let stand until a strong tea has formed, about 10 minutes. Remove tea bags; reserve. Return water to the boil. Add the lemon and duck halves. Simmer covered 15 minutes.

5 · Meanwhile, remove the tea leaves from the bags and combine in a small bowl with the rice,.

6 · Remove ducklings from the pot and pat dry with paper towels. Spread the spiced scallion-ginger mixture over the tops. Rub in with the back of a spoon.

7 · Sprinkle the tea leaves–rice mixture over the hot coals. For gas, place in a drip pan directly on the lava rocks. Brush the grid lightly with oil.

8 · Place the duck halves skin side up on the grid and prick all over with a fork. Cover-cook over hot or high heat with the vents *completely closed* 10 minutes. Open the vents and cover-cook 5 minutes longer. Remove cover and prick the skin once more. Turn the duck halves skin side down and grill until crisp and done, about 10 minutes.

Serves 4.

GRILLED DUCK BREASTS
WITH ROASTED PEPPER MAYONNAISE

Nouvelle cuisine chefs have been serving rare duck breast for some time. That notion transposed to the grill is decidedly better than it sounds—particularly when the rosy meat is amended with a scarlet pepper mayonnaise, served warm or cold. Make the mayonnaise mixture in the morning. I never bother to preheat the grill for roasting the peppers in the sauce. I take the lazy way out and roast them in the oven.

Roasted Pepper Mayonnaise

1 red bell pepper
1 green bell pepper
2 egg yolks
1 tablespoon wine vinegar
Juice of ½ lemon
½ teaspoon soy sauce
Pinch of ground white pepper
1½ teaspoons Dijon mustard
1 cup vegetable oil
½ cup olive oil
Dash of hot pepper sauce
1 shallot, finely minced
1 tablespoon boiling water

2 whole duck breasts, skinned, boned, halved, and lightly pounded
½ cup red wine
Vegetable oil

1 · To make the Roasted Pepper Mayonnaise: Cook the peppers in boiling salted water 2 minutes. Drain. Roast on a foil-lined baking sheet in a 350-degree oven for 50 minutes. Cool. (Or grill covered over direct heat until charred and soft, about 30 minutes. Carefully wrap the charred peppers in paper towels and place in a plastic bag. Cool.)

2 · Peel the peppers with a sharp knife. Remove seeds. Finely chop.

3 · Beat the egg yolks in a large bowl until light. Slowly beat in the vinegar, lemon juice, soy sauce, white pepper, and mustard.

Beat in the oils, 1 tablespoon at a time, until thick. Add the hot pepper sauce, shallot, boiling water, and peppers. Chill.

4 · Place the pounded duck breasts in a large shallow glass or ceramic dish. Pour the wine over the breasts. Let stand covered 3 hours.

5 · Preheat the grill.

6 · To serve the mayonnaise slightly warm, place in the top of a double boiler over hot water, stirring often.

7 · If using presoaked wood chips or chunks (chips for gas), or other flavorings, sprinkle them on the hot coals or lava rocks. Brush the grid lightly with oil.

8 · Grill the duck breasts over hot or high heat until golden and crisp, 2 to 3 minutes per side. Do not overcook; the meat should be rosy pink inside. Serve with the Roasted Pepper Mayonnaise.

Serves 4.

SCREWDRIVER DUCK

The inspiration for this orange-filled duckling is Persian, but the secret of its supercrispness is borrowed from the Chinese. The bird is aerated and then bathed in pure vodka to dry out the fat. As the duck continues to release fat as it cooks, a drip pan is imperative on the grid. Double the drip pan, as you will have to change it for a clean start halfway through the cooking. And always keep an inch of water in the pan to keep the grease from splattering. For charcoal grills, have partially lit coals ready to add to the grill after the first 50 minutes.

1 duckling, about 4½ pounds, well chilled
½ cup vodka, approximately
   Juice of 1 lemon
1 clove garlic, bruised
   Salt and freshly ground pepper
1 large orange, sliced
   Vegetable oil

1 · Pull all fat from the cavity and neck area of the duckling. Prick the skin at ½-inch intervals along the thighs, back, and lower breast. Rub the duck all over with ¼ cup vodka. Either tie the duck

to hang (over a bowl), or place on a rack in a roasting pan. Let stand in a cool place (do not refrigerate if at all possible) overnight, basting occasionally with more vodka.

2 · Preheat the grill.

3 · Wipe the duck off with damp paper towels. Rub inside and out with the lemon juice, garlic, and salt and pepper. Place the orange slices inside the cavity of the duck.

4 · If using presoaked wood chips or chunks (chips for gas), or other flavorings, sprinkle them over the hot coals or lava rocks. Place a drip pan in the center of the grid and add 1 inch water. Place an oil-rubbed roasting rack in the pan and place the duck on its side on the rack. Do not allow the duck to touch the water. Cover-cook over medium-hot heat with vents about halfway open for 25 minutes. Turn the duck on its other side and cover-cook another 25 minutes.

5 · Remove the rack with the duck and exchange a clean drip pan (with water) for the first one with the duck fat, being careful not to spill it into the coals. (Replenish coals at this time if using a charcoal grill.) Place the duck breast side up and continue to cover-cook with the vents open until the juices run clear when pricked with a fork, about 1 hour. Let stand 10 minutes before cutting into halves.

Serves 2.

Pork

IF PORK IS king of barbecue (and it is), the sovereignty comes with good reason. No other meat takes to smoke so felicitously, nor is prepared with less sweat. And while fresh hams and large pork roasts do require prolonged periods of cookery, pork chops, pork medallions, and boneless pork tenderloins cook fast and are easy to prepare in advance of the fire.

Many Americans have what I deem "pork paranoia." They righteously overcook pork products in the dread fear of trichinosis. Even meat thermometers suggest that an internal temperature of 180 degrees be reached before a cut of pork is deemed ready for consumption. However, it was established way back in 1919 that trichinae (pork worms) are killed at the internal temperature of 137 degrees, and it is generally accepted today that 170 degrees on a meat thermometer is more than a sufficient safeguard. In Iowa, where pork is truly big business, many cooks insist that for full-bodied flavor the meat should register no more than 155 degrees, but I will leave the elective of a medium-rare cutlet up to you. Do bear in mind, however you slice it, pork will continue to cook once it is removed from the grill, so any trace of pink will disappear as it rests.

I unflaggingly use a covered cooker for all pork, as the meat dehydrates quickly when cooked in the open air.

For the duplicated taste of down-home barbecued pork (Southern style), a water smoker is the only appliance that does the trick, in my opinion, for this type of grill allows one to cook the pork until it reaches the shatter-with-a-fork stage without irrevocably drying out the meat.

Hickory, maple, and oak are the classic flavoring woods that complement pork, but fruitwoods, herbs, and garlic are equally bliss. A general timing and cooking chart for pork follows.

PORK CHART

CUT OF PORK ·	TECHNIQUE* ·	TIMES AND SUGGESTIONS† ·
LOIN/RIB CHOPS (1 inch thick)	*Grilling:* Hot to sear meat. Then *Covered Cooking* with medium-hot direct heat.	Sear 1 minute per side. Sear edges. Then cook covered until juices run clear, about 8 minutes per side (internal temp.: 170°).
PORK ROASTS **TENDERLOIN** (about ¾ pound)	*Grilling:* Hot to sear meat. Then *Covered Cooking* with medium-hot, direct heat.	Sear 2 minutes per side. Then cook covered 15 minutes 1st side; 10 minutes 2nd side or until juices run clear (internal temp.: 170°).
BONELESS ROLLED ROAST (about 4 pounds)	*Covered Cooking:* Medium-hot with indirect heat.	Cook on a rack, basting often, until juices run yellow, about 25 minutes per pound (internal temp.: 170°).
LOIN ROAST (about 4 pounds)	*Covered Cooking:* Medium-hot with indirect heat.	Cook on a rack, basting often, until juices run yellow, about 22 minutes per pound (internal temp.: 170°).
HAM (fully cooked) (about 4 pounds)	*Covered Cooking:* Medium-hot with direct heat.	Cook about 1 hour to warm through (internal temp.: 140°).
HAM (cooked) (about 4 pounds)	*Covered Cooking:* Medium-hot with direct heat.	Foil-bake 45 minutes. Then cook covered 30 minutes (internal temp.: 170°).
HAM STEAK (1 inch thick)	*Covered Cooking:* Hot with direct heat.	Cook covered 10 minutes per side.

RIBS

SPARERIBS
(¾ to 1 pound per person)

Covered Cooking: Medium-hot with direct heat. (Alternate method: medium-hot with indirect heat, then direct heat.)

Parboil or foil-bake (see page 164). Then grill covered, with sauce, until crisp, about 6 minutes per side. (Alternate method: grill over indirect 1½ hours, then direct 6 minutes per side.)

COUNTRY-STYLE RIBS
(¾ to 1 pound per person)

Covered Cooking: Medium-hot with direct heat.

Parboil or foil-bake (see page 164). Then grill covered, with sauce, until crisp, about 6 minutes per side.

BABY BACK RIBS
(¾ to 1 pound per person)

Covered Cooking: Medium-hot with direct heat. (Alternate method: medium-hot with indirect heat, then direct heat.)

Parboil or foil-bake (see page 164). Then grill covered, with sauce, until crisp, about 6 minutes per side. (Alternate method: grill over indirect, 1¼ to 1½ hours, then direct, 6 minutes per side.)

KABOBS
(1-inch cubes)

Grilling: Medium-hot with direct heat.

Grill 3 minutes per side for a total of 12 minutes.

* For gas or electric grills, use the high setting for hot, the medium setting for medium-hot. Use the cooler edges of the grid in case of flare-up.

For charcoal grills, hot refers to the 2-second hand test (see page 43). Use the 3- to 4-second test for medium-hot and the 5-second test for medium. To lower the temperature of coal, raise the grid, use the outside edges of the briquets, or cover with cover vents partially closed.

† Times may vary depending on outdoor temperature and velocity of wind.

Pork Chops

$\mathcal{Q}$ MUCH OF THE fresh pork we find in the butcher's case is cut from the pork loin, which includes a variety of chops. Meat sliced from the front of the loin is known as *blade pork chops*. These generally are the strange-looking, large flat pieces one never knows quite what to do with. From the nether end of the loin, near the ham, comes the sirloin. Sirloin pork chops are the ones that have a small round bone, slightly off-center, embedded in the meat. But while butchers assure us the quality of the meat from one end of a loin to the other is virtually alike (aside from varying degrees of fat content), the most sought after, tender chops by far come from the center section. Loin chops (bone in or boneless) and rib chops both come from the center loin. Speaking as a hearty eater, I prefer pork chops at least 1 inch thick, but supermarket cuts average about ¾ inch thick, which is just as suitable for the grill as the heftier cuts.

As with other quick-cooking meats (a ¾-inch-thick loin chop will be done in 15 minutes), wood chips provide more than adequate flavoring for the amount of smoke necessary during the cooking process.

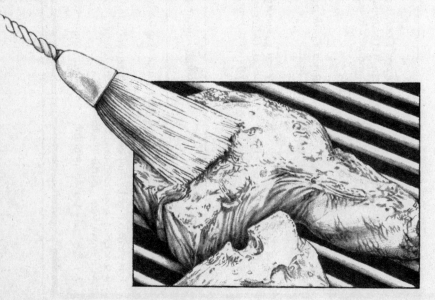

THE CLASSIC PORK CHOP

My classic pork enhancer, on or off the grill, is always garlic and mustard. A quick rub of the former and a healthy dab of the latter will turn a mere chop into a choice entrée.

    4 pork chops, 1 inch thick
    1 clove garlic, bruised
    4 teaspoons Dijon mustard
      Vegetable oil
      Salt and freshly ground pepper

1 · Trim all but ¼ to ½ inch fat from the edges of the pork chops. Slash remaining fat with a knife at 1-inch intervals. Rub the chops well with bruised garlic. Rub ½ teaspoon mustard into each top and bottom. Let stand covered 1 hour.

2 · Preheat the grill.

3 · If using presoaked wood chips, or other flavorings, sprinkle them over the hot coals or lava rocks. Brush the grid lightly with oil.

4 · Sear the chops over hot or high heat 1 minute per side, including edges. Then cover-cook with the vents open over medium-hot heat 8 minutes per side. Sprinkle with salt and pepper before serving.

Serves 4.

DEVILED CHOPS

More mustard variations. This version employs a country-style Dijon mustard (with seeds) in concert with cayenne pepper and basil for a devilishly different taste.

    4 pork chops, 1 inch thick
    4 tablespoons country-style Dijon mustard (with seeds)
    2 teaspoons olive oil
    ¼ cup finely slivered fresh basil leaves
    ½ teaspoon freshly ground pepper
    ¼ teaspoon cayenne pepper
      Vegetable oil

1 · Trim all but ¼ to ½ inch fat from the edges of the pork chops. Slash remaining fat with a knife at 1-inch intervals.

2 · In a small bowl, combine the mustard, olive oil, basil, and peppers. Spread this mixture over the pork chops. Let stand covered 1 hour.

3 · Preheat the grill.

4 · If using presoaked wood chips, or other flavorings, sprinkle them over the hot coals or lava rocks. Brush the grid lightly with vegetable oil.

5 · Sear the chops over hot or high heat 1 minute per side, including edges. Then cover-cook with vents open over medium-hot heat 8 minutes per side.

Serves 4.

APPLE-DAPPLED CHOPS

The next recipe is dependent on a thick, rough-textured apple sauce. Best if homemade, the apple sauce not only adds savor, but actually sears to the flesh as it cooks. Serve with more apple sauce on the side.

    Homemade Apple Sauce (recipe follows)
4 pork chops, 1 inch thick
1 large clove garlic, bruised
    Vegetable oil

1 · Make the Homemade Apple Sauce.

2 · Trim all but ¼ to ½ inch fat from the edges of the pork chops. Slash remaining fat with a knife at 1-inch intervals. Rub the chops well with garlic. Spread apple sauce over each chop, about 1 tablespoon per side. Let stand 1 hour.

3 · Preheat the grill.

4 · If using presoaked wood chips, or other flavorings, sprinkle them over the hot coals or lava rocks. Brush the grid lightly with oil.

5 · Sear the chops over hot or high heat for 1 minute on the fatty edge only. Then cover-cook with the vents open over medium-hot heat *10* minutes per side. Serve remaining apple sauce on the side.

Serves 4.

HOMEMADE APPLE SAUCE

  4 tart green apples, peeled, cored and sliced
      Juice of ½ lemon
      Finely slivered peel of ½ lemon
  ½ cup light brown sugar

1 · Combine the ingredients in a medium saucepan. Cook over medium heat, mashing frequently, until thick, but not too smooth.

Makes about 1 pint.

CHOPS À L'ORANGE

Citrus is a natural meat tenderizer. For proof have the following marinade: a syrup of orange juice, honey, and vinegar that will turn even a lackluster cut of meat supple after an hour's marination.

  ½ cup orange juice
  4 teaspoons honey
  4 teaspoons vinegar
  ½ teaspoon finely slivered orange peel
  4 pork chops, 1 inch thick
      Vegetable oil

1 · Combine the orange juice, honey, and vinegar in a small saucepan. Heat to boiling; reduce heat. Simmer until thick and syrupy, about 8 minutes. Stir in the orange peel.

2 · Trim all but ¼ to ½ inch fat from the edges of the pork chops. Slash remaining fat with a knife at 1-inch intervals. Brush the orange syrup over all sides of the chops. Let stand 1 hour.

3 · Preheat the grill.

4 · If using presoaked wood chips, or other flavorings, sprinkle them over the hot coals or lava rocks. Brush the grid lightly with oil.

5 · Sear the chops over hot or high heat 1 minute per side, including edges. Then cover-cook with vents open over medium-hot heat 8 minutes per side.

Serves 4.

POPPY CHOPS

Along the Danube, poppy seeds flavor every dish from bread to ice cream. One of the most engaging Austro-Hungarian notions for a seeded pork chop makes a highly original nominee for the grill.

4 pork chops, 1 inch thick
1 clove garlic, crushed
4 teaspoons olive oil
4 teaspoons poppy seeds
Vegetable oil
Salt and freshly ground pepper

1 · Trim all but ¼ to ½ inch fat from the edges of the pork chops. Slash remaining fat with a knife at 1-inch intervals.

2 · In a small bowl, mash the garlic with the olive oil until a paste is formed. Rub over both sides of the chops. Sprinkle each side with ½ teaspoon poppy seeds. Let stand covered 1 hour.

3 · Preheat the grill.

4 · If using presoaked wood chips, or other flavorings, sprinkle them over the hot coals or lava rocks. Brush the grid lightly with oil.

5 · Sear the chops over hot or high heat 1 minute per side, including edges. Then cover-cook with vents open over medium-hot heat 8 minutes per side. Sprinkle with salt and pepper before serving.

Serves 4.

SNAP CHOPS

For a pork chop with definitive zing, consider a prefire rubdown made of horseradish, paprika, soy sauce, and honey.

1 teaspoon Hungarian hot paprika
4 tablespoons prepared horseradish
2 teaspoons soy sauce
2 teaspoons honey
4 pork chops, 1 inch thick
Vegetable oil

1 · In a small bowl, combine the paprika, horseradish, soy sauce, and honey. Mix well.

2 · Trim all but ¼ to ½ inch fat from the edges of the pork chops. Slash remaining fat with a knife at 1-inch intervals. Spread the horseradish mixture over both sides of the chops. Let stand covered 1 hour.

3 · Preheat the grill.

4 · If using presoaked wood chips, or other flavorings, sprinkle them over the hot coals or lava rocks. Brush the grid lightly with oil.

5 · Sear the chops over hot or high heat 1 minute per side, including edges. Then cover-cook with the vents open over medium-hot heat 8 minutes per side.

Serves 4.

CHOP SCOTCH

Simple things are almost always the most ingenious. Take the happy notion of basting pork with a wee drop of smoky Scotch whisky, for example. Smoke with smoke makes the ultimate blend.

    4 pork chops, 1 inch thick
    1 large clove garlic, bruised
    6 tablespoons Scotch whisky
      Vegetable oil

1 · Trim all but ¼ to ½ inch fat from the edges of the pork chops. Slash remaining fat with a knife at 1-inch intervals. Rub the chops well with garlic. Sprinkle the Scotch over both sides of the chops. Let stand covered 1 hour.

2 · Preheat the grill.

3 · If using presoaked wood chips, or other flavorings, sprinkle them over the hot coals or lava rocks. Brush the grid lightly with oil.

4 · Sear the chops over hot or high heat 1 minute per side, including edges. Then cover-cook with vents open over medium-hot heat 8 minutes per side.

Serves 4.

CHA SHIU

In China, pork is invariably spit-roasted, and basted, in brick ovens. A translation from the classic Cantonese below is untraditionally amended with a jot of pure (made in the USA) chili sauce.

 1 clove garlic, crushed
 ½ teaspoon freshly ground pepper
 ½ teaspoon finely grated ginger root
 4 teaspoons soy sauce
 4 teaspoons honey
 4 teaspoons dry sherry
 ½ teaspoon five-spice powder (available in the gourmet department of most supermarkets; see note)
 4 teaspoons chili sauce
 4 pork chops, 1 inch thick
 Vegetable oil

1 · In a small bowl, combine the garlic, pepper, ginger, soy sauce, honey, sherry, five-spice powder, and chili sauce. Mix well.

2 · Trim all but ¼ to ½ inch fat from the edges of the pork chops. Slash remaining fat with a knife at 1-inch intervals. Spread the chili mixture over both sides of the chops. Let stand covered 1 hour.

3 · Preheat the grill.

4 · If using presoaked wood chips, or other flavorings, sprinkle them over the hot coals or lava rocks. Brush the grid lightly with oil.

5 · Sear the chops over hot or high heat 1 minute per side, including edges. Then cover-cook with vents open over medium-hot heat 8 minutes per side.

Serves 4.

Note: If five-spice powder is not available in your local supermarket, you can make it at home. Combine 1 teaspoon ground cinnamon, 1 teaspoon crushed aniseed, ¼ teaspoon crushed fennel seed, ¼ teaspoon freshly ground pepper, and ⅛ teaspoon ground cloves. Store in an airtight container. (Makes about 2½ teaspoons.)

VIETNAMESE BARBECUED PORK MEDALLIONS

Pork medallions are nothing more than a round slice of meat cut from the loin, often just a boneless chop. This Vietnamese rendition incorporates nuoc mam *sauce in the marinade. Available in most Oriental groceries these days, you can also make it yourself. See page 85.*

     2 cloves garlic, crushed
     3 shallots, minced
     ¼ cup peanut oil
     3 tablespoons *nuoc mam* sauce
     2 tablespoons sugar
     ¼ teaspoon bouillon powder
     ¼ teaspoon freshly ground pepper
     8 pork medallions, each about ½ inch thick
       Vegetable oil
     ¼ cup coarsely chopped, unsalted dry-roasted peanuts

1 · In a small bowl, combine the garlic, shallots, peanut oil, nu'o'ć mám sauce, sugar, bouillon powder, and pepper. Mix well and spread over the medallions. Let stand covered 1 hour.

2 · Preheat the grill.

3 · If using presoaked wood chips, or other flavorings, sprinkle them over the hot coals or lava rocks. Brush the grid lightly with oil.

4 · Place the medallions on the grid and cover-cook with the vents open over hot or high heat about 5 minutes per side. Serve sprinkled with chopped peanuts.

Serves 4.

Pork Roasts

ONE OF THE superior cuts of pork, perfect for the outdoor grill, is the tenderloin. Cut from the center and sirloin portions of the loin, this long, narrow filet is usually 1½ to 2 inches thick. A lean and solid meat, the tenderloin will cook outdoors in 25 to 30 minutes. Fairly inexpensive, tenderloins weigh from ½ to ¾ pounds on the average. Canadian imports run somewhat larger (about 1 pound).

More familiar pork roasts are, of course, cut from the center of the loin. A pork loin roast, sometimes called a rib roast, contains a narrow strip of meat on the outside of the ribs (unless the butcher has removed it) which is in fact the narrow end of the tenderloin. This roast is also sold boned, rolled, and tied.

In the kitchen, sizable pork cuts are often bypassed by hurried chefs because they require protracted cooking times. At the backyard grill, however, these same cuts roast in much abbreviated time sequences, and what is even more tonic for the cook, provide surcease from a hot stove during the summer months.

RED PEPPERED TENDERLOIN

Flame-roasted red pepper is what gives this pork tenderloin its incredibly pungent savor.

    1 small red bell pepper
    1 clove garlic, peeled
    ¼ cup heavy or whipping cream
    ¼ cup unsalted butter
    1 tablespoon tomato paste
    ¼ teaspoon chopped fresh sage
    ½ teaspoon Hungarian hot paprika
      Salt
    2 pork tenderloins, about ¾ pound each
      Vegetable oil

1 · Place the pepper over a gas flame (or on a grill or under the broiler) until charred all over. Carefully wrap pepper in paper towels and place in a plastic bag. Let stand until cool. Rub the charred skin from the pepper with paper towels. Core the pepper; roughly chop.

2 · Place the pepper, garlic, and cream in the container of a food processor or blender. Process until smooth.

3 · Melt the butter in a medium saucepan over medium-low heat. Whisk in the tomato paste and the pepper-garlic puree. Add the sage, paprika, and salt to taste. Cook, without boiling, until hot. Set aside to cool.

4 · Coat the tenderloins with the red pepper sauce. Let stand covered 1 hour.

5 · Preheat the grill.

6 · If using presoaked wood chips or chunks (chips for gas), or other flavorings, sprinkle them over the hot coals or lava rocks. Brush the grid lightly with oil.

7 · Sear the tenderloins over medium-hot heat 2 minutes per side. Then cover-cook with vents open over medium-hot heat, basting every 5 minutes, for 15 minutes. Turn the tenderloins over and continue to cover-cook until done, about 10 minutes longer. Let stand 10 minutes before carving.

Serves 4.

SOUTHWESTERN TENDERLOIN

While beef is still the number one choice among Southwestern cooks, the northern Mexican style of marinating pork has developed an entire school of adherents in the rest of the country. Adventurous souls may wish to substitute hot jalapeño peppers for all or part of the milder variety called for below.

> 1 cup Bloody Mary mix
> Juice of ½ lemon
> 1 tablespoon prepared horseradish
> 1 tablespoon Dijon mustard
> 2 tablespoons finely chopped mild canned green chiles
> ½ teaspoon freshly ground pepper
> 2 pork tenderloins, about ¾ pound each
> Vegetable oil

1 · Combine the Bloody Mary mix, lemon juice, horseradish, mustard, chiles, and pepper in a bowl. Mix well. Spoon this mixture over both sides of the tenderloins. Let stand covered 4 hours.

2 · Preheat the grill.

3 · If using presoaked wood chips or chunks (chips for gas), or other flavorings, sprinkle them over the hot coals or lava rocks. Brush the grid lightly with oil.

4 · Sear the tenderloins over medium-hot heat 2 minutes per side. Then cover-cook with vents open over medium-hot heat, basting every 5 minutes, for 15 minutes. Turn the tenderloins over and continue to cover-cook until done, about 10 minutes longer. Let stand 10 minutes before carving.

Serves 4.

SAUCY LOIN OF PORK WITH APPLES

Another bequest from Ruth and Skitch Henderson, this old-fashioned pork roast (baked apples and all) makes a remarkable Sunday dinner cooked outdoors at any time of year. (Charcoal users will need partially lit coals at the ready to stoke the fire.)

1 boneless loin of pork, about 4 pounds, rolled and tied
1 clove garlic, bruised
½ cup Dijon mustard
¼ cup honey
  Juice of ½ lemon
½ teaspoon chopped fresh marjoram, or ¼ teaspoon dried
¼ cup applejack or apple brandy
1 tablespoon cider vinegar
  Dash of hot pepper sauce
½ teaspoon freshly ground pepper
4 to 6 juicy red apples
3 to 4 tablespoons unsalted butter, softened
  Ground cinnamon
4 to 6 teaspoons brown sugar

1 · Rub the pork well with garlic.

2 · Combine all ingredients from mustard through the pepper in a medium bowl. Mix well. Coat the pork with about ½ cup of this mixture. Let stand 3 hours. Cover and reserve remaining basting mixture.

3 · Preheat the grill.

4 · If using a charcoal grill, spread the coals apart and place a drip pan in the center. If using presoaked wood chips or chunks, sprinkle them over the hot coals. If using a gas grill, place the drip pan on one side of the grill directly on the lava rocks and add any presoaked chips to the pan.

5 · Place the pork roast on a rack directly over the drip pan. Cover-cook with vents about halfway open over medium-hot heat, basting often with remaining sauce, about 25 minutes per pound or until the internal temperature reads 170 degrees on a meat thermometer. (Add more heated coals after 45 minutes if using a charcoal grill.) Let roast stand 15 minutes before carving.

6 · Meanwhile, while the pork is roasting, rub each apple with 1 teaspoon softened butter. Sprinkle each lightly with cinnamon. Sprinkle each with a teaspoon of brown sugar. Enclose each apple in an aluminum-foil packet and place on the grid with the pork about 30 minutes before the pork is done. To serve, place the apples upright on a serving dish. With a sharp knife, make a cross at the top of each apple, about ¾ inch deep, and pour any liquid from the foil packets over the top. Dot with the remaining butter.

Serves 4 to 6.

AMAGANSETT PORK ROAST

The Store in Amagansett, almost at the tip end of Long Island, was the very first purveyor of carryout cuisine in the United States. The Store flourished gastronomically from 1966 to 1976. It was a wonderful place. I know, because I did my culinary apprenticeship there. The following pork roast, a Store classic, gets its extraordinarily mellow flavor from a vegetable topping, seasoned liberally with caraway seeds and sprigs of fresh thyme. (As the pork is long-cooked, charcoal users will need partially lit coals at the ready to add to the fire.)

    1 loin of pork, about 4 pounds
    1 clove garlic, bruised
      Salt and freshly ground pepper
    3 tablespoons Dijon mustard
    ½ cup unsalted butter, melted
    1 small onion, finely chopped
    1 medium carrot, chopped
    2 tablespoons caraway seeds
    2 sprigs fresh thyme

1 · Rub the pork well with garlic. Sprinkle with salt and pepper. Spread the mustard over the top. Let stand 1 hour.

2 · Preheat the grill.

3 · Place 3 tablespoons melted butter in a small skillet and cook the onion and carrot over medium-low heat 5 minutes. Place the pork flat (bones down) on a roasting rack. Spoon the onion and carrots over the top. Pat down with the back of the spoon. Sprinkle with caraway seeds. Lay the thyme over the top.

4 · If using a charcoal grill, spread the coals apart and place a drip pan in the center. If using presoaked wood chips or chunks, sprinkle them over the hot coals. If using a gas grill, place the drip pan on one side of the grill directly on the lava rocks and add any presoaked chips to the pan.

5 · Carefully place the rack with the pork directly over the drip pan. Cover-cook with vents about halfway open over medium-hot heat, basting occasionally with melted butter, about 22 minutes per pound or until the internal temperature reads 170 degrees on a meat thermometer. (Add more heated coals after 45 minutes if using a charcoal grill.) Let roast stand 15 minutes before carving.

Serves 4.

GARLIC STRIPED PORK LOIN

Carole Lalli, my editor and friend, has an unusual method for preparing a pork roast. She cuts a series of slashes in the thick side of the meat and lines each with finely slivered garlic and fresh oregano leaves. Roast pork never had it so good.

1 loin of pork, about 4 pounds
1 large clove garlic, cut into fine slivers
   Small fresh oregano leaves (about 33)
1 teaspoon olive oil
   Freshly ground pepper

1 · Place the loin of pork bone side down on a work surface. Using a sharp knife, cut a series of slashes on the bony top portion, between each bone, about 2 inches long and ¼ inch deep. Cut an alternating series of slashes, over the bones, along the thickest part of the meat. You should have 11 or 12 vertical slashes. Place 2 slivers of garlic and about 3 oregano leaves into each slash. Brush the meat with olive oil. Sprinkle with pepper. Tie the meat in two places: around the bony tips and around the meaty bottom. Let stand 1 hour.

2 · Preheat the grill.

3 · If using a charcoal grill, spread the coals apart and place a drip pan in the center. If using presoaked wood chips or chunks, sprinkle them over the hot coals. If using a gas grill, place the drip pan on one side of the grill directly on the lava rocks and add any presoaked chips to the pan.

5 · Place the pork on a rack directly over the drip pan. Cover-cook with vents about halfway open over medium-hot heat, about 22 minutes per pound or until the internal temperature reads 170 degrees on a meat thermometer. (Add more heated coals after 45 minutes if using a charcoal grill.) Let roast stand 15 minutes before carving.

Serves 4.

SOUTH-OF-THE-BORDER BUTTERFLIED PORK

The secret ingredient in this Mexican specialty is juniper berries mingled with fresh cilantro. Freely adapted from Maggie Klein's The Feast of the Olive *(Aris Books, 1983), I use a boneless loin roast, which is a snap for even a neophyte to butterfly. Merely cut the meat slightly more than halfway deep lengthwise—until both wings can be opened flat, like a butterfly.*

    1 boneless pork loin, about 2¼ pounds, butterflied
    1 clove garlic, crushed
    1 small onion, minced
    1 teaspoon sugar
    ¼ cup olive oil
    3 tablespoons tarragon wine vinegar
    ⅛ teaspoon hot pepper sauce
    5 juniper berries, crushed
    ¼ cup finely chopped fresh cilantro (Chinese parsley)
      Vegetable oil

1 · Place the butterflied pork in a shallow glass or ceramic dish.

2 · Combine the garlic, onion, sugar, olive oil, vinegar, hot pepper sauce, juniper berries, and cilantro in a medium bowl. Mix well. Spread over both sides of the pork. Let stand covered 2 hours.

3 · Preheat the grill.

4 · If using presoaked wood chips or chunks (chips for gas), or other flavorings, sprinkle them over the hot coals or lava rocks. Brush the grid lightly with vegetable oil.

5 · Place the pork on the grid and spoon any extra marinade over the top. Cover-cook with vents open over hot or high heat, about 20 minutes per side or until the internal temperature reads 170 degrees on a meat thermometer. Let roast stand 10 minutes before carving.

Serves 4 to 6.

Ham

SPECIALTY HAMS—you know, the old-fashioned cob-smoked variety cured for months and months—were once the pride of our nation's tables. Sad to say, the last remnants of true smokehouse hams must be mail-ordered from Virginia, Vermont, or Wisconsin these days, at fancy tariffs in the bargain. That's the bad news. The good news is that any ham at all can be transformed to a reasonably accurate facsimile of a real old-time toothsome hock after a stint on the grill.

"Ham" is a misnomer to many consumers. So-called fresh hams (like picnic shoulders) which automatically require hours of cooking time, inevitably end up in my water smoker (see pages 276–77) because that is the most cost-efficient *and* delectable way I know to prepare one properly. True ham, however, if it is labeled as such, must, by law, be cut from the leg of the animal.

Just because you buy a ham that bears the tag "smoked" does not necessarily imply it is smoked to your taste. Many such products do not visit the smokehouse for more than 24 hours. But flavoring woods and chips on the grill can make up for the manufacturer's translation.

All ham is alternately marked "cooked," "fully cooked," or "ready to eat." A "cooked" ham means only that it has been heated to an internal temperature of 137 degrees, just enough to kill trichinae. A "fully cooked" or "ready to eat" ham is generally heated internally to 155 degrees to 160 degrees. All canned hams are cooked to at least 150 degrees internally and most require refrigeration, even in the can. Do not buy a canned ham that is not refrigerated unless it is marked "sterilized," though God knows what that means.

Go heavier with the wood chunks or chips when cooking ham than you normally do. After all, the smoky taste *is* what is important here. Dried twigs from maple trees, and an occasional dried corncob, will also do wonders for ham.

MAPLE- AND COB-SMOKED HAM

This recipe calls for a "fully cooked" ham, and is ready to eat when the internal temperature hits the "warmed through" stage, about 140 degrees on a meat thermometer. If you can't find maple chips, hickory or oak can be substituted. The corncob? Even dreary winter corn found in supermarkets will do. Scrape the corn first, of course, and hang the cob in a warm place to dry. Then presoak before using.

   1 "fully cooked" ham, about 4 pounds
     Whole cloves
   2 tablespoons Dijon mustard
   1 clove garlic, crushed
  ¼ cup Chinese duck sauce (sweet and sour or plum sauce)
   1 tablespoon orange juice
     Maple chips, presoaked
   1 dried corncob, presoaked
     Vegetable oil

1 · Score the top (fatty side) of the ham in a diamond pattern. Insert whole cloves at each intersection.

2 · Combine the mustard, garlic, duck sauce, and orange juice in a small bowl. Spread over the ham. Let stand at least 2 hours.

3 · Preheat the grill.

4 · If using a charcoal grill, bank the hot coals at one end of the grill. Place a drip pan at the other end. Sprinkle the chips over the coals and add the corncob. If using a gas grill, place the drip pan (doubled) at one side of the grill directly on the lava rocks and add the chips and corncob to the pan. Brush the grid lightly with oil.

5 · Place the ham on the grid and cover-cook with vents halfway open over medium-hot heat about 1 hour or until the internal temperature reads 140 degrees on a meat thermometer. (Add more presoaked wood chips after 30 minutes for a smokier taste, if desired.) Let the ham stand 20 minutes before carving.

Serves 6 to 8.

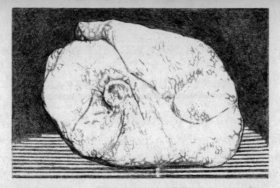

BEER-SOAKED HAM WITH MUSTARD SAUCE

The following devise also calls for "fully cooked" ham, but any ham labeled "cooked" may be used as well, as the hock virtually steams in beer before it is coated with mustard sauce (made with more beer) and finished over direct heat. Adapted from Bert Greene's award-winning book, Honest American Fare *(Contemporary Books, 1981), it is indeed a winner.*

     Beery Mustard Sauce (see page 319)
1 "fully cooked" ham, about 4 pounds
     Whole cloves
½ cup brown sugar
½ cup beer
     Vegetable oil

1 · Make the Beery Mustard Sauce.

2 · Preheat the grill.

3 · Score the top (fatty side) of the ham in a diamond pattern. Insert whole cloves at each intersection. Press the sugar over the top.

4 · Place the ham in an aluminum-foil pan and pour the beer over the top. (This may also be done by foil wrapping.) Cover tightly with foil.

5 · If using presoaked wood chips or chunks (chips for gas), sprinkle them over the hot coals or lava rocks.

6 · Place the ham on the grid and cover-cook with vents halfway open 45 minutes. Remove the grid. (If using a charcoal grill, add more hot coals to the grate.) Brush the grid lightly with oil.

7 · Remove the ham from the pan. Spread ⅓ cup mustard sauce over the top and sides. Place the ham on the grid and cover-cook with vents open 30 minutes. Let stand 20 minutes before carving.

Serves 6 to 8.

SMOKED PORK BUTT STEAKS

Technically not ham, but processed in the same manner, smoked pork butt (sometimes called a cottage roll) can weigh anywhere from 1 to 4 pounds. An excellent buy for the money, pork butts have a tendency to be salty, so I parboil them first before cutting them into steaks.

1 pork butt, casing removed, about 2 pounds
1 clove garlic, bruised
4 teaspoons Dijon mustard
½ cup tomato juice or V-8
  Vegetable oil

1 · Cook the pork butt in boiling water for 30 minutes. Drain and cool.

2 · Using a sharp knife, peel the tough outer skin off the pork butt. Cut into 6 1-inch-thick steaks. Rub all sides with bruised garlic and place the steaks in a glass or ceramic dish. Combine the mustard and the tomato juice or V-8. Coat both sides of the pork butt steaks with the mixture. Let stand 1 hour.

3 · Preheat the grill.

4 · If using presoaked wood chips or chunks (chips for gas), or other flavorings, sprinkle them over the hot coals or lava rocks. Brush the grid lightly with oil.

5 · Place the steaks on the grid and cover-cook with vents open over hot or high heat 10 minutes per side.

Serves 6.

HOLY SMOKE

Deep-dyed pork lovers in North Carolina are so fervid about their culinary preference, it shouldn't come as a surprise to discover there is even a church named to honor the hot stuff.

Barbecue Church (south of Sanford on route 87), one of the oldest Presbyterian churches in the United States, was founded in 1757 and is still going strong. Rumor has it, this edifice got its name by contiguous geography. Erected on the banks of Barbecue Creek, the church was dubbed "barbecue" because morning mist rising on the water reminded new arrivals from the West Indies of smoke rising from barbecue pits at home.

The church's culinary connection is not entirely coincidental. Every Sunday in November (harvest season) a barbecue supper is held for parishioners. On that day, according to Rev. J. Waldo Dodson, pastor of the two-hundred-member church, ushers merely pass plates to collect compliments.

Pork Ribs

PORK RIB LOVERS should be advised there are three distinct types found at meat counters: spareribs, country-style ribs, and baby back ribs. Spareribs, by far the most popular and easily available, are taken from the animal's midriff and include both breastbone and rib bones. Country-style and baby backs are both taken from the loin, country-style from the blade end and the baby backs, the most toothsome of all, from the center.

Cooking ribs on an outdoor grill poses two serious problems for a neophyte chef. The first is ridding the ribs of excess fat; the second, taking caution not to burn any sweet-laced sauce that inevitably bedecks them on a barbecue.

One way to "degrease" ribs efficiently is to roast them on a rack in the oven for an hour prior to the outdoor grill. But it is sizzling hot work at best. There are several less steamy alternatives. My preferred method is to parboil the ribs until almost tender on the stove—and finish them later (sauced) on the grill. Ribs may be parboiled in advance (up to 24 hours prior to the grill), cooled, then marinated in sauce and refrigerated until the fire is ready.

For chewy, crunchy ribs, consider marinating them first, then cooking them over indirect heat—basting every 15 minutes—until they are tender. Then grill over direct heat until crisp. A jot of caution is advised here: keep a steady eye on the grill, so the ribs do not overcook or dry out.

Pork ribs may also be foil-wrapped prior to the fire and cooked on the grill over direct heat until they are tender—then ultimately drained, sauced, and grilled.

Use wood chunks in the fire (except on gas grills) if you opt for the latter two methods. Wood chips are recommended for the parboiling method as the grilling time is brief and chips have more immediate smoke concentration.

OLD-FASHIONED SPARERIBS

Parboiling ribs is perhaps the easiest (and most old-fashioned) way to prepare ribs. If you are preparing them in advance, parboil the ribs for 10 minutes less than the time specified (see note below), as the pork will continue to cook as it cools. Like everyone else, I dearly love gooey barbecue sauce on my ribs. My preferences for this recipe are (in alphabetical order): All-American, Amish Sticken', LBJ BBQ, Nathalie Dupree's Coca-Cola, and Ohio Valley Soothing Syrup (see pages 299, 304, 303, 301, 302).

    4 pounds meaty pork ribs
    1 medium onion stuck with 2 cloves
   ¼ cup soy sauce
    2 teaspoons dried marjoram
    1 teaspoon salt
   ½ teaspoon freshly ground pepper
       Barbecue sauce of choice (see above)
       Vegetable oil

1 · Place the ribs in a large pot (do not cut into sections if possible). Cover with cold water. Add the onion with cloves, soy sauce, marjoram, salt, and pepper. Heat to boiling; reduce heat. Simmer uncovered, turning once, until ribs are tender, about 1 hour for large ribs.

2 · Preheat the grill.

3 · When ribs are tender, transfer to a large shallow dish. Brush with sauce.

4 · If using presoaked wood chips or chunks (chips for gas), or other flavorings, sprinkle them over the hot coals or lava rocks. Brush the grid lightly with oil.

5 · Grill the ribs over *medium* heat, basting often with more sauce, until crisp, about 6 minutes per side. Serve the extra sauce (reheated), on the side.

Serves 4 to 6.

Note: If parboiled in advance, heat on the grill—covered—10 minutes per side.

GROWN-UP RIBS

This rib concoction is dubbed "grown-up" because the ribs retain some of their pungent "porkiness" when foil-wrapped in the method described below. While tomato still plays a key role in the marinade and subsequent basting sauce, this topping is by no means sweet or gooey either. Just downright good.

1 small onion, roughly chopped
1 clove garlic, chopped
1 large tomato, seeded, and roughly chopped
½ red bell pepper, seeded, and roughly chopped
1 teaspoon salt
½ teaspoon freshly ground pepper
½ teaspoon Hungarian hot paprika
¼ teaspoon ground turmeric
¼ cup light brown sugar
¾ cup beer
¼ cup apple cider vinegar
1 tablespoon Worcestershire sauce
¼ teaspoon hot pepper sauce
4 pounds meaty pork ribs
  Vegetable oil

1 · Combine all ingredients from the chopped onion through the hot pepper sauce in the container of a food processor or blender. Process until smooth. Place the ribs in a large shallow glass or ceramic dish. Pour 1 cup of the marinating sauce over the ribs. Let stand covered 2 hours.

2 · Preheat the grill.

3 · Transfer the ribs to 2 large sheets of heavy-duty aluminum foil. Fold up the edges and pour about ½ cup marinade over the ribs. Fold the top two edges of the foil together and seal. Fold up the ends and seal.

4 · If using presoaked wood chips or chunks (chips for gas), sprinkle them over the hot coals or lava rocks.

5 · Place the foil packets with ribs on the grid and cover-cook with vents halfway open over medium-hot heat for 1½ hours. (If using a charcoal grill, add more preheated coals after about 45 minutes.)

6 · Remove the ribs from the foil packets and drain. Then grill the ribs over medium heat, basting often with more sauce, until crisp, about 6 minutes per side.

Serves 4 to 6.

GEORGIA RIBS

Called Georgia-style ribs because their geographic heritage is famed for peaches, the following recipe is loosely adapted from one found in The American Table *by Richard Johnson (Morrow, 1984). Both sweet and sour, and tangy as well, this sauce makes a good choice for ribs cooked over indirect heat, with no prior preparation other than several hours' marination.*

    1 medium onion, finely chopped
    1 cup peach preserves
    1 tablespoon ketchup
    ¼ cup brown sugar
    1 teaspoon Hungarian sweet paprika
    ¼ cup cider vinegar
    ¼ cup Worcestershire sauce
    1 teaspoon dry mustard
    ¼ teaspoon hot pepper sauce
    4 pounds meaty pork ribs
      Vegetable oil

1 · Combine all ingredients from the chopped onion through the hot pepper sauce in a saucepan. Heat to boiling; reduce heat. Simmer uncovered 10 minutes. Place the ribs in a large shallow glass or ceramic dish. Pour the sauce over the ribs. Let stand covered 2 hours.

2 · Preheat the grill.

3 · If using a charcoal grill, bank the coals at one end of the grate and place a large drip pan (or two small ones) at the other end. Sprinkle any presoaked wood chips or chunks over the hot coals. If using a gas grill, place a large drip pan at one end of the grill directly on the lava rocks. Place any presoaked chips in the pan. Brush the grid lightly with oil.

4 · Place the ribs on the grid directly over the drip pan. Cover-cook with vents halfway open, basting often with extra sauce, until tender, about 1½ hours. (Charcoal users will have to add more preheated coals to the fire after 45 minutes.)

5 · When ribs are tender, move over direct heat. Grill, basting once on each side, until crisp.

Serves 4 to 6.

SHANGHAI-STYLE RIBS

Chinese-style spareribs are traditionally grilled in individual portions, which means a chef must be on constant alert to keep the ribs from drying out. To my taste these ribs always cry out for the classic accompaniments most always served in Cantonese restaurants, which are, of course, a sweet and sour sauce (duck or plum varieties) which can be found on grocery shelves everywhere, and truly hot mustard which can be approximated by adding two-thirds of dry mustard to one-third cream and, optionally, a splash of vodka—or whiskey—until smooth.

    4 pounds meaty pork ribs
    1 tablespoon plus ¼ cup Hoisin sauce
  2½ tablespoons oyster sauce
  2½ tablespoons soy sauce
  2½ tablespoons honey
  1½ tablespoons peanut oil
    2 tablespoons dry sherry
    3 cloves garlic, minced
    2 teaspoons chili sauce
    2 teaspoons chili powder
   ⅛ teaspoon ground ginger
     Vegetable oil

1 · Cut the ribs into individual pieces and place in a large pot. Add water to cover; add 1 tablespoon Hoisin sauce. Heat to boiling; reduce heat. Simmer uncovered 30 minutes. Drain.

2 · Preheat the grill.

3 · Meanwhile, combine ¼ cup Hoisin sauce with all the ingredients through ginger in a bowl. Brush this mixture over the parboiled ribs.

4 · If using wood chips or chunks (chips for gas), or other flavorings, sprinkle them over the hot coals or lava rocks. Brush the grid lightly with oil.

5 · Grill the ribs over medium heat, basting often with remaining sauce, until crisp on all sides.

Serves 4 to 6.

Pork Kabobs

VIRTUALLY ANY CUT of pork will do for kabobs, but most precut varieties come from the loin. Pork kabobs, cut into 1-inch cubes, will grill in about 3 minutes per side for a total of 12 minutes.

Because of the brief cooking time, wood chips are more than sufficient flavoring adjuncts.

SKEWERED PORK AND PEPPERS

Pork and peppers are such a classic (and classy) combination that it only seems fitting to include them on a skewer. I use yellow peppers for color and delicate flavor as well. The marinade is dappled with molasses which makes this recipe a study of alternating sweet and sour.

>   2 medium yellow bell peppers
>   2½ tablespoons Dijon mustard
>   ¼ cup chili sauce
>   4 teaspoons molasses
>   1½ pounds boneless pork, cut into 1-inch cubes
>   Vegetable oil

1 · Cut the peppers in half, and then cut each half into 1-inch-square pieces. Cook in boiling salted water 3 minutes. Rinse under cold running water; drain. Set aside.

2 · Combine the mustard, chili sauce, and molasses in a large bowl. Stir the pork into this mixture. Let stand covered 30 minutes.

3 · Preheat the grill.

4 · Divide the meat equally in fours. You should have about 8 pieces per portion. Divide the pepper squares into fours. Starting with a pepper, place the meat, alternating with peppers, on 4 skewers, ending up with meat on each skewer.

5 · If using presoaked wood chips or chunks (chips for gas), or other flavorings, sprinkle them over the hot coals or lava rocks. Brush grid lightly with oil.

6 · Grill the kabobs uncovered over hot or high heat, basting often with extra marinade, 3 minutes per side.

Serves 4.

FRUITED PORKABOBS

Nectarines teamed with lean pork makes a fresh and light outdoor entrée dieters will adore. Particularly if the pork is initially marinated in Edie Acsell's zesty marinating sauce. As noted earlier, Edie is a cooking teacher/author in Colorado, and her sauce is unbeatable.

> 1 clove garlic, minced
> 2 tablespoons safflower oil
> 2 tablespoons tomato juice
> 2 tablespoons soy sauce
> 2 tablespoons brown sugar
> ⅛ teaspoon freshly ground pepper
> 1½ pounds boneless pork, cut into 1-inch cubes
> 8 nectarines, cut in half across, pits removed
> Vegetable oil

1 · Combine the garlic, safflower oil, tomato juice, soy sauce, brown sugar, and pepper in a small bowl. Pour this mixture over the pork cubes. Let stand 1 hour.

2 · Preheat the grill.

3 · Divide the meat equally in fours. You should have about 8 pieces per portion. Starting with a nectarine half, place the meat, alternating with nectarines (4 nectarine halves per skewer) on 4 skewers, ending up with a nectarine half on each skewer.

4 · If using presoaked wood chips or chunks (chips for gas), or other flavorings, sprinkle them over the hot coals or lava rocks. Brush grid lightly with oil.

5 · Grill the kabobs uncovered over hot or high heat, basting often with extra marinade, 3 minutes per side.

Serves 4.

Lamb

AS NOTED EARLIER, lamb in any guise is an excellent nominee for the grill. Why lamb is not more popular in this country (where some of the best in the world is raised) is beyond me. Unless it is the common myth that lamb has a "muttony" undertaste that is offputting—even to bonafide meat lovers. However, as all lamb on the market these days is "baby lamb" (less than one year old with a delicate, fresh flavor), there is no reason to pass up one of life's true gustatory pleasures.

When buying lamb, look for meat that is fine-textured, firm, and pink. The older the lamb, the redder the meat and, parenthetically, the stronger and more insistent the flavor.

Lamb cooks quickly and should be eaten slightly pink at the center for the fullest flavor and softest texture. Marinating lamb prior to the grill will keep the meat from drying out.

Go easy on flavoring woods, as the baby lamb is delicate in taste and easily overpowered. A touch of mesquite or hickory wood, herbs, spices, and even grapevines are good flavoring adjuncts. A general timing and cooking chart for lamb follows.

LAMB CHART ∾

CUT OF LAMB ·	TECHNIQUE* ·	TIMES AND SUGGESTIONS† ·
CHOPS (1 to 1½ inches thick)	**Grilling:** Hot to sear meat; medium-hot for grilling with direct heat.	Sear 1 minute per side. Sear edges. *Rare:* 4 to 6 minutes per side. *Med.:* 5 to 7 minutes per side.
STEAKS (cut from the leg) (1 inch thick)	**Grilling:** Hot to sear meat; medium-hot for grilling with direct heat.	Sear 1 minute per side. Sear edges. *Rare:* 4 minutes per side. *Med.:* 5 minutes per side.
LEG OF LAMB **Bone In** (4 pounds or less)	**Covered Cooking:** Medium-hot with indirect heat.	Marinate 3 hours. Cook, basting occasionally. *Rare:* 18 to 20 minutes per pound (internal temp.: 135°). *Med.:* 20 to 22 minutes per pound (internal temp.: 150°). Let stand 10 minutes before serving.
Butterflied (from a whole 5- or 6-pound leg)	**Covered Cooking:** Medium-hot with direct heat.	Marinate 6 hours or overnight. Cook covered. *Rare:* 12 minutes per side (internal temp.: 135°). *Med.:* 15 minutes per side (internal temp.: 150°).

LAMB ROASTS

RACK OF LAMB (about 2¼ pounds)	*Covered Cooking:* Medium-hot with direct heat.	Cook meaty side down for 10 minutes. Turn meat over and cook. *Rare:* 10 minutes longer (internal temp.: 135°). *Med.:* 14 minutes longer (internal temp.: 150°).
BONELESS, ROLLED ROASTS (about 4 pounds)	*Covered Cooking:* Medium-hot with direct heat.	Marinate 6 hours. Cook on a rack, basting often. *Rare:* 20 minutes per pound (internal temp.: 135°). *Med.:* 22 minutes per pound (internal temp.: 150°).
KABOBS FROM LEG (cut in 1¼-inch cubes)	*Grilling:* Medium-hot with direct heat.	Marinate 2 hours or overnight. Grill 3 minutes per side for a total of 12 minutes for medium-rare.

* For gas or electric grills, use the high setting for hot, the medium setting for medium-hot. Use the 3- to 4-second test for medium-hot and the 5-second test for medium. To lower the temperature of coal, raise the grid, use the outside edges of the briquets, or cover with cover vents partially closed.

For charcoal grills, hot refers to the 2-second hand test (see page 43).

† Times may vary depending on outdoor temperature and velocity of wind.

Lamb Chops

ᔕ THERE ARE SEVERAL different kinds of lamb chops one is likely to encounter in a butcher's meat case. The two most expensive cuts come from the loin of the animal and are dubbed "loin chops" and "English-cut chops."

The loin, with its small T-bone, is probably the most familiar. The English cut is exactly the same; however, it is rounded, sliced from a full loin which has not been severed at the chine bone.

Rib chops, taken from the "rack" section, are equally choice cuts that are extremely delectable though generally less hefty in size.

There are also various chops from the lamb shoulder (notably blade chops and arm chops) that are flavorful, if not as tender, but as they are considerably lower tabbed, worthy of a buyer's attention.

I use wood chips for lamb chops and only a small handful at that. Lamb cannot stand up to a heavy dose of smoke.

CLASSIC CHOPS

For this prejudiced palate, a rub of garlic and a pinch of curry are matchless seasonings for any cut of lamb.

    4 lamb chops, 1 inch thick
    1 clove garlic, bruised
      Curry powder
      Vegetable oil
      Salt and freshly ground pepper

1 · Trim all but ¼ to ½ inch fat from the edges of the lamb chops. Slash remaining fat with a knife at 1-inch intervals. Rub the chops well with bruised garlic. Sprinkle a pinch of curry powder over each side of the chops and rub in. Let stand covered 1 hour.

2 · Preheat the grill.

3 · If using presoaked wood chips, or other flavorings, sprinkle them over the hot coals or lava rocks. Brush the grid lightly with oil.

4 · Sear the chops over hot or high heat 1 minute per side, including edges. Then grill over medium-hot heat 4 minutes per side

for rare, 5 minutes per side for medium-rare. Sprinkle with salt and pepper before serving.

Serves 2 to 4.

MINTED CHOPS

If you can find a good brand of mint jelly (the kind with mint leaves in it) at your gourmet grocer, use it for the next recipe. If not, transform the supermarket variety into Almost Homemade (recipe follows).

    4 lamb chops, 1 inch thick
    ½ cup mint jelly
      Vegetable oil
      Salt and freshly ground pepper

1 · Trim all but ¼ to ½ inch fat from the edges of the lamb chops. Slash remaining fat with a knife at 1-inch intervals. Spoon 1 tablespoon mint jelly over each side of the lamb chops. Let stand covered 1 hour.

2 · Preheat the grill.

3 · If using presoaked wood chips, or other flavorings, sprinkle them over the hot coals or lava rocks. Brush the grid lightly with oil.

4 · Sear the chops over hot or high heat 1 minute per side, including edges. Then grill over medium-hot heat 4 minutes per side for rare, 5 minutes per side for medium-rare. Sprinkle with salt and pepper before serving.

Serves 2 to 4.

ALMOST HOMEMADE MINT JELLY

    1 jar (12 ounces) apple-mint jelly
    ¼ cup green creme de menthe
    1 tablespoon tarragon wine vinegar
    ½ cup chopped fresh mint

1 · Place the apple-mint jelly in a large bowl. Whisk in the creme de menthe with a large wire whisk. Beat in the vinegar and mint leaves until smooth. Chill thoroughly before serving.

Makes about 1½ cups.

GROUNDHOG CHOPS

Punxsutawney, Pennsylvania, is the home of Phil the Groundhog, whose shadow keeps us in meteorological suspense yearly. It is also the home of Elaine Light, who put together a charming cookbook titled, The New Gourmets and Groundhogs, *Groundhog Press, 1982, from which this recipe was adapted.*

    4 lamb chops, 1 inch thick
    1 tablespoon Dijon mustard
    2 tablespoons olive oil
    3 tablespoons white wine
    2 teaspoons chopped parsley
    2 teaspoons chopped fresh mint
    1 teaspoon chopped fresh oregano
      Vegetable oil
      Salt and freshly ground pepper

1 · Trim all but ¼ to ½ inch fat from the edges of the lamb chops. Slash remaining fat with a knife at 1-inch intervals. Combine the mustard, olive oil, wine, parsley, mint, and oregano. Spread over the chops. Let stand covered 1 hour.

2 · Preheat the grill.

3 · If using presoaked wood chips, or other flavorings, sprinkle them over the hot coals or lava rocks. Brush the grid lightly with vegetable oil.

4 · Sear the chops over hot or high heat 1 minute per side, including edges. Then grill over medium-hot heat 4 minutes per side for rare; 5 minutes per side for medium-rare. Sprinkle with salt and pepper before serving.

Serves 2 to 4.

LAMB CHOPS PROVENÇAL STYLE

When it comes to seasoning lamb, it seems the French do more (and do it better) than any other nationality of cooks in the world. For instance, rosemary and crushed allspice turn this ordinary chop into a Côté Exceptionale.

    4 lamb chops, 1 inch thick
    1 large clove garlic, crushed
   10 allspice berries, crushed
    ½ teaspoon finely chopped rosemary leaves
    2 tablespoons olive oil
      Vegetable oil

1 · Trim all but ¼ to ½ inch fat from the edges of the lamb
chops. Slash remaining fat with a knife at 1-inch intervals. Combine
the garlic, allspice, and rosemary in a small bowl or mortar. Crush
together with the back of a spoon or a pestle. Stir in the olive oil.
Spread over the chops. Let stand covered 1 hour.
2 · Preheat the grill.
3 · If using presoaked wood chips, or other flavorings, sprinkle
them over the hot coals or lava rocks. Brush the grid lightly with
vegetable oil.
4 · Sear the chops over hot or high heat 1 minute per side, including edges. Then grill over medium-hot heat 4 minutes per side
for rare, 5 minutes per side for medium-rare.

Serves 2 to 4.

"SUPER" CHOPS

*What makes these chops "super" is a secret ingredient: a jot of
anchovy paste added to the marinade.*

    4 lamp chops, 1 inch thick
    4 teaspoons tomato paste
    ½ teaspoon anchovy paste
    1 teaspoon minced fresh basil
    1 teaspoon olive oil
      Vegetable oil
      Freshly ground pepper

1 · Trim all but ¼ to ½ inch fat from the edges of the lamb
chops. Slash remaining fat with a knife at 1-inch intervals. Combine
the tomato paste, anchovy paste, basil, and olive oil. Spread over
the chops. Let stand covered 1 hour.
2 · Preheat the grill.

3 · If using presoaked wood chips, or other flavorings, sprinkle them over the hot coals or lava rocks. Brush the grid lightly with vegetable oil.

4 · Sear the chops over hot or high heat 1 minute per side, including edges. Then grill over medium-hot heat 4 minutes per side for rare, 5 minutes per side for medium-rare. Sprinkle with pepper before serving.

Serves 2 to 4.

SHIRLEY SARVIS'S LAMB LOIN ROASTS

Shirley Sarvis is a talented and innovative wine authority from San Francisco who conducts seminars that match and mix the flavors of various vintages and dishes. The "roasts" in her recipe are really chops, but so thick (2½ inches), they are literally roasted over indirect heat.

  4 large loin lamb chops, each 2½ inches thick
    Salt and freshly ground pepper
  4 large cloves garlic, cut into slivers
  2 tablespoons olive oil
    Vegetable oil

1 · Trim all but ¼ to ½ inch fat from the edges of the lamb chops. Slash remaining fat with a knife at 1-inch intervals. Rub the chops well with salt and pepper. Poke a hole in the center of each chop and insert a sliver of garlic. Combine the olive oil with 2 tablespoons vegetable oil. Brush over the chops. Sprinkle each side with remaining slivers of garlic. Let stand covered 6 hours.

2 · Preheat the grill.

3 · If using a charcoal grill, spread the coals apart and place a drip pan in the center. If using presoaked wood chips, sprinkle them over the hot coals. If using a gas grill, place the drip pan on one side of the grill directly on the lava rocks and add any presoaked chips to the pan. Brush the grid lightly with vegetable oil.

4 · Sear the chops, being very careful, over hot or high heat 2 minutes per each edge. Then grill the chops 4 minutes per side. Move the chops over the drip pan and cover-cook with vents two-thirds of the way open 4 minutes per side for rare, 5 to 6 minutes per side for medium-rare.

Serves 4.

Lamb Steaks

❧ LAMB STEAKS, CUT from the sirloin end (the fat end) of a leg of lamb, have a texture similar to beefsteak and are a marvel on the grill. Most butchers will cut lamb steaks only when they already have an order for a half roast leg, so it is advisable to call and place your order in advance.

Lamb steaks are generally cut about 1 inch thick, and timing on the grill exactly matches those for chops. Again, just a small portion of wood chips for flavoring is advised.

JUDITH'S LAMB STEAKS

Judith Weber, literary agent and friend, introduced me to grilled lamb steaks awhile back. Now I am a convert to the cause. Anyone who likes a lamb chop will absolutely love lamb in steak form.

> 4 lamb steaks, 1 inch thick
> ¼ cup red wine
> 1 tablespoon olive oil
> 1½ teaspoons chopped fresh oregano
> 1 teaspoon chopped fresh thyme
> 1 large clove garlic, minced
>   Vegetable oil
>   Salt and freshly ground pepper

1 · Trim all but ¼ to ½ inch fat from the edges of the lamb steaks. Slash remaining fat with a knife at 1-inch intervals. Combine the wine, olive oil, oregano, thyme, and garlic. Spread over both sides of the lamb steaks. Let stand covered 2 hours.

2 · Preheat the grill.

3 · If using presoaked wood chips, or other flavorings, sprinkle them over the hot coals or lava rocks. Brush the grid lightly with vegetable oil.

4 · Sear the steaks over hot or high heat 1 minute per side, including edges. Then grill over medium-hot heat 4 minutes per side for rare, 5 minutes per side for medium-rare. Sprinkle with salt and pepper before serving.

Serves 4.

GRILLED LAMB STEAKS WITH OLIVE BUTTER

The best recipes often stem from extraordinary coincidences. The following sage-flecked lamb (and its accompaniment of Olive Butter) is a dish invented when a mild summer caused a sagebush to grow like weeds—and a friend in California sent a half-dozen jars of home-grown olives the same month. Do not make this dish unless you have fresh sage to spare.

    4 lamb steaks, 1 inch thick
    1 clove garlic, bruised
    4 teaspoons olive oil
  20 large fresh sage leaves, roughly chopped
      Vegetable oil
      Olive Butter (see page 317)

1 · Trim all but ¼ to ½ inch fat from the edges of the lamb steaks. Slash remaining fat with a knife at 1-inch intervals. Rub the steaks well with garlic on both sides. Brush both sides with olive oil. Press the chopped sage leaves, equally on both sides of the steaks. Let stand covered 1 hour.

2 · Preheat the grill.

3 · If using presoaked wood chips, or other flavorings, sprinkle them over the hot coals or lava rocks. Brush the grid lightly with vegetable oil.

4 · Sear the steaks over hot or high heat 1 minute per side, including edges. Then grill over medium-hot heat 4 minutes per side for rare, 5 minutes per side for medium-rare. Serve with about 1 tablespoon Olive Butter placed on the top of each steak. Serve extra butter on the side.

Serves 4.

Leg of Lamb

LEG OF LAMB is equal to lamb chops in any summer popularity contest at the grill. The leg may be roasted whole, but these days many barbecue enthusiasts choose to have it alternately boned and butterflied. Not only does a butterflied lamb cook in one quarter the time required for a whole leg, but the problem of carving the meat at the table has been virtually eliminated.

It is essential to marinate butterflied or whole legs of lamb overnight in order to keep the meat moist during the cooking. Like all other cuts, leg of lamb should be served medium-rare.

A few wood chunks, or a handful of chips, will give lamb an extra dimension. Garlic cloves, dried spices (presoaked), and lemon peel are also excellent options for flavoring lamb.

LEMON ROAST LEG OF LAMB

When choosing a bone-in lamb for the grill, I advise you to select a half or three-quarter leg weighing no more than 4 pounds. This will keep the cooking time under 1½ hours. Garlic and lemon in tandem are the flavor architects of this roast.

½ or ¾ leg of lamb, 4 pounds or less
1 clove garlic, cut into slivers
  Peel of 1 lemon, cut into slivers
  Vegetable oil
¼ cup unsalted butter, melted
  Juice of ½ lemon

1 · With an ice pick, poke holes in the surface of the lamb and insert slivers of garlic, alternating with slivers of lemon peel. Let stand 3 hours.

2 · Preheat the grill.

3 · If using a charcoal grill, spread the coals apart and place a drip pan in the center. If using presoaked wood chips, sprinkle them over the hot coals. If using a gas grill, place the drip pan on one side

181

of the grill directly on the lava rocks and add any presoaked chips to the pan. Brush the grid lightly with oil.

4 · Place the lamb on the grid over the drip pan and cover-cook with vents three-quarters open over medium-hot heat, basting occasionally with melted butter and lemon juice, 18 to 20 minutes per pound for rare (internal temperature: 135 degrees), 20 to 22 minutes per pound for medium (internal temperature: 150 degrees). (Charcoal users will have to add more prelit coals after the first 45 minutes.)

Serves 4 to 6.

JODY GILLIS'S BUTTERFLIED LAMB

Jody Gillis is a protean cook, teacher, and general espouser of the good life in Santee, California. Her comment (sent along with the following recipe) sums up her culinary philosophy: "This is the most *elegant way to serve lamb and wonderfully tasty besides!"*

    1 leg of lamb, 5 to 6 pounds, boned and butterflied
    3 cloves garlic, crushed
      Vegetable oil
    ½ cup dry sherry
    1 teaspoon crushed cumin seeds
    2½ teaspoons chopped fresh rosemary
    1 teaspoon salt
    ½ teaspoon freshly ground pepper

1 · Place the lamb in a shallow glass or ceramic dish. Combine the garlic with ½ cup vegetable oil, the sherry, cumin, rosemary, salt, and pepper. Mix well. Pour over lamb. Refrigerate covered overnight. Let stand at room temperature 1 hour before cooking.

2 · Preheat the grill.

3 · If using presoaked wood chips or chunks (chips for gas), or other flavorings, sprinkle them over the hot coals or lava rocks. Brush the grid lightly with oil.

4 · Place the lamb on the grid and cover-cook with vents open over medium-hot heat 12 minutes per side for rare, 15 minutes per side for medium-rare. Let stand 10 minutes before serving.

Serves 6 to 8.

BUTTERMILK BUTTERFLIED LAMB

Buttermilk and lamb are a classic partnership—largely because the acid in the former tames the muscle fiber in the latter, resulting in a velvety soft bite. This version, dappled with fresh rosemary, stems from the sheep region of the West.

　　1　leg of lamb, 5 to 6 pounds, boned and butterflied
　　2　cloves garlic, minced
　　2　sprigs fresh rosemary
　　1　tablespoon Dijon mustard
　　1　teaspoon soy sauce
　½　teaspoon crushed, dried hot red peppers
　¼　teaspoon freshly ground pepper
　　3　cups buttermilk
　　　Vegetable oil

1 · Place the lamb in a shallow glass or ceramic dish. Add the garlic and rosemary sprigs to the dish. Combine the mustard, soy sauce, hot peppers, and freshly ground pepper in a bowl. Stir in the buttermilk and pour over the lamb. Refrigerate covered overnight. Let stand at room temperature 1 hour before cooking.

2 · Preheat the grill.

3 · If using presoaked wood chips or chunks (chips for gas), or other flavorings, sprinkle them over the hot coals or lava rocks. Brush the grid lightly with oil.

4 · Place the lamb on the grid and cover-cook with vents open over medium-hot heat 12 minutes per side for rare, 15 minutes per side for medium-rare. Let stand 10 minutes before serving.

Serves 6 to 8.

PIQUANT PRODIGAL BUTTERFLIED LAMB

*Another classic coalition: yoghurt and lamb. As in the prior but-
termilked butterfly, lactic acid tenderizes the meat before it hits
the grill. Incidentally, the sauces called for below accompany both
dishes with great distinction.*

  1 leg of lamb, 5 to 6 pounds, boned and butterflied
  1 pound plain yoghurt
  4 cloves garlic, crushed
  ½ cup chopped fresh mint
  ¼ teaspoon freshly ground pepper
    Vegetable oil
    Cold Cucumber Sauce or Hot Spicy Mint Sauce (see page
      318 or 311)

1 · Place the lamb in a shallow glass or ceramic dish. Combine
the yoghurt, garlic, mint, and pepper. Spread over both sides of the
lamb. Refrigerate covered overnight. Let stand at room temperature 1 hour before cooking.

2 · Preheat the grill.

3 · If using presoaked wood chips or chunks (chips for gas), or
other flavorings, sprinkle them over the hot coals or lava rocks.
Brush the grid lightly with oil.

4 · Place the lamb on the grid and cover-cook with vents open
over medium-hot heat 12 minutes per side for rare, 15 minutes per
side for medium-rare. Let stand 10 minutes before serving, with
Cold Cucumber Sauce and/or Hot Spicy Mint Sauce.

Serves 6 to 8.

Lamb Roasts

WITHOUT QUESTION, THE most elegant roasted lamb is the rack (or rib roast). Racks of lamb generally have 8 ribs, and serve a scant 2 to 3 people. Be sure to have your butcher cut through the chine bone, however, for easy carving after the rack is roasted.

Boneless, rolled lamb roasts are also impressive cover-cooked on a grill. The tenderest is cut from the loin area and is marketed as either a boneless loin roast or a rolled double roast (from the saddle). A boned-and-rolled leg of lamb is also a tonic choice for roasting. Shoulder roasts, less expensive and somewhat less tender than the aforementioned cuts, will do nicely on the grill but require an extended period of prior marination.

Again, keep adjunctive flavoring woods to a minimum.

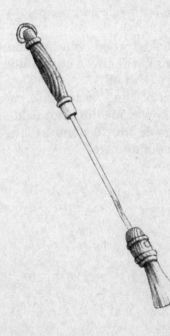

ROAST RACK OF LAMB

Lamb is a meat of exceptional flavor—and that flavor is often at its best totally unadorned. Or almost totally—as in the case of the following rack of lamb, merely smudged with garlic, oil, and parsley.

1 8-rib rack of lamb, about 2¼ pounds
2 cloves garlic, crushed
  Vegetable oil
1 teaspoon minced fresh thyme
1 cup minced fresh parsley
  Salt and freshly ground pepper

1 · Trim all but ¼ inch fat from the meaty side of the lamb. Rub the meat thoroughly with crushed garlic. Brush with about 1½ tablespoons oil. Sprinkle the thyme over the top and sides of the meat. Press the parsley over the entire rack, pressing firmly with your hands. Sprinkle with salt and pepper.

2 · Preheat the grill.

3 · If using presoaked wood chips or chunks (chips for gas), or other flavorings, sprinkle them over the hot coals or lava rocks. Brush the grid lightly with oil.

4 · Place the rack of lamb on the grid, meat side down. Cover-cook with vents open over medium-hot heat 10 minutes. Continue to cover-cook, meat side up, 10 minutes longer for rare, about 14 minutes longer for medium-rare.

Serves 2 to 4.

KHAROOF MIHSHEE
(Stuffed Lamb Persian Style)

Persians dote on excuses for feasts. The birth of a male child, a betrothal, marriage, even a funeral is occasion enough for a great dish to be prepared. This lamb-stuffed roast lamb, for example.

        2 tablespoons unsalted butter
        ½ cup minced onion
        1 pound ground lamb
        1 cup cooked rice
     1½ tablespoons chopped fresh dill
        ½ teaspoon salt
        ¼ teaspoon freshly ground pepper
        ½ teaspoon crushed, dried hot red peppers
           Pinch of ground mace
           Pinch of ground cinnamon
        1 egg, lightly beaten
        ¼ cup toasted pine nuts (pignolias)
        1 boneless, butterflied lamb roast, about 4 pounds
           Vegetable oil

1 · Melt the butter in a large skillet over medium-low heat. Add the onion; cook 2 minutes. Add the ground lamb and cook, breaking up the meat with a wooden spoon, until the meat just begins to lose its color, about 1 minute, no longer. Transfer to a large bowl.

2 · Add the cooked rice to the lamb mixture along with the dill, salt, pepper, hot peppers, mace, cinnamon, egg, and pine nuts. Mix thoroughly.

3 · Lay the rolled roast on a work surface and press the stuffing over the meat, leaving an inch all the way around. Roll up the meat and tie around with string at 1-inch intervals. Then tie the long way in 2 places to secure the meat. Brush lightly with oil.

4 · Preheat the grill.

5 · If using presoaked wood chips or chunks (chips for gas), or other flavorings, sprinkle them over the hot coals or lava rocks. Brush the grid lightly with oil.

6 · Place the lamb roast on the grid. Cover-cook with vents open over medium-hot heat for 15 minutes per each of its 4 sides. Let stand 12 minutes before serving.

Serves 6 to 8.

Lamb Kabobs

THE MEAT MOST often used for lamb kabobbery is the sirloin portion of the leg, the same cut that produces a lamb steak. Since some butchers will, on occasion, substitute lesser cuts (like shoulder), I advise you to be very specific when ordering. In my opinion, there is nothing worse than biting into a chunk of tough (or sinewy) meat after it is showily apportioned from a skewer.

Use chips if wood is your preference for flavoring.

KEFTA

Kefta is the North African version of sausage and is much dependent on a curious alignment of diverse flavorings like cinnamon and garlic. Be forewarned. These sausages are addictive. Though Moroccans actually skewer kefta *before grilling, I find them too fragile and usually cook them in a hinged wire basket.*

> 1½ pounds ground lamb
> ½ pound ground beef
> ¼ pound ground veal
> 2 cloves garlic, mashed
> 1 medium onion, finely chopped
> ½ cup bread crumbs
> Pinch of allspice
> 1 tablespoon chopped fresh mint
> 2 tablespoons chopped fresh parsley
> Dash of hot pepper sauce
> 1 egg, lightly beaten
> ½ teaspoon salt
> ⅛ teaspoon freshly ground pepper
> 3 to 4 tablespoons water
> Vegetable oil

1 · Combine the ground lamb with all ingredients through the pepper. Mix thoroughly. Add just enough water to moisten the meat. Continue to mix until stiff.

2 · Form the meat mixture into sausages, each about 3 inches long and ¾ inch thick. Do not make them too small or they will break. Place on a lightly oiled platter. Refrigerate 1 hour.

3 · Preheat the grill.

4 · Remove *kefta* from refrigerator and place in a well-oiled hinged wire basket. Brush both sides of the meat lightly with oil.

5 · If using presoaked wood chips or other flavorings, sprinkle them over the hot coals or lava rocks. Brush the grid lightly with oil.

6 · Grill the *kefta* in the basket over hot or high heat 8 to 10 minutes per side.

Serves 4 to 6.

TRADITIONAL ARMENIAN SHISH KEBOB

"Shish" is the Arabic term for a skewer and "kebob" means meat. Somehow the term got turned around and the word kebob or kabob implies anything on a skewer. The concept of skewered, fire-roasted meat developed back in the time of Alexander the Great—when hungry foot soldiers, gathered round a blazing conflagration, cooked dinner at sword's point.

        Juice of 1 large lemon
        Juice of 1 lime
    ¼ cup olive oil
    2 tablespoons grated onion
    1 clove garlic, crushed
    1 teaspoon crushed, dried hot red peppers
    2 teaspoons salt
    2 teaspoons turmeric
    1 teaspoon ground coriander
    1 teaspoon ground ginger
 1½ pounds lamb, cut into 1¼-inch cubes
    8 small white onions
    8 cherry tomatoes
        Vegetable oil

1 · Combine all ingredients from lemon juice through ginger in a large glass or ceramic bowl. Mix well. Stir in the lamb cubes. Cover and let stand 2 hours.

2 · Meanwhile, peel the onions and cut a cross in each root end to keep them from falling apart. Cook in boiling water 3 minutes. Rinse under cold running water; drain. Pat dry.

3 · Preheat the grill.

4 · Divide the meat equally in fours. You should have about 5 pieces per portion. On each skewer, place a piece of meat, then onion, meat, tomato, meat, onion, meat, tomato, ending with meat. Brush lightly with marinade.

5 · If using presoaked wood chips, or other flavorings, sprinkle them over the hot coals or lava rocks. Brush the grid lightly with vegetable oil.

6 · Grill the kabobs over hot or high heat 3 minutes per side.

Serves 2 to 4.

KEY WEST KABOBS

From the low country of Florida (Key West) comes the following "easy as falling off a log" kabob. The ingredients? Merely orange marmalade, vinegar, and a good imagination.

   1 clove garlic, minced
   ½ cup orange marmalade
   ¼ cup white wine vinegar
   ¼ teaspoon cayenne pepper
     Vegetable oil
1½ pounds lamb, cut into 1¼-inch cubes
   3 medium zucchini, cut into 16 ¾-inch-thick slices
     Sugar
   8 large seedless orange sections

1 · Combine the garlic, marmalade, vinegar, cayenne, and 2 teaspoons oil in a large bowl. Mix thoroughly. Stir in the lamb cubes. Cover and let stand 2 hours.

2 · Preheat the grill.

3 · Brush the zucchini slices lightly with oil. Pat sugar onto each orange section.

4 · Divide the meat equally in fours. You should have about 5 pieces per portion. On each skewer, place a piece of meat, then zuc-

chini, meat, orange, zucchini, meat, zucchini, orange, meat, zucchini, ending with meat. Brush lightly with marinade.

5 · If using presoaked wood chips, or other flavorings, sprinkle
them over the hot coals or lava rocks. Brush the grid lightly with
oil.

6 · Grill the kabobs over hot or high heat 3 minutes per side.

Serves 2 to 4.

INDOCHINA SKEWERED LAMB

*Southeast Asian cuisine is the most imaginative and delicate in
the Orient. Do not take my word alone as gospel. Instead try the
following marinated lamb. Do not skip the honey walnut topping,
spooned over the cooked meat and vegetables. It is totally essential to this eloquent fare.*

       2 tablespoons black bean sauce (available in the gourmet
           department of most supermarkets)
      ½ teaspoon dry mustard
       2 tablespoons dry sherry
       2 tablespoons soy sauce
       1 tablespoon sesame oil
      1½ pounds lamb, cut into 1¼-inch cubes
      ½ cup roughly chopped walnuts
       2 tablespoons honey
       2 teaspoons vinegar
      16 small radishes, peeled
       4 small hot green Italian peppers, seeded, deveined, and cut
           in half lengthwise
         Vegetable oil

1 · Combine the black bean sauce with the mustard, sherry, soy
sauce, and sesame oil in a large bowl. Mix well. Stir in the lamb
cubes. Cover and let stand 2 hours.

2 · Preheat the grill.

3 · Combine the walnuts, honey, and vinegar in a bowl. Mix
well; reserve.

4 · Divide the meat equally in fours. You should have about 5
pieces per portion. On each skewer, place a piece of meat, then rad-

ish, meat, pepper, radish, meat, radish, pepper, meat, radish, ending with meat. Brush lightly with vegetable oil.

5 · If using presoaked wood chips, or other flavorings, sprinkle them over the hot coals or lava rocks. Brush the grid lightly with oil.

6 · Grill the kabobs over hot or high heat 3 minutes per side. Spoon some of the walnut mixture over each portion after it has been removed from the skewer.

Serves 2 to 4.

HOT OFF THE GRILL

If you are the "average American" who grills first and groans later, this is a tally of what viands you're likely to conspicuously consume in a year. (These are U.S. Department of Agriculture statistics rounded to the nearest pound.)

Beef:	95 pounds
Pork:	54 pounds
Chicken:	43 pounds
Fish:	13 pounds
Turkey:	9 pounds
Veal:	3 pounds
Lamb:	2 pounds

Sausage

IT HAS BEEN estimated that there are between five and six hundred different types of sausage being ground out in the world today. Sausage, according to the American Meat Institute, is "a mixture of meat and other foodstuffs, in a natural or artificial casing or tube," which pretty much leaves the door wide open for sausage makers.

All sausages however, do fall into one of the following categories: fresh, smoked, cooked, new conditioned, dried, and cooked specialties.

Fresh: This basically refers to any link made of uncooked meat, period. For instance, such diverse items as ordinary breakfast sausage, scrapple, Boudin Blanc, bratwurst, weisswurst, and Italian sausages, whether sweet or mild, fall into this category.

Smoked: These sausages are made from cured meats (and other products) and, of course, are smoked before they are found brightening up a meat case. There are *cooked* smoked sausages such as ye old hot dog, knockwurst, Vienna sausage, bologna, kielbasa, and mortadella; and *uncooked* varieties as well, including some country-style pork sausage, some mettwurst, and cotechina.

Cooked: Cooked wursts are made from either fresh or cured meats, but must be fully cooked before they are sold; for instance, liverwurst, braunschweiger, teawurst, and blood sausage.

New Conditioned: Mostly ready-to-eat, these sausages are composed of meat and curing agents. They are all uniformly cured, but some are smoked as well. This group includes French sauccison d'ail, cooked salami, pepperoni, cervelat, soppressata, Thuringer, and summer sausage.

Dried: These sausages are made from fresh meat to which spices and various seasonings have been added. They are cured and dried, but not necessarily cooked. Italian dry salami falls into this category, which needs no cooking, as well as Spanish chorizo, which most definitely must be cooked before it is eaten.

Cooked Specialties: This classification was obviously designed for anything and everything that does not fit in the other five subdivisions. It includes headcheese, blood pudding, and haggis.

Sausages (of practically any stripe) make quick and easy work for the griller. Fresh sausages, however, *must* be poached, steamed (foil-wrapped on the grill), or cooked over indirect heat, before they are grilled over direct heat to brown. Grilling a fresh sausage over direct heat without prior treatment (to reduce the fat content) will cause constant conflagration and/or burnt weiners! Prick all fresh sausages several times with a fork before cooking to help release the excess fat and prevent the casings from bursting. Precooked sausages need no special handling.

Because of the abbreviated cooking times, wood chips are adequate for adding to the coals or lava rocks. Choose hearty woods, like hickory, maple, or oak. A general timing and cooking chart for sausage follows.

SAUSAGE CHART

TYPE OF SAUSAGE ·	TECHNIQUE* ·	TIMES AND SUGGESTIONS† ·
FRESH BEEF OR LAMB	**Grilling:** Medium-hot, direct heat.	(Poach, steam, or grill indirect.) Prick skins, grill 5 minutes per side. (Use edges of coals if sausage flares up.)
FRESH PORK OR VEAL	**Grilling:** Medium-hot, direct heat. Then *Covered Cooking* with medium, direct heat.	(Poach, steam, or grill indirect.) Prick skins, grill 5 minutes per side. Then cook 2½ minutes per side.
DRIED, UNCOOKED	**Covered Cooking:** Medium-hot, indirect heat. Then *Grilling* with medium, direct heat.	Prick skins, cook over pan for 10 minutes. Then grill over direct heat 5 minutes.
PRECOOKED	**Grilling:** Medium-hot, direct heat.	Grill 8 to 10 minutes.

* For gas or electric grills, use the medium setting for medium-hot. Use the cooler edges of the grid in case of flare-up.
For charcoal grills, medium-hot refers to the 3- to 4-second hand test (see page 43). To lower the temperature of coal, raise the grid, use the outside edges of the briquets, or cover with cover vents partially closed.

† Times may vary depending on outdoor temperature and velocity of wind.

GRILLED, POACHED ITALIAN SAUSAGES

*Though fresh sausages may be cover-cooked first over a drip pan
for 10 minutes prior to direct grilling, poaching them in advance
in a flavored liquid (in this case red wine) adds a bright new dimension as well as eliminates the need for indirect cooking.*

  1 cup red wine
  1 cup water
  8 sweet Italian sausages, about 1½ pounds
    Vegetable oil

1 · Preheat the grill.

2 · Meanwhile, combine the wine and water in a skillet large
enough to hold the sausages in a single layer. Heat to boiling; reduce heat. Prick the sausages and gently poach in the liquid 3 minutes per side. Drain.

3 · If using presoaked wood chips or other flavorings, sprinkle
them over the hot coals or lava rocks. Brush the grid lightly with
oil.

4 · Grill the sausages over medium-hot heat 5 minutes per side,
using the outer edges of the grid in case of flare-up. Then cover-
cook with vents open 5 minutes longer, turning the sausages once.

Serves 4.

LACED LINKS

*Italian sausages, wrapped in wilted green onion ends, look (and
taste) fabulous when they come off the grill.*

  2 cups water
  3 lemon slices
  3 sprigs parsley
  1 tablespoon celery leaves
 32 scallion tops—the part above the white bulb, which should
     be reserved for another purpose
  8 sweet or hot Italian sausages, about 1½ pounds
    Vegetable oil

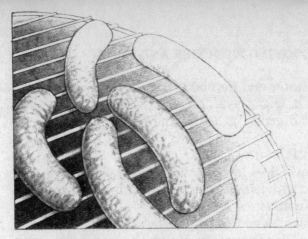

1 · Preheat the grill.

2 · Meanwhile, combine the water, lemon slices, parsley, and celery leaves in a skillet large enough to hold the sausages in a single layer. Heat to boiling; reduce heat. Dip the green onion ends in the hot liquid until just wilted; set aside. Prick the sausages and gently poach in the liquid 3 minutes per side. Drain.

3 · Wrap each sausage with 4 onion ends, tucking each tip underneath to secure. Brush each sausage lightly with oil.

4 · If using presoaked wood chips or other flavorings, sprinkle them over the hot coals or lava rocks. Brush the grid lightly with oil.

5 · Grill the sausages over medium-hot heat 5 minutes per side, using the outer edges of the grid in case of flare-up. Then cover-cook with vents open 5 minutes longer, turning the sausages once.

Serves 4.

FRESH FENNEL WITH FENNEL SAUSAGE

Fresh fennel is a natural ally to fresh Italian sausage with its delicate seasoning of fennel seeds. A drop of anise-flavored Pernod in the poaching liquid underscores the licoricey amalgam.

2 cups water
2 tablespoons Pernod
8 sweet or hot Italian sausages, about 1½ pounds
2 small heads fennel, cut crosswise into ¼-inch-thick slices
2 tablespoons lemon juice
2 tablespoons olive oil
Freshly ground pepper
Vegetable oil

1 · Combine the water and Pernod in a skillet large enough to hold the sausages in a single layer. Heat to boiling; reduce heat. Prick the sausages and gently poach in the liquid 3 minutes per side. Drain.

2 · Preheat the grill.

3 · Place the fennel slices in a fish basket (use 2 if necessary). Sprinkle on both sides with lemon juice; brush both sides with olive oil and then sprinkle both sides with pepper.

4 · If using presoaked wood chips or other flavorings, sprinkle them over the hot coals or lava rocks. Brush the grid lightly with vegetable oil.

5 · Place the sausages on the outer edges of the grid. Place the fish basket(s) with fennel in the center. Grill over medium-hot heat 5 minutes per side. Then cover-cook with vents open 5 minutes longer, turning sausages and fennel once.

Serves 4.

GRILLED SHRIMP AND SAUSAGES BEDDED ON RED, RED RICE

This recipe for smoky, fresh shrimp and sausage served atop peppery red rice is a gastronomic inspiration, created by Bert Greene, the noted food writer, author, and television personality. Note that the rice should be prepared in advance through step 3, and completed (and kept warm in a low oven) no more than 20 minutes before the shrimp and sausage hit the grill.

    Red, Red Rice (recipe follows)
16 large fresh shrimp, shelled and deveined
 3 tablespoons olive oil
 2 tablespoons chopped fresh basil
½ teaspoon freshly ground pepper
1½ cups dry white wine
1½ pounds hot Italian sausage
    Vegetable oil

1 · Make the Red, Red Rice through step 3. Set aside.

2 · Place the shrimp in a glass or ceramic bowl. Add the olive oil, basil, and pepper. Toss well. Cover and let stand 30 to 45 minutes.

3 · Heat the wine to boiling in a skillet large enough to hold the

sausages in a single layer. Reduce heat. Prick the sausages and gently poach in the wine 3 minutes per side. Drain.

4 · Preheat the grill.

5 · Finish the Red, Red Rice. Keep warm in a low oven. Prick the sausages once more and place the shrimp on skewers.

6 · If using presoaked wood chips or other flavorings, sprinkle them over the hot coals or lava rocks. Brush the grid lightly with vegetable oil.

7 · Place the sausages on the grid. Cover-cook with vents open over hot or high heat 5 minutes, turning once. Remove cover and grill 5 minutes longer. Turn the sausages over and add the shrimp to the grill. Grill the shrimp for 2½ minutes per side.

8 · To serve, place a mound of Red, Red Rice on a plate. Place a sausage in the middle and top with 4 shrimp.

Serves 4.

RED, RED RICE

1 cup long-grain rice
1 large red bell pepper
3 tablespoons unsalted butter
1 teaspoon olive oil
¼ cup thinly sliced scallion bulbs
Salt and freshly ground pepper

1 · Add the rice to a large pot of boiling, salted water. Stir once while water returns to boil; boil 12 minutes. Drain rice into a colander. Place the colander over steaming water and cover the rice with one sheet of paper towel. Steam 15 minutes.

2 · Meanwhile, char the pepper over a gas flame, under a broiler, or on a preheated grill. Wrap the charred pepper in paper towels and place in a plastic bag to cool for 5 minutes. Rub off the charred skin with paper towels. Seed the pepper and roughly chop.

3 · Heat 2 tablespoons butter with the oil in a large skillet over medium heat. Add the scallions; cook 2 minutes, but do not brown. Add the pepper and cook 1 minute longer. Transfer mixture to a food processor and process until smooth.

4 · Add the rice to the same skillet with the remaining tablespoon of butter. Add the processed scallions and peppers, and toss until well mixed and the rice takes on a red hue. Add salt and pepper to taste. Keep warm in a low oven until ready to serve.

Serves 4.

GRILLED GARLIC SAUSAGE

Perhaps the most famous French sausage, sauccison d'ail is coated with a rough mix of ground pepper and allspice to complement the exquisite bite of its garlicky flavor.

> French sauccison d'ail, 1 to 1¼ pounds
> 1 tablespoon walnut oil
> 1½ tablespoons black peppercorns, crushed
> ½ teaspoon allspice berries, crushed
> Vegetable oil

1 · Prick the sausage and rub with the walnut oil. Place the crushed peppercorns and allspice berries on a plate and roll the sausage in this mixture. Let stand 1 hour.

2 · Preheat the grill.

3 · If using presoaked wood chips, or other flavorings, sprinkle them over the hot coals or lava rocks. Brush the grid lightly with vegetable oil.

4 · Place the sausage on the grid. Cover-cook with vents open over medium-hot heat 10 minutes. Turn the sausage over and cover-cook 5 minutes longer. Serve, sliced on the diagonal.

Serves 4.

BEER-POACHED POLISH SAUSAGE

Sausage and beer are longtime confederates, served in tandem at pubs and cafés around the world. In this instance, however, they are together in a pot prior to grilling.

> 12 ounces beer
> Kielbasa (Polish) sausage, 1 to 1¼ pounds
> Vegetable oil
> Juice of 1 lemon

1 · Preheat the grill.

2 · Place the beer in a skillet large enough to hold the sausage. Heat to boiling; reduce heat. Prick the sausage and gently poach it in the beer 4 minutes per side. Drain.

3 · If using presoaked wood chips or other flavorings, sprinkle

them over the hot coals or lava rocks. Brush the grid lightly with oil.

4 · Brush the sausage lightly with oil. Grill over medium-hot heat 5 minutes per side.

5 · To serve: Split the sausage down the center or cut into thick wedges. Sprinkle with lemon juice before serving.

Serves 4.

GRILLED TOMATOED SAUSAGE

I use kielbasa in the following recipe as well, but Poltava, Ukrainian-style sausage, is equally salubrious.

Polish or Ukrainian sausage, 1 to 1¼ pounds
1 tablespoon tomato paste
1 teaspoon country-style Dijon mustard (with seeds)
1 teaspoon vodka
½ teaspoon olive oil
Vegetable oil

1 · Prick the sausage and cook in boiling water 10 minutes.

2 · Combine the tomato paste, mustard, vodka, and olive oil in a bowl. Mix well. Spread over the sausage. Let stand 1 hour.

3 · Preheat the grill.

4 · If using presoaked wood chips or other flavorings, sprinkle them over the hot coals or lava rocks. Brush the grid lightly with vegetable oil.

5 · Grill the sausage over medium-hot heat 5 minutes per side.

6 · To serve: Split the sausage down the center or cut into thick wedges.

Serves 4.

SOPPRESSATA STEAKS

A rosemary coating adds distinction to this thick-sliced, spicy sausage. For the grill, I prefer a coarse-textured salami like Italian soppressata, but its smoother cousin, Milano salami, will make an admirable stand-in. This dish stands on its own at a mixed-grill cookout, but also makes a fine first course sliced on a bed of lettuce.

> 4 1-inch thick slices soppressata or Milano salami
> 4 teaspoons olive oil
>   Freshly ground pepper
> 3 tablespoons chopped fresh rosemary leaves
>   Vegetable oil

1 · Brush the salami slices with olive oil on both sides. Sprinkle both sides with pepper. Pat the rosemary leaves over both sides as well. Let stand 1 hour.

2 · Preheat the grill.

3 · If using presoaked wood chips or other flavorings, sprinkle them over the hot coals or lava rocks. Brush the grid lightly with vegetable oil.

4 · Grill the sausages over medium-hot heat 5 minutes per side.

Serves 4.

SKEWERED CHORIZOS AND POTATO CUBES

What gives a Spanish chorizo its unusal stamp (and color) is the oil of annatto, a yellowish-red seasoning made from the pulp seeds of the annatto tree. Though dried, chorizos are uncooked, and the interior chunks of fat must be drained before grilling directly over the coals. In this case use indirect heat.

> 4 large potatoes, peeled and cut into 1½-inch cubes
> 8 chorizos
>   Vegetable oil
>   Red wine vinegar

1 · Preheat the grill.

2 · Cook the potato cubes in boiling, salted water 7 minutes. Drain.

3 · Arrange the chorizos and potatoes on 4 skewers: 2 chorizos and 3 potato cubes per skewer. Prick the chorizos and brush lightly with oil.

4 · If using a charcoal grill, spread the coals apart and place a

drip pan in the center. If using presoaked wood chips, or other flavorings, sprinkle them over the hot coals. If using a gas grill, place
the drip pan on one side of the grill directly on the lava rocks and
add any presoaked chips to the pan. Brush the grid lightly with oil.

5 · Place the skewers on the grid directly over the drip pan.
Cover-cook with vents open over medium-hot heat 10 minutes. Remove cover and grill over direct heat 5 minutes per side. Serve
sprinkled with red wine vinegar.

Serves 4.

BLACKENED WURST

*The following recipe will convert even die-hard liverwurst phobes
to its culinary cause. Supercrusty on the outside, satiny smooth
within, the wurst must be sliced* after *grilling so remember to request an uncut chunk from your butcher.*

    8 ounces calves liverwurst (I prefer Schaller & Weber)
      Vegetable oil
      Freshly ground pepper
    3 tablespoons malt vinegar

1 · Preheat the grill.
2 · Brush the liverwurst lightly with oil.
3 · If using presoaked wood chips or other flavorings, sprinkle
them over the hot coals or lava rocks. Brush the grid lightly with
oil.
4 · Grill the sausage over hot or high heat 2 minutes per side, or
until well burnished. Cover-cook with vents open, turning once, 4
minutes longer. Sprinkle with pepper and vinegar before serving;
cut into slices.

Serves 4.

CRISPY KNOCKWURST

*The Bavarian hot dog, in all its seared glory, but with a Franco-
Italian twist.*

¼ cup Dijon mustard
1 tablespoon freshly grated Parmesan cheese
½ teaspoon freshly ground pepper
1 teaspoon olive oil
4 knockwursts
  Vegetable oil

1 · Preheat the grill.

2 · Combine the mustard, cheese, pepper, and olive oil in a bowl. Spread this mixture over the knockwursts. Let stand 20 minutes.

3 · If using presoaked wood chips or other flavorings, sprinkle them over the hot coals or lava rocks. Brush the grid lightly with vegetable oil.

4 · Grill the sausages over hot or high heat for 8 minutes, rotating every 2 minutes.

Serves 4.

HAM-WRAPPED KNOCKWURST

This is a German bequest from Munich. Thin shards of dill pickle are ham-wrapped around each link and grilled for a short period. The ham? Black Forest, of course.

4 thin slices Black Forest ham, about 4 inches by 5 inches
4 knockwursts
2 large dill pickles, cut lengthwise into ⅛-inch-thick slices
  Vegetable oil

1 · Preheat the grill.

2 · Spread the ham flat on a work surface. Place a knockwurst near one end of the ham slice. Place a pickle slice on either side of the knockwurst. Roll up. Secure with toothpicks if necessary to hold in place. Brush lightly with oil.

3 · If using presoaked wood chips or other flavorings, sprinkle them over the hot coals or lava rocks. Brush the grid lightly with oil.

4 · Grill the sausages over hot or high heat for 8 minutes, rotating every 2 minutes.

Serves 4.

Fish and Shellfish

NOTHING IS MORE eminently suited to outdoor cookery than fish and shellfish because these gifts of the sea require virtually minutes of cooking time over hot coals (or lava rocks). Marinades add variety to fish preparation, but should be used with discretion—for flavoring only, never for tenderizing. Overmarinated fish will disintegrate on the fire. An hour's marination (at the most) is usually sufficient for most fresh- and saltwater denizens.

Cubed fish chunks make arrestingly flavored kabobs, and hand-chopped fish steaks can be converted into totally new-tasting croquettes. Let your imagination and taste buds be your guide.

A grill basket for delicate filets and shellfish that might otherwise slip through the grid is a *must* for any serious fish lover—and surprisingly not expensive either.

As with other "fast cooked foods," I use wood chips only with fish and shellfish. Alder and mesquite are my preferences. However, don't forget that herbs, garlic, lemon peel, and dried seaweed make spectacular alternatives to chips. A general timing and cooking chart for fish and shellfish follows.

FISH AND SHELLFISH

TYPE OF FISH OR SHELLFISH .	TECHNIQUE* .	TIMES AND SUGGESTIONS† .
FISH FILETS	*Grilling:* Hot with direct heat.	Marinate up to 30 minutes. Grill in a basket on the grid 1½ to 2 minutes per side.
FISH STEAKS	*Grilling:* Hot with direct heat.	Marinate up to 1 hour. Grill on grid 10 minutes per inch of thickness, turning once, basting occasionally.
KABOBS	*Grilling:* Hot with direct heat.	Marinate up to 30 minutes. Grill 10 minutes per inch, turning frequently.
SHRIMP	*Grilling:* Hot with direct heat.	Marinate up to 1 hour. Grill on a skewer, 3 to 5 minutes per side.
DRESSED FISH	*Grilling:* Hot with direct heat; or *Covered Cooking* with medium-hot, direct heat.	Grill unstuffed fish in a basket 10 minutes per inch. Foil-wrap or cover-cook stuffed fish 10 minutes per inch.

CLAMS (steamers)	*Covered Cooking:* Hot with direct heat.	Cook on grid until shells pop open, 10 to 12 minutes, turning once.
MUSSELS	*Covered Cooking:* Hot with direct heat.	Cook in a basket until shells pop open, 8 to 10 minutes, turning once.
LOBSTER OR CRAB (freshly killed)	*Covered Cooking:* Hot with direct heat.	Cook on grid 12 to 15 minutes for lobster; 10 to 12 minutes for crab—turning once.

* For gas or electric grills, use the high setting for hot, the medium setting for medium-hot. Use the cooler edges of the grid in case of flare-up.

For charcoal grills, hot refers to the 2-second hand test (see page 43). Use the 3- to 4-second test for medium-hot and the 5-second test for medium. To lower the temperature of coal, raise the grid, use the outside edges of the briquets, or cover with cover vents partially closed.

† Times may vary depending on outdoor temperature and velocity of wind.

Filets

FISH FILETS ARE the quickest, though certainly not the easiest, cut of fish to grill. And while filets vary in thickness and density, you will rarely ever grill a filet more than 2 minutes per side.

Filets may or may not be skinned depending on the porosity of the fish. Flatfish is always sold skinless, while bluefish filets, for example, usually have the skin intact. Needless to say, it is the skinless filets that create serious problems for the outdoor cook. Skin is a natural binder that will hold even a fragile fish together as it is grilled. To avoid the dire possibility that a skinless filet could fall through the grid at its flake-with-a-fork stage, I invariably make use of a small fish basket, or a larger hinged grill basket, depending on the quantity of filets I am cooking. However, do make sure to oil these baskets well before using.

There are two ways to grill a fish filet: on an uncovered grid over direct heat or over indirect heat. I like as much color as possible on mine and almost always work over direct heat. However, using indirect heat allows the chef the luxury of cooking the filets slowly and greatly reduces the risk of drying the fish out. Either method works well for any of the following recipes.

FLOUNDER FILETS WITH RED BUTTER SAUCE

Flounder or any other member of this flatfish family (gray sole, lemon sole, Dover sole, petrale, rex, rock, plaice, halibut, sanddab, and turbot) is still just flounder. Some are large, some are small; but all make super good eating, especially when teamed with a red butter sauce.

> 4 large (or 8 small) flounder filets
> ½ cup red butter sauce (see Beurre Rouge, page 311)
> 2 tablespoons chopped fresh chives
>   Vegetable oil

1 · Preheat the grill.

2 · Coat each side of each filet (large) with 1 tablespoon red butter (Beurre Rouge). Sprinkle both sides with chives.

3 · If using presoaked wood chips or other flavorings, sprinkle them over the hot coals or lava rocks. Brush the grid lightly with oil.

4 · Place the fish filets in an oiled basket and grill over hot or high heat 1½ to 2 minutes per side.

Serves 4.

BLUEFISH FILETS WITH MUSTARD

Bluefish are common off the Atlantic coast and are said to be more ferocious predators than sharks. There is a common theory that the farther north a bluefish migrates the darker its taste. Many people do pass on this fish because it is so strongly flavored, though very fresh bluefish is not really so—buy carefully. Fileted, however, and blanketed in French mustard, the fish can be surprisingly tame.

4 small bluefish filets (about 3 ounces each)
6 tablespoons Dijon mustard
Vegetable oil

1 · Preheat the grill.

2 · Coat each side of each filet with ¾ tablespoon mustard. Let stand 30 minutes.

3 · If using presoaked wood chips or other flavorings, sprinkle them over the hot coals or lava rocks. Brush the grid lightly with oil.

4 · Place the fish filets in an oiled basket and grill over hot or high heat 1½ to 2 minutes per side.

Serves 2.

BLUEFISH WITH HORSERADISH

A tinge of tangy horseradish offsets any objectionable oiliness in the fish's flavor.

    4 small bluefish filets (about 3 ounces each)
       Vegetable oil
    5 tablespoons plus 1 teaspoon prepared horseradish
    4 teaspoons chopped fresh parsley

1 · Preheat the grill.

2 · Lightly brush the filets on both sides with vegetable oil. Coat each side of each filet with 2 teaspoons horseradish. Sprinkle each side with ½ teaspoon parsley.

3 · If using presoaked wood chips or other flavorings, sprinkle them over the hot coals or lava rocks. Brush the grid lightly with oil.

4 · Place the fish filets in an oiled basket and grill over hot or high heat 1½ to 2 minutes per side.

Serves 2.

MONKFISH WITH SAUCE ROUILLE

Another predatory species, monkfish, is another name for goose-fish, an ugly creature that up until recently was often discarded by American fishermen, yet prized as a delicacy in other parts of the world (in France it is lotte) because of its lobsterlike flavor. Only the tail of monkfish is eaten, and though technically not a filet, it is herein treated as such.

    1½ cups Processor Rouille (see page 314)
    1½ pounds monkfish, 1 to 1½ inches thick
        Vegetable oil

1 · Preheat the grill.

2 · Spread the Rouille over both sides of the monkfish. Let stand 30 minutes.

3 · If using presoaked wood chips or other flavorings, sprinkle them over the hot coals or lava rocks. Brush the grid lightly with oil.

4 · If the fish is in several small pieces, place in an oiled basket. If in one piece, grill directly on the grid over hot or high heat 5 to 7½ minutes per side.

Serves 4.

SEATTLE INDIAN BAKED SALMON

Indians of the Puget Sound know their salmon. Though tradition-ally "baked" on alderwood branches over an open fire, this Indian recipe has been adapted for the grill, using, naturally, alderwood chips. The salmon is cleaned and boned, then fileted, but still con-nected along the back. Your fishmonger, incidentally, knows this cut as a butterfly *filet. I generally use the tail section of a large salmon. This preparation begins the day before serving.*

    1 boned tail section of salmon, about 4 pounds (or a 5-pound
       salmon), butterfly fileted
 1½ tablespoons light brown sugar
    2 tablespoons vinegar (I use balsamic)
    3 tablespoons olive oil
  ½ teaspoon kosher salt
  ¼ teaspoon freshly ground pepper
  ¼ cup chopped fresh dill
      Vegetable oil

1 · Open the salmon up and sprinkle the flesh with brown sugar and vinegar. Close the salmon. Refrigerate covered overnight.

2 · About 2 hours before grilling the salmon, combine the olive oil, salt, pepper, and dill in a bowl. Mash together. Remove the salmon from the refrigerator and spread the dill mixture over the *skin* of the salmon. Let stand covered at room temperature.

3 · If using presoaked alderwood chips, sprinkle over the hot coals or lava rocks. Brush the grid lightly with vegetable oil.

4 · Open the salmon and place skin side down on the grid. Cover-cook with the vents open over medium-hot heat until the flesh flakes when pierced with a fork, 10 minutes per inch of thick-ness. Use two spatulas to get the salmon off the grid, or cut along the back and remove the fish in two pieces.

Serves 6 to 8.

Fish Steaks

❧ LARGE, ROUND-BODIED fish are usually available "steaked" as they say in the fish trade. These fish are scaled, gutted, and cut across vertically into pieces ranging from 1 to 1½ inches in thickness. In most species, the backbone is left in to keep the fish together during cooking. However, removing the bone and the surrounding bitter dark meat in oily fish (such as bluefish) makes for a pleasanter taste experience. These days, many fishmongers do this excision automatically.

Marination and basting are imperatives when it comes to grilling fish steaks over direct heat. Not just for flavor either, but more importantly to keep the outer flesh moist, until the centers are perfectly cooked. The standard time for grilling fish steaks is 10 minutes (total) per inch of thickness.

PEPPER SWORDFISH WITH COLD CUCUMBER SAUCE

Swordfish, which thrives around the world in tropical and temperate seas, is a fairly elusive beast whose supply is always exceeded by demand; hence the high tariff. Swordfish meat is firm textured and highly distinctive in flavor. Best of all it takes to the grill like it takes to water. A commoner and good substitute for swordfish is the similarly textured mako shark.

      4 swordfish steaks, 1 inch thick
      1 clove garlic, bruised
      ¼ cup olive oil, approximately
      ⅓ cup black peppercorns
      2 teaspoons allspice berries
        Vegetable oil
        Cold Cucumber Sauce (see page 318)

1 · Rub the swordfish steaks on both sides with bruised garlic. Brush each side of each fish steak with 1 teaspoon olive oil. Crush the peppercorns with the allspice berries and pat evenly over both sides of the fish steaks. Let stand covered 1 hour.

2 · Preheat the grill.

3 · If using presoaked wood chips or other flavorings, sprinkle them over the hot coals or lava rocks. Brush the grid lightly with vegetable oil.

4 · Grill the fish steaks over hot or high heat, drizzling once with remaining olive oil, 5 minutes per side. Serve with Cold Cucumber Sauce.

Serves 4.

RUSSET SWORDFISH

The following recipe for swordfish, doused in a tangy tomatoey marinade, goes equally well with the Cold Cucumber Sauce (see above).

    4 swordfish steaks, 1 inch thick
    ½ cup olive oil
    ½ cup dry white wine
    2 large cloves garlic, crushed
    2 sprigs fresh thyme, minced
    1 large tomato, seeded and finely chopped
    ½ teaspoon salt
    ¼ teaspoon freshly ground pepper
      Vegetable oil

1 · Place the swordfish steaks in a shallow glass or ceramic dish.

2 · Combine the olive oil, wine, garlic, thyme, tomato, salt, and pepper in a bowl. Mix well. Pour over the fish. Let stand covered, turning once, 1 hour.

3 · Preheat the grill.

4 · If using presoaked wood chips or other flavorings, sprinkle them over the hot coals or lava rocks. Brush the grid lightly with vegetable oil.

5 · Grill the fish steaks over hot or high heat, basting with remaining marinade, 5 minutes per side.

Serves 4.

GRILLED TUNA STEAKS
WITH ROASTED PEPPER MAYONNAISE

Fresh tuna is still somewhat of an oddity in the United States where most Americans know only the canned variety. Tuna is a meaty fish that is decidedly enhanced by smoke cookery. The two fresh varieties most highly sought after are the albacore and yellowfin. Served with a smoky, peppery mayonnaise on the side, a simple tuna steak becomes an eloquent entrée.

Roasted Pepper Mayonnaise

    1 red bell pepper
    1 green bell pepper
    2 egg yolks
    1 tablespoon wine vinegar
       Juice of ½ lemon
    ½ teaspoon soy sauce
       Pinch of ground white pepper
  1½ teaspoons Dijon mustard
    1 cup vegetable oil
    ½ cup olive oil
       Dash of hot pepper sauce
    1 shallot, finely minced
    1 tablespoon boiling water

For grilling the fish

    1 small clove garlic, minced
    2 teaspoons lemon juice
    ¼ teaspoon dried oregano
    ⅛ teaspoon freshly ground pepper
    1 tablespoon chopped fresh parsley
  1½ teaspoons anchovy paste
    3 tablespoons unsalted butter, softened
    4 tuna steaks, 1 inch thick
       Vegetable oil

1 · To make the Roasted Pepper Mayonnaise: Cook the peppers in boiling, salted water 2 minutes. Drain. Roast on a foil-lined baking sheet in a 350 degree oven for 50 minutes. (Or grill covered over direct heat until charred and soft, about 30 minutes. Carefully

wrap the charred peppers in paper towels and place in a plastic bag.) Cool.

2 · Peel the peppers with a sharp knife. Remove seeds. Finely chop.

3 · Beat the egg yolks in a large bowl until light. Slowly beat in the vinegar, lemon juice, soy sauce, white pepper, and mustard. Beat in the oils, 1 tablespoon at a time, until thick. Add the hot pepper sauce, shallot, boiling water, and peppers. Chill.

4 · To prepare the fish steaks: Mash the garlic with the lemon juice in a medium bowl. Stir in the oregano, black pepper, parsley, and anchovy paste. Beat in the butter until smooth. Spread over the fish steaks; let stand 1 hour.

5 · Preheat the grill.

6 · If using presoaked wood chips or other flavorings, sprinkle them over the hot coals or lava rocks. Brush the grid lightly with oil.

7 · Grill the fish steaks over hot or high heat 5 minutes per side. (Watch for flare-up because of the butter.) Serve with the Roasted Pepper Mayonnaise.

Serves 4.

HINT-OF-GINGER BLUEFISH STEAK

As noted earlier, if the bone and encircling dark meat of a bluefish steak has not been removed, do not hesitate to ask your fishmonger to do it. The dark flesh is the "bitter" part of a bluefish that most diners object to. Ginger and soy, incidentally, complement this fish immeasurably.

    4 bluefish steaks, 1 inch thick
   ¾ cup soy sauce
   ¼ cup dry sherry
   1 small carrot, peeled and minced
   1 clove garlic, minced
   1 tablespoon minced sweet red pepper
1½ teaspoons minced ginger root
   2 small scallions, finely chopped
   1 teaspoon grated lemon peel
     Vegetable oil

1 · Place the bluefish steaks in a shallow glass or ceramic dish.

2 · Combine the soy sauce, sherry, carrot, garlic, sweet red pepper, ginger root, scallions, and lemon peel in a medium bowl. Pour over the fish steaks. Let stand covered 1 hour.

3 · Preheat the grill.

4 · If using presoaked wood chips or other flavorings, sprinkle them over the hot coals or lava rocks. Brush the grid lightly with oil.

5 · Grill the fish steaks over hot or high heat, basting with remaining marinade, 5 minutes per side.

Serves 4.

LEMON-BASTED FISH STEAKS

Marinating fish steaks in a lemon-based marinade is a classic method for preparing fish steaks to be grilled. Use swordfish, tuna, or bluefish.

    ¼ cup lemon juice
    ½ cup olive oil
    1 small clove garlic, minced
      Pinch of dried oregano, crushed
    ½ teaspoon finely grated lemon peel
      Salt and freshly ground pepper
    4 fish steaks, 1 inch thick
      Vegetable oil

1 · Preheat the grill.

2 · Place the lemon juice in a small bowl. Slowly whisk in the olive oil. Whisk in the garlic, oregano, lemon peel, and salt and pepper to taste. Pour over the fish steaks. Let stand covered 30 minutes.

3 · If using presoaked wood chips or other flavorings, sprinkle them over the hot coals or lava rocks. Brush the grid lightly with vegetable oil.

4 · Grill the fish steaks over hot or high heat, basting with remaining marinade, 5 minutes per side.

Serves 4.

BOURBON STEAKS

Straight bourbon, believe it or not, has a remarkably tonic effect on a fish steak, most notably cuts of swordfish and tuna, though halibut or turbot, when available at the market, make awfully good alternatives.

    4 fish steaks, 1 inch thick
    1 cup bourbon
      Vegetable oil
      Salt and freshly ground pepper

1 · Place the fish steaks in a shallow glass or ceramic dish. Pour the bourbon over the fish steaks. Let stand covered 1 hour.

2 · Preheat the grill.

3 · If using presoaked wood chips or other flavorings, sprinkle them over the hot coals or lava rocks. Brush the grid lightly with oil.

4 · Remove the fish steaks from the marinade and pat dry. Lightly brush with oil. Grill over hot or high heat, basting once with oil 5 minutes per side. Sprinkle with salt and pepper before serving.

Serves 4.

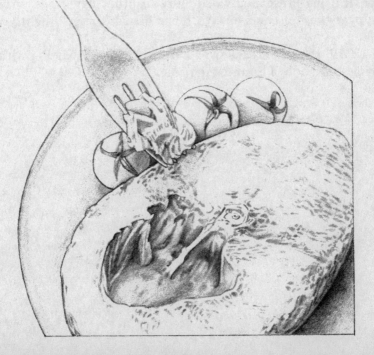

MARINATED SALMON STEAKS

Salmon is second only to swordfish in the piscine popularity sweepstakes. The version below for long-marinated salmon is freely adapted from the Cafe Beaujolais *cookbook by Margaret Fox and John Bear (Ten Speed Press, 1984). Margaret is the very talented owner of the redoubtable Cafe Beaujolais in Mendocino, California.*

½ cup dry white wine
½ cup soy sauce
¼ cup water
2 tablespoons light brown sugar
1 small white onion, minced
1 small clove garlic, crushed
⅛ teaspoon hot pepper sauce
¼ teaspoon freshly ground pepper
4 salmon steaks, 1 inch thick
Vegetable oil

1 · Combine the wine, soy sauce, water, sugar, onion, garlic, hot pepper sauce, and pepper in a bowl. Pour over the fish steaks. Refrigerate covered 3 hours. Let stand at room temperature 30 minutes before grilling.

2 · Preheat the grill.

3 · If using presoaked wood chips or other flavorings, sprinkle them over the hot coals or lava rocks. Brush the grid lightly with oil.

4 · Grill the fish steaks over hot or high heat, basting with remaining marinade, 5 minutes per side.

Serves 4.

Fish Kabobs and Croquettes

BITE-SIZED FISH are what I call fun food. Any firm-fleshed fish that can be effortlessly cut up for steak is perfectly suited to the skewer. And, in fact, almost all the preceding recipes for fish steaks may be adapted for kabob cookery. Sea scallops, as well as shrimp, are at their very best grilled this way.

And while there is a certain degree of advance preparation required for fish croquettes, these succulent seaburgers are relatively easy to grill. I generally cook croquettes right on the grid, but they may also be grilled in a hinged basket. Any firm-fleshed, distinctive-flavored fish can be used in a croquette, but consider crab or lobster meat (picked over but uncooked) for a very special treat.

TUNA KABOBS

If you have only eaten tuna from a can, try fresh tuna in conjunction with onions, endive, and cherry tomatoes.

1½ pounds fresh tuna, cut into 1-inch cubes
½ cup lemon juice
⅓ cup olive oil
2 tablespoons sesame oil
½ teaspoon salt
¼ teaspoon freshly ground pepper
1 large shallot, grated
1 tablespoon oyster sauce
8 small white onions
4 small endive, root trimmed
8 cherry tomatoes
Vegetable oil

1 · Place the tuna cubes in a medium bowl. Combine the lemon juice, olive oil, sesame oil, salt, pepper, shallot, and oyster sauce in a separate bowl. Mix well. Pour over the tuna. Let stand covered 1 hour.

219

2 · Preheat the grill.

3 · Meanwhile, peel the onions and cut across in each root end to keep them from falling apart. Cook in boiling water 3 minutes. Rinse under cold running water. Drain.

4 · Divide the tuna cubes into 4 equal portions. Arrange on skewers, alternating with onions, endive, and cherry tomatoes. Brush the vegetables lightly with marinade.

5 · If using presoaked wood chips or other flavorings, sprinkle them over the hot coals or lava rocks. Brush the grid lightly with vegetable oil.

6 · Grill the tuna kabobs over hot or high heat, basting often with marinade, 2½ minutes per side for a total of 10 minutes.

Serves 4.

SKEWERED SCALLOPS

Scallops have infinite variety of texture and taste. The ones most suited to a skewer are sea scallops taken off the Atlantic shore, and rock scallops, harvested in limited quantities off the Pacific. Either variety takes on an Oriental caste in a soy'd marinade, partnered with crunchy snow peas.

1½ pounds sea scallops
⅔ cup soy sauce
4 teaspoons finely slivered lime peel
½ cup lime juice
3 cloves garlic, minced
2 tablespoons Dijon mustard
½ cup peanut oil
½ cup finely chopped scallions
½ teaspoon freshly ground pepper
1 pound snow peas, trimmed
Vegetable oil

1 · Preheat the grill.

2 · Place the scallops in a large bowl. Combine the soy sauce, lime peel, lime juice, garlic, mustard, peanut oil, scallions, and pepper in a separate bowl. Mix well. Pour over the scallops. Let stand covered 30 minutes.

3 · Cook the snow peas in boiling water 1 minute. Rinse under cold running water. Drain; pat dry with paper towels.

4 · Divide the scallops into 4 equal portions. Arrange on skewers, alternating with snow peas. Brush lightly with marinade.

5 · If using presoaked wood chips or other flavorings, sprinkle them over the hot coals or lava rocks. Brush the grid lightly with vegetable oil.

6 · Grill the scallop kabobs over hot or high heat, basting often with marinade, 3 minutes per side for a total of 12 minutes.

Serves 4.

THE COACH HOUSE GRILLED SHRIMP

Grilling shrimp kabob style is virtually imperative to keep this delicate member from falling through the grid. The following recipe is a culinary bequest from one of New York's most esteemed restaurants, the Coach House in Greenwich Village.

16 large shrimp, shelled and deveined but tails left intact
1 cup dry white wine
3 large shallots, minced
2 large cloves garlic, minced
2 tablespoons olive oil
2 tablespoons lemon juice
1½ tablespoons Dijon mustard
10 peppercorns, crushed
Vegetable oil

1 · Place the shrimp in a medium glass or ceramic bowl. Combine the wine, shallots, garlic, olive oil, lemon juice, mustard, and peppercorns in a separate bowl. Pour over the shrimp. Refrigerate covered 3 hours. Let stand at room temperature 30 minutes before grilling.

2 · Preheat the grill.

3 · Drain the marinade from the shrimp into a saucepan. Place over high heat and heat to boiling; boil until reduced to ⅓ cup, about 10 minutes. Meanwhile, place the shrimp on skewers.

4 · If using presoaked wood chips or other flavorings, sprinkle them over the hot coals or lava rocks. Brush the grid lightly with vegetable oil.

5 · Grill the shrimp over hot or high heat 3 to 5 minutes per side (depending on size). Drizzle with reduced marinade before serving.

Serves 4 as an appetizer.

CLOAKED SHRIMP

My favorite grilled shrimp recipe, and truly an all-American classic, is a direct adaptation of the wonderfully spicy appetizers served at the rustic Settlement Inn, north of San Antonio, Texas.

    1 tablespoon unsalted butter
    1 small onion, finely chopped
    ¾ cup ketchup
    3 tablespoons Worcestershire sauce
    2 tablespoons A.1. Steak Sauce
    1 tablespoon cider vinegar
    3 tablespoons brown sugar
    ¼ cup water
      Dash of hot pepper sauce
   16 large shrimp, shelled and deveined
    5 ⅓ strips thin bacon
      Vegetable oil

1 · Melt the butter in a medium saucepan over medium-low heat. Add the onion. Cook 5 minutes but do not brown. Stir in the ketchup, Worcestershire sauce, A.1. sauce, vinegar, sugar, water, and hot pepper sauce. Heat to boiling; reduce heat. Simmer uncovered 20 minutes. Cool.

2 · Preheat the grill.

3 · Place the shrimp in the barbecue sauce and let stand 30 minutes.

4 · Cut each whole strip of bacon into thirds. Remove the shrimp from the sauce and wrap each in a piece of bacon (stretching the bacon if necessary). Secure with water-soaked toothpicks. Place shrimp on skewers.

5 · If using presoaked wood chips or other flavorings, sprinkle them over the hot coals or lava rocks. Brush the grid lightly with oil.

6 · Grill the shrimp over hot or high heat until bacon is crisp, about 3 minutes per side. Serve with remaining barbecue sauce (reheated), on the side.

Serves 4 as an appetizer.

SALMON CROQUETTES

Fresh fish croquettes, in this case composed of raw salmon, are relatively easy to prepare—and a tonic surprise to the taste buds as well. They may be grilled either directly on the grid or placed in an oiled hinged grill basket. Do not let the raw croquettes stand longer than 15 minutes after they are formed. Fresh fish croquettes should be eaten "hot off the grill."

    1 pound salmon, finely chopped
    ½ cup chopped fresh parsley
    2 teaspoons chopped fresh thyme
    4 anchovy fillets, minced
    1 large shallot, minced
    3 teaspoons capers, chopped
    1 teaspoon prepared horseradish
    2 teaspoons country-style Dijon mustard (with seeds)
    ⅛ teaspoon hot pepper sauce
    2 tablespoons lemon juice
    1 egg, beaten
    ¼ cup fresh bread crumbs
    Salt and freshly ground pepper
    Vegetable oil

1 · Preheat the grill.

2 · In a large bowl, combine all ingredients from the salmon through the salt and pepper in the order listed. Mix thoroughly. Form the mixture into 8 balls. Place the balls on a lightly greased plate. Flatten slightly with a spatula. Brush the tops lightly with oil.

3 · If using presoaked wood chips or other flavorings, sprinkle them over the hot coals or lava rocks. Brush the grid lightly with oil.

4 · Grill the fish croquettes directly on the grid or placed in an oiled hinged grill basket, over hot or high heat for 3 minutes per side.

Serves 4.

Whole Fish

A WHOLE FISH that has been gutted and scaled, with its gills removed, is known as *dressed*. When the head is also removed, it becomes *pan-dressed*. Some of the most popular fish commonly "dressed to grill"—heads on—are trout, coho salmon, sablefish, bass, red snapper, rockfish, and sole. However, any fish that will fit horizontally on the grid may be successfully grilled—whether it be stuffed or *au naturel*.

Fish weighing 2 pounds or less will fit into a fish basket, which should be part of any deep-dyed fish-lovers barbecue equipment. Large fish (5 pounds) like bass and salmon are trickier to grill, but the richer flavor is worth the effort of some extracurricular navigation by the chef.

SESAME SPECKLED BUTTERFISH

Butterfish (so called because of its high fat content) is a small, but highly flavorful fish indigenous to the Northeast where about 10 million pounds per year are consumed. Its West Coast counterpart is known as Pacific or "California" pompano, though in truth neither species is related to the true pompano found only in the Southeast Atlantic and the Gulf of Mexico. Speaking of which, note that pompano would make an excellent stand-in for this Korean-influenced recipe.

> 3 tablespoons soy sauce
> 2 teaspoons sugar
> 3 tablespoons toasted sesame seeds, crushed
> 1 tablespoon sesame oil
> 1 large clove garlic, minced
> 1 teaspoon finely grated ginger root
> 2 teaspoons chili sauce
> 4 small butterfish, dressed
> 3 tablespoons all-purpose flour, approximately
> Vegetable oil

1 · Combine all the ingredients from soy sauce through chili sauce in a small bowl. Mix well.

224

2 · Pat the butterfish dry with paper towels. Dust with flour. Spoon the marinade over both sides of each fish. Let stand 40 minutes.

3 · Preheat the grill.

4 · If using presoaked wood chips or other flavorings, sprinkle them over the hot coals or lava rocks. Brush the grid lightly with vegetable oil.

5 · Grill the butterfish, either directly on the grid or in an oiled hinged fish basket, over hot or high heat 4 minutes per side.

Serves 2.

TARRAGON STRIPED FLOUNDER WITH PERNOD CREAM

Any flat sweet fish (petrale, sand dabs, sole, etc.) that has been pan-dressed adapts itself nicely to the following recipe.

> 2 small flounders, pan-dressed
> ¼ cup Pernod
> Tarragon leaves from 4 large fresh sprigs
> 1 cup heavy or whipping cream
> Salt and freshly ground pepper
> Vegetable oil

1 · Preheat the grill.

2 · Rub each flounder with 1 tablespoon Pernod. Place tarragon leaves along both sides of each fish in a stripe pattern. Let stand 30 minutes.

3 · Meanwhile, combine the cream with the remaining 2 tablespoons Pernod in a small saucepan. Heat to boiling; reduce heat. Simmer until reduced to ½ cup, about 10 minutes. Add salt and pepper to taste. Keep warm over low heat.

4 · If using presoaked wood chips or other flavorings, sprinkle them over the hot coals or lava rocks. Brush the grid lightly with oil.

5 · Grill the flounders, either directly on the grid or in an oiled hinged basket, over hot or high heat 4 minutes per side. Serve with the Pernod cream sauce.

Serves 2.

RED-HOT FLOUNDER WITH NASTURTIUM BUTTER

Red hot to the eye, rather than to the palate, is this dish's sole precept. No flat fish ever had a better partner than the zesty Nasturtium Butter served on the side. If nasturtiums are scarce in your garden, use small geranium leaves or even arugula or watercress leaves in a pinch.

Nasturtium Butter

¼ cup unsalted butter, softened
1 small shallot, minced
⅛ teaspoon hot pepper sauce
½ cup nasturtium leaves, torn
   Salt

2 small flounders, pan-dressed
2 tablespoons walnut oil
4 teaspoons Hungarian hot paprika
1 teaspoon dry mustard
⅛ teaspoon freshly ground pepper
1 clove garlic, minced
   Vegetable oil

1 · To make the Nasturtium Butter: In a medium bowl, whisk the butter with the shallot, hot pepper sauce, and nasturtium leaves until well mixed. Whisk in salt to taste. Cover and refrigerate. Remove from refrigerator at least 30 minutes before serving.

2 · Preheat the grill.

3 · Pat the flounders dry with paper towels. Rub each side of each fish well with walnut oil. Combine the paprika, mustard, pepper, and garlic in a small bowl. Sprinkle this mixture over both sides of each fish. Let stand 30 minutes.

4 · If using presoaked wood chips or other flavorings, sprinkle them over the hot coals or lava rocks. Brush the grid lightly with vegetable oil.

5 · Grill the flounders, either directly on the grid or in an oiled hinged basket, over hot or high heat 4 minutes per side. Serve with the Nasturtium Butter.

Serves 2.

GRILL-POACHED SNAPPER DRESSED WITH FENNEL

Snappers come in various shades and cognomens: gray, mutton, red, silk, and yellowtail. All make superior eating, especially when stuffed with a dressing of fresh Italian fennel and prosciutto. I foil-bake these fish on the grill to make outdoor life simpler.

> 2 tablespoons unsalted butter
> 1 small white onion, finely chopped
> 1 medium fennel bulb, trimmed and chopped (about 2½ cups)
> 1 teaspoon chopped fresh chives
> ⅓ cup chopped prosciutto
> 2½ tablespoons minced fresh parsley
> 1½ teaspoons plus 2 tablespoons Pernod
> ½ teaspoon freshly ground pepper
> 2 snappers (each about 1¼ pounds), dressed and boned
> 1 cup sour cream
> ¼ cup finely chopped fennel fronds
> Salt and freshly ground pepper

1 · Melt the butter in a large skillet over medium-low heat. Add the onion; cook 2 minutes. Stir in the fennel, chives, and prosciutto. Cook covered 5 minutes. Remove from the heat. Stir in the parsley, 1½ teaspoons Pernod, and the pepper. Cool.

2 · Preheat the grill.

3 · Rub 2 large sheets of heavy-duty aluminum foil with oil. Place a snapper on each sheet. Spoon the fennel dressing into the

fish cavities. Bring up the edges of the foil and fold the top and ends together to form tight enclosures.

4 · If using presoaked wood chips or chunks (chips for gas), sprinkle them over the hot coals or lava rocks.

5 · Place the fish packets on the grid and cover-cook with vents open until the fish flakes when pierced with a fork, 20 to 25 minutes.

6 · Meanwhile, combine the sour cream with the chopped fennel fronds and 2 tablespoons Pernod in a bowl. Add salt and pepper to taste.

7 · To serve, carefully unwrap the fish and flip or slide them onto a serving platter. Pour the juices over the top. Serve with the sour cream sauce.

Serves 4.

PAELLA-STUFFED STRIPED BASS

Striped bass is one of the most savory fish in the world and a "striper" is sheer heaven stuffed most pertinently with a saffron-riced version of Spanish paella. Grilling a bass, however, can be sheer hell! It takes two confederates to flip the heavy fish over during cooking, and a double pair of hands, as well, to get it off the grill. But this dish is worth every hair-raising moment, I promise you.

  1 striped bass (about 5 pounds), dressed, boned, and tail removed (so it will fit on the grill)
  2 tablespoons vodka
2½ tablespoons unsalted butter
  1 medium yellow onion, minced
  1 clove garlic, minced
    Pinch of saffron
  2 chorizos (Spanish sausages), chopped
 ½ fresh hot green pepper, seeded, deveined and minced
  1 small tomato, seeded and chopped
2½ cups cooked rice, hot
  1 tablespoon sliced black olives
 ½ teaspoon chopped fresh thyme
  2 teaspoons chopped fresh parsley
    Salt and freshly ground pepper
    Vegetable oil

1 · Rinse the bass with fresh water; pat dry with paper towels. Open the fish and rub the flesh with the vodka. Close the fish and refrigerate covered 2 hours. Remove from refrigerator about 30 minutes before grilling.

2 · Preheat the grill.

3 · Melt the butter in a large skillet over medium-low heat. Cook the onions 2 minutes. Add the garlic and saffron; cook 1 minute. Stir in the chorizos and hot green pepper. Cook, stirring occasionally, until sausages have exuded their grease, about 5 minutes. Stir in the tomato; cook 2 minutes longer. Transfer to a large bowl and fold in the rice, olives, thyme, and parsley. Add salt and pepper to taste.

4 · Spoon the paella stuffing into the cavity of the fish. Tie the fish around with string every 1½ inches to keep stuffing in place. Use toothpicks to seal edges if necessary. Brush lightly with oil.

5 · If using presoaked wood chips or chunks (chips for gas), or other flavorings, sprinkle them over the hot coals or lava rocks. Brush the grid lightly with oil.

6 · Place the stuffed bass on the grid. Cover-cook with vents about three-quarters open over medium-hot heat 15 minutes. Using 2 spatulas (and a friend), flip the fish over. (Gently push the fish back to the center of the grill if you have flipped too far.) Cover-cook until the flesh flakes when pricked with a fork, 15 minutes longer. Using 2 long spatulas (and friend) carefully lift the fish onto a serving platter. Remove strings and toothpicks before serving.

Serves 6 to 8.

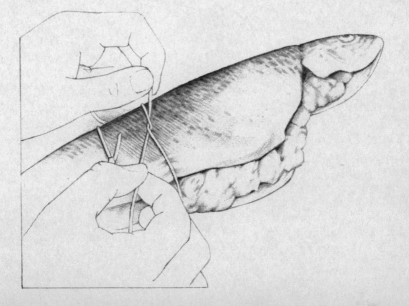

Shellfish

IT IS NO secret that smoke does wonders for shellfish—or is it the other way around? Shellfish can be grilled whole or cut apart and will generally cook in 5 to 15 minutes, depending on the size and type. Crab, lobster, and shrimp will take on a reddish hue and be firm to the touch when thoroughly cooked. Bivalves like mussels and clams essentially cook in their own juices and will open when they are ready. The following recipe for a Seafood Mixed Grill covers all the basic procedures needed for a successful "aboveboard clambake" on any outdoor grill.

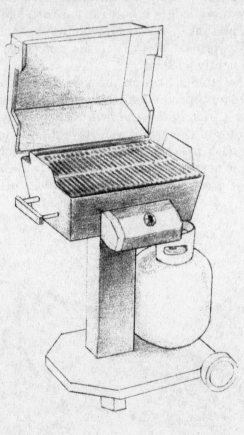

SEAFOOD MIXED GRILL

Planning a seafood mixed grill for a large group of people requires thoughtful planning. Having two grills helps, but is not a necessity, but a friend in the kitchen is. Manpower is definitely a prerequisite to getting all the food on the table at one time. Since an essential part of this dish requires the use of baskets (which take up grid space), the food must be cooked in relays, which is where the friend comes in. While the cook is busy at the grill, it is up to his kitchen aide to fetch and arrange the various components on a large heatproof platter (or a pair of them). All the cooked seafood should be kept in a warm (not hot) oven until every last bivalve and crustacean comes off the grill. (Charcoal users, go heavy on the coals!)

24 steamer clams, scrubbed
24 mussels, scrubbed and beards removed
2 tablespoons cornstarch
10 tablespoons unsalted butter, softened
1 cup lightly toasted wheat germ
2 teaspoons seasoned pepper
8 soft-shell crabs, cleaned
4 teaspoons Hungarian hot paprika
½ teaspoon salt
½ teaspoon freshly ground pepper
1½ pounds weakfish filets, about ½ inch thick
32 shrimp (about 2 pounds), shelled and deveined
2 tablespoons olive oil
2 teaspoons minced fresh basil
2 teaspoons minced fresh chives
2 to 3 1½-pound lobsters
Vegetable oil
Melted butter
Tomato Sauce in the Nice Style (see page 315)

1 · Place the clams in a large pot of cold water. Place the mussels in another pot of cold water. Stir 1 tablespoon cornstarch into each pot. (The bivalves will clean themselves.) Let stand 30 minutes. Drain and rinse under cold running water. Place the mussels and clams in separate pots of cold water and set aside.

2 · Melt 1 stick of butter in a medium saucepan. Transfer to a bowl. Combine the wheat germ and seasoned pepper in another

shallow bowl. Dip the soft-shell crabs in the butter and then coat with the wheat germ mixture. Set aside.

3 · Combine the remaining 2 tablespoons butter with the paprika, salt, and freshly ground pepper in a small bowl. Mix well. Rub this mixture over both sides of the weakfish filets. Let stand covered.

4 · Place the shrimp in a large bowl. Combine the olive oil, basil, and chives in another bowl. Mix well. Pour over the shrimp. Let stand covered.

5 · Preheat the grill.

6 · Place each lobster shell side up. Using a sharp heavy knife, cut through the shell where the tail joins the body to kill the lobster quickly. Turn the lobster over and split in half lengthwise, without cutting all the way through. Remove the sac from behind the head and the lungs. Leave any coral (roe) intact.

7 · Drain the mussels and clams. Place the mussels in an oiled hinged basket. Place the weakfish filets in two oiled fish baskets. Place the shrimp on skewers.

8 · If using presoaked wood chips or other flavorings, sprinkle over the hot coals or lava rocks. Brush the grid lightly with oil.

9 · Place the clams around the edge of the grid. Place the lobsters, flesh side up, in the center. Cover-cook with vents open over hot or high heat 5 minutes. Turn the clams, and then the lobsters, over. Place the grill basket with the mussels on top of the lobsters. Cover and cook until the clams and mussels open and the lobster is firm to the touch, about 10 minutes. Remove and transfer to a warm oven.

10 · Brush the grid lightly with oil.

11 · Place the soft-shell crabs around the edge of the grid. Grill 1 minute. Place the skewered shrimp in the center of the grid; grill 3 minutes. Turn the crabs and shrimp over. Remove the shrimp after 3 minutes, the crab after 4 minutes. Transfer to a warm oven.

12 · Again brush the grid lightly with oil. Grill the fish filets in the center of the grid until the flesh flakes when pierced with a fork, about 4 to 5 minutes per side.

13 · To serve: Using sharp poultry shears, cut the large lobster claws from the body, and cut the body into six pieces. Cut the weakfish into pieces. Arrange the seafood over one or two large platters. Serve with melted butter and Tomato Sauce for dipping.

Serves 8 to 10.

Vegetables

᚜ IN TIMES PAST, no one considered preparing vegetables on the outdoor grill. Roast potatoes and fresh corn on the cob were the only exceptions. Nowadays, however, everything from asparagus to zucchini is considered fare game by the backyard chef. All manner of arresting vegeteria are being skewered or foil-wrapped and cooked over hot coals or lava rocks with exceedingly palate-pleasing results. Needless to say, some vegetables require a lot of prepreparation before hitting the grill (such as parboiling) and most decidedly need anointment with butter or oil-based marinades.

Certain vegetables like potatoes or winter squash may be cooked directly in the coals (this is known as ember cooking), but for the most part, grilled vegetables are prepared right on the grid, alongside the main course. And, therefore, specific instructions as to grilling techniques have been omitted from the following recipes. If you are grilling only vegetables, use presoaked wood chips sprinkled over the hot coals or lava rocks, and remember to oil the grid before the cooking begins.

Be sure to plan the timing of the vegetable to be served with the main course. For instance, potatoes should be cooked completely and kept warm around the sides of the grid if you are grilling steaks or chops as well. Even quick-grilled veggies should precede grilled entrées on the grid. It is easier to keep the vegetables on hold than a steak which is to be served rare.

If you plan to serve quick-grilled vegetables with large cuts of meat that require cover cooking, you will have to reverse the order and grill the vegetables after the meat comes off the grill and the juices are settling. Charcoal-grill users will have to stoke and replenish the coals to keep the heat up. A general timing and cooking chart for some of the more grillable vegetables follows.

VEGETABLE CHART ❧

VEGETABLE ·	TECHNIQUE* ·	TIMES AND SUGGESTIONS† ·
ASPARAGUS	*Grilling:* Hot with direct heat, then medium with direct heat.	Grill over hot heat 10 minutes. Then medium for 10 minutes.
BROCCOLI	*Covered Cooking:* Medium with direct heat.	Cut stalks in half lengthwise. Grill 10 minutes per side.
CORN	*Covered Cooking:* Medium-hot with direct heat.	Foil-wrap and cook 20 minutes. Husk-roast for 15 minutes.
EGGPLANT	*Grilling:* Medium, with direct heat.	Grill ¼-inch slices 6 to 7 minutes per side.
ENDIVE	*Covered Cooking:* Medium-hot with direct heat.	Cook, halved or whole, 4 minutes per side.
GREEN BEANS	*Covered Cooking:* Hot with direct heat.	Cook, tossing occasionally, in foil pan on grid.
OKRA	*Grilling:* Hot with direct heat.	Grill on skewers 3 to 4 minutes per side.
ONIONS	*Ember Cook* or *Covered Cooking* with medium, direct heat.	Ember-cook in coals 20 to 30 minutes. Or cook on grid 30 minutes.
PEPPERS	*Covered Cooking:* Hot or medium-hot with direct heat.	Foil-wrap or cover-cook 15 to 20 minutes.

POTATOES	***Covered Cooking:*** Medium-hot with direct heat.	Rub with butter or oil. Cook 45 to 55 minutes.
SQUASH (summer)	***Grilling:*** Hot with direct heat.	Grill 4 minutes per side.
SQUASH (winter)	***Ember Cook*** or ***Covered Cooking*** with medium, direct heat.	Ember-cook for 45 minutes. Or cover cook about 50 minutes.
TOMATOES	***Grilling:*** Hot with direct heat. Or ***Covered Cooking*** with hot, direct heat.	Grill cherry tomatoes 2 minutes per side. Cook larger tomatoes 5 to 10 minutes.

* For gas or electric grills, use the high setting for hot, the medium setting for medium-hot. Use the cooler edges of the grid in case of flare-up.

For charcoal grills, hot refers to the 2-second hand test (see page 43). Use the 3- to 4-second test for medium-hot, and the 5-second test for medium. To lower the temperature of coal, raise the grid, use the outside edges of the briquets, or cover with cover vents partially closed.

† Times may vary depending on outdoor temperature and velocity of wind.

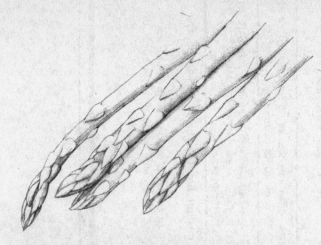

GRILLED HERBED ASPARAGUS

Asparagus has been part of culinarians' diets since Roman times—but as far as I know, no one has ever before herbed and grilled one in just this manner before. They will now! Fresh asparagus, unfortunately, is only available in late May and June.

    1 pound fresh asparagus
    ¼ cup olive oil
    4 large fresh basil leaves, chopped
    ⅛ teaspoon chopped fresh thyme
    1 teaspoon chopped fresh parsley
    1 small scallion, minced

1 · Break the tough bottoms off the asparagus spears by bending each spear until it snaps. Peel the stems. Place the asparagus in a shallow glass or ceramic dish.

2 · Combine the remaining ingredients and pour over the asparagus. Toss to coat. Let stand covered 30 minutes.

3 · Grill the asparagus over hot or high heat for 10 minutes, turning once. Continue to cook, turning several times, over medium heat (use the outer edges of the grid) until crisp-tender, about 10 minutes.

Serves 4.

BROCCOLI EN ROUILLE

Broccoli is a vegetable often bypassed in summer except in salads and on platters of raw crudités. Dipping a stalk in provincial pepper mayonnaise prior to the fire, and grilling till crisp, will raise its status immeasurably.

3 large uniform stems broccoli, about 1½ pounds
1¼ cups Processor Rouille (see page 314)

1 · Using a sharp knife, trim any leafy stems from the broccoli and peel the stalk, smoothing the bumps as you peel. Trim all but 3½ inches of the stalk from the broccoli. Hold each stalk with the flowerets down vertically on a cutting board and cut each stalk in half, slicing right through the flowerets.

2 · Place the broccoli in a large glass or ceramic dish. Spoon the Rouille over the top. Toss to coat. Let stand covered 30 minutes.

3 · Cover-cook with vents open over medium, direct heat (use the outer edges of the grid) 10 minutes per side.

Serves 4 to 6.

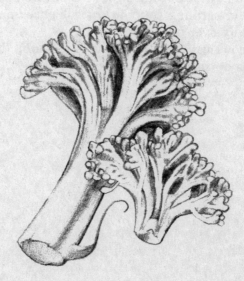

GRILLED BROCCOLI PARMA STYLE

Italians have known about this combination—broccoli sprinkled with freshly grated Parmesan cheese—for generations. Their dining instinct provided the inspiration for one of the best grilled vegetables I know.

> 3 large uniform stems broccoli, about 1½ pounds
> ⅓ cup olive oil
> Juice of 1 large lemon
> ¼ teaspoon salt
> ⅛ teaspoon freshly ground pepper
> ¾ cup freshly grated Parmesan cheese

1 · Using a sharp knife, trim any leafy stems from the broccoli and peel the stalks, smoothing the bumps as you peel. Trim all but 3½ inches of the stalk from the broccoli. Hold each stalk with the flowerets down vertically on a cutting board and cut each stalk in half, slicing right through the flowerets.

2 · Place the broccoli in a large glass or ceramic dish. Combine the oil, lemon juice, salt, and pepper in a bowl. Mix well and pour over the broccoli. Toss to coat. Let stand covered 30 minutes.

3 · Just before grilling, toss the broccoli once more and sprinkle the cheese evenly over both sides.

4 · Cover-cook with vents open over medium, direct heat (use the outer edges of the grid) 10 minutes per side.

Serves 4 to 6.

GRILLED CORN

This is my version of the wonderful summer dish I was raised on in Colorado as prepared by my mother, Mildred Schulz. Hers is baked in the oven, however; and the corn was grown by my father outside our kitchen door. It's a simple conversion to do it on the grill. Merely husk and clean the corn. Rub it with softened, unsalted butter, sprinkle each cob with about a teaspoon of cold water, and wrap it in aluminum foil. Another popular method for grilling corn is to roast it in its own green husks. To do this first carefully peel back the green leaves and remove the silk. Add the butter, anoint with the water, and re-form the leaves, tying the tops with kitchen twine. Then presoak in cold water for 10 minutes before grilling to keep the husks from catching fire.

    8 ears fresh corn
    ¼ cup unsalted butter, approximately
    Cold water

1 · Prepare each corncob, using either of the above methods. Rub each cob with 1½ teaspoons butter and sprinkle with about 1 teaspoon cold water. Wrap in foil, or reshape the husk.

2 · Cover-cook with vents open over medium-hot heat, turning frequently, 15 minutes for the husk version, about 20 minutes for the foil version. Serve with lots of butter and salt and freshly ground pepper.

Serves 4.

GRILLED GARLICKED EGGPLANT

Eggplant has a natural affinity for garlic on or off the grill. But it is an imperative to presalt this vegetable and allow it to sit in a colander at least a half hour's time before cooking.

> 2 small (not baby) eggplant
> Salt
> ⅓ cup olive oil
> 1 large clove garlic, minced
> 3 tablespoons chopped fresh basil

1 · Cut each eggplant lengthwise into ¼-inch-thick slices. Sprinkle with salt and place in a colander. Let stand 30 minutes or longer. Brush off the salt and pat off excess moisture.

2 · Combine the oil, garlic, and basil. Brush over the eggplant slices.

3 · Grill the eggplant over medium, direct heat until tender, 6 to 7 minutes per side, until deeply browned, but take care, as they char quickly.

Serves 4.

JUDY BLAHNIK'S SESAME GRILLED ENDIVE

Belgian endive is one of the surprises of outdoor cooking. The easiest way to grill endive is to cut it in half, lightly oil, and coat with sesame seeds that toast as the stalk cooks. This recipe is a culinary invention of Judy Blahnik, any outdoor cook's best friend, and this one's cooking associate.

> 3 large Belgian endive
> 2 tablespoons olive oil
> Salt and freshly ground pepper
> 2 teaspoons sesame seeds

1 · Lightly trim but do not remove the root ends of the endive. Cut the heads in half lengthwise. Brush each piece with 1 teaspoon olive oil. Sprinkle with salt and pepper to taste; coat each with sesame seeds.

2 · Cover-cook with vents open over medium-hot, direct heat until just barely tender, about 4 minutes per side.

Serves 4 to 6.

GOAT-CHEESE-STUFFED ENDIVE

Goat cheese and endive are very compatible allies. The trick here is to half-cut the stalk (like a hinged door), stuff it with cheese, then re-form and tie it so that the cheese melts as a tart dressing over the fire.

> 4 ounces white goat cheese (I use a French Montrachet)
> 2 tablespoons olive oil
> 1 teaspoon fresh thyme leaves, or ¼ teaspoon dried
> 4 large Belgian endive
>   Salt and freshly ground pepper

1 · Cut the goat cheese into four 1-ounce-size pieces. Place in a flat glass or ceramic dish. Cover with olive oil and sprinkle with thyme leaves. Let stand covered 2 hours.

2 · With a sharp knife, cut into the endive vertically from tip to stem without slicing all the way through, so it may be opened like a hinge book.

3 · Cut each piece of cheese in half. Using a bowl scraper, spread half the cheese in the center of each endive. Then using your fingers, lift up an outside leaf from one side, and then the other, smearing cheese inside—so the endive is stuffed near the outside surface as well. Tie the endive at its midriff with kitchen twine to keep it well closed. Brush each with some of the leftover marinade. Sprinkle with salt and pepper.

4 · Cover-cook with vents open over medium-hot, direct heat 4 minutes per side.

Serves 4.

BROASTED GREEN BEANS

Green beans are so crisp and delicate when cooked over a grill they are worth a mite of ingenuity. I cook them in an improvised wok (actually an aluminum-foil drip pan) that allows them to brown over high heat while they are concurrently being flavored with swirling smoke.

1 pound green beans, ends trimmed
¼ cup olive oil
3 tablespoons fresh sage leaves, chopped
½ teaspoon coarse salt
Freshly ground pepper

1 · Place the beans in an aluminum-foil pan (or make one out of heavy-duty foil). Add the oil, sage, salt, and pepper to taste. Toss well.

2 · Cover-cook with vents open over hot or high heat, tossing occasionally, until just tender, about 20 minutes.

Serves 4.

LETTUCE AND CHEESE PANCAKES

This is a recent invention for the outdoor grill that makes a sensational lunch or brunch pick-me-up—or an appetizer, especially if the main dish is simply broiled or grilled fish. Easy to perform, it must be done in a hinged grill basket.

20 separated lettuce leaves (2 to 3 small heads Bibb or Boston lettuce)
2 tablespoons olive oil
2 tablespoons red wine vinegar
¼ pound smoked mozzarella cheese (without rind), grated
Salt and freshly ground pepper

1 · Wash the lettuce leaves. Pat dry with paper towels. Arrange 10 leaves, overlapping, in a circle over the bottom of a lightly oiled hinged grill basket.

2 · Combine the oil and vinegar. Sprinkle 1 tablespoon of this mixture over the lettuce leaves. Sprinkle the grated cheese over the lettuce. Sprinkle the cheese with salt and pepper to taste.

3 · Place 5 lettuce leaves over the top of the cheese. Sprinkle with 1 tablespoon oil and vinegar mixture. Place remaining leaves on top. Sprinkle with another tablespoon oil and vinegar mixture. Turn the basket over and sprinkle the other side with mixture.

4 · Grill the lettuce pancake, in the basket, over hot or high, direct heat 2 minutes. Turn over and grill 3 minutes longer. Serve immediately, cut into wedges, or allow to cool slightly before serving.

Serves 4.

SKEWERED OKRA

Okra is not everyone's favorite vegetable because it has a tendency to become viscous during long periods of cookery. Not so on the grill. Each tender morsel is as crunchy and flavorsome as a French-fried potato.

8 ounces medium-sized okra, tops lightly trimmed
1 large clove garlic, roughly chopped
1 medium tomato, seeded
1 teaspoon chopped fresh basil
¼ cup vegetable oil
  Pinch of salt
¼ teaspoon freshly ground pepper

1 · Place the okra in one layer in a shallow glass or ceramic dish.

2 · Combine the remaining ingredients in the container of a food processor or blender. Process until smooth. Pour over the okra. Let stand covered 1 hour.

3 · Arrange the okra on skewers and grill over hot or high heat, basting frequently with any remaining tomato mixture, until golden brown, 3 to 4 minutes per side.

Serves 4.

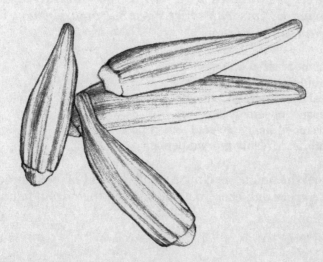

CHARCOAL-ROASTED ONIONS

The onion, in my opinion, is at its absolute best when it is char-coal-roasted deep in the fire. However, as it is not possible to ember-cook onions on a gas grill, it is advisable to apply the procedure for grilling found in the recipe that follows.

    4 large sweet yellow or red onions

1 · Soak the onions in cold water 30 minutes.

2 · Place the onions directly in the hot coals (ember cooking). Allow 20 to 25 minutes for tender onions if you are cover cooking, 30 to 35 minutes if you are grilling.

3 · To serve: Either peel the skin from the onions with a sharp knife and fork and serve whole, or place each onion on the root end and slice downward without cutting all the way through the root end, into 4 equal quarters. Open the onion and gently press out.

Serves 4.

MOROCCAN GRILLED ONION SALAD

Moroccans bake onions in a mixture of oil and lemon juice. The following recipe, adapted by a friend from Northern Italy, augments the ingredients with sweet, aged balsamic vinegar. It makes an aromatic difference too.

    4 medium-sized onions
    1 tablespoon olive oil
    1 teaspoon balsamic vinegar
    2 teaspoons lemon juice
    ½ teaspoon finely slivered lemon peel
      Salt and freshly ground pepper

1 · Peel the onions, leaving a small amount of stem intact at the tops. Cut a cross into each root end to keep them from falling apart.

2 · Combine the oil, vinegar, lemon juice, and lemon peel in a small bowl. Brush this mixture over the onions. Let stand 30 minutes.

3 · Cover-cook with vents open over medium, direct heat (use the outer edges of the grid) 15 minutes. Turn onions over and cover-cook until tender, about 15 minutes longer.

4 · Cool the onions slightly and cut into ⅓-inch slices. Sprinkle with salt and pepper. Serve slightly warm, room temperature, or lightly chilled.

Serves 2 to 4.

PACKET POACHED PEPPERS

The following bouquet of tricolored peppers is braised in oil, vinegar, and rosemary in a loose pouch of aluminum foil over direct heat. Smoke gives this dish its quintessential flavor.

1 large red bell pepper
1 large green bell pepper
1 large yellow bell pepper
6 tablespoons olive oil
¼ cup red wine vinegar
1½ teaspoons chopped fresh rosemary
    Salt and freshly ground pepper

1 · Core and seed the peppers. Cut into ¼-inch-wide strips. Place in a medium bowl. Add the oil, vinegar, and rosemary. Toss well.

2 · Place the peppers on a medium sheet of heavy-duty aluminum foil. Bring up the long edges of the foil and seal at the top. Seal the short edges.

3 · Place the foil packet on the grid and cover-cook over medium-hot heat, until tender, 15 to 20 minutes.

4 · Carefully unwrap the peppers, draining off excess liquid. Transfer to a serving dish; sprinkle with salt and pepper to taste.

Serves 4.

"Barbecued" Potatoes

A long-favored way to outdoor-cook a potato is to butter and roast it over (medium) direct heat. What gives it bite, however, is a fast rub with barbecue sauce.

    4 medium-sized baking potatoes
    3 tablespoons unsalted butter, melted, or 3 tablespoons any
        tomato-based barbecue sauce

1 · Scrub the potatoes and prick all over with a fork. Brush each potato with melted butter or barbecue sauce.

2 · Cover-cook with vents open over medium, direct heat (use the outer edges of the grid) until tender, 45 to 55 minutes.

Serves 4.

Dilled New Potatoes

For a faster-cooked potato on the grill, parboil a batch first and allow them to marinate in olive oil and dill prior to the flame.

   10 to 12 small new red potatoes
   ¼ cup olive oil
   2½ tablespoons chopped fresh dill

1 · Cook the potatoes in boiling salted water for 5 minutes. Rinse under cold running water; drain.

2 · Place the potatoes in a shallow glass or ceramic dish. Pour the oil over the potatoes; sprinkle with dill. Toss well. Let stand 1 hour.

3 · Cover-cook with vents open over medium-hot, direct heat, turning every 5 minutes, until tender, 15 to 20 minutes.

Serves 4.

GRIDLOCKED POTATOES

These potato halves, incised for faster cooking and deeper flavor prior to the fire, make the best accompaniment to steak I know.

  4 baking potatoes
  ¼ cup unsalted butter, melted

1 · Scrub the potatoes and cut in half lengthwise. Using a sharp knife, make crosshatch slashes ¼ inch deep and ¼ inch apart in the flesh of each potato half, without cutting into the skin. The end result should be a grid pattern. Brush each half with 1½ teaspoons butter, gently pushing the edges of the potatoes together toward the center, to open the "grid work."

2 · Cover-cook with vents open over medium-hot, direct heat until tender, about 35 minutes.

Serves 4.

MUSTARD ROASTED POTATOES

The following roasted potato dish (cooked in a hinged grill basket) is like an innovative hot potato salad.

  1½ pounds new red potatoes
  ½ cup Dijon mustard
  2 tablespoons red wine vinegar
  1 teaspoon sugar
  2 large yellow onions, cut into ¼-inch-thick rounds
     Freshly ground pepper

1 · Cook the potatoes in boiling, salted water 5 minutes. Rinse under cold running water; drain. Cut into ½-inch-thick slices. Coat the slices well with mustard.

2 · Combine the red wine vinegar and sugar and sprinkle over the onions. Combine the potatoes and onions. Toss lightly to mix.

3 · Place the potato and onion mixture in a hinged grill basket and grill over medium-hot, direct heat until tender, about 10 minutes per side.

Serves 4 to 6.

SASSY SNOW PEAS

Snow peas, marinated for a half hour before the fire, are, like the green beans, wok-cooked in an aluminum-foil pan that crisp-cooks them with smoke as well as fire.

    1 small clove garlic, minced
    2 tablespoons safflower oil
    2 tablespoons tomato juice
    2 tablespoons soy sauce
    2 tablespoons brown sugar
    ⅛ teaspoon freshly ground pepper
    ½ pound fresh snow peas, trimmed

1 · Combine the garlic, oil, tomato juice, soy sauce, brown sugar, and pepper in a medium bowl. Add the snow peas. Toss to coat. Let stand 30 minutes.

2 · Place the snow peas with marinade in an aluminum-foil drip pan (or make a container out of heavy-duty aluminum foil). Place the pan on the grid over hot or high, direct heat and cook, tossing occasionally, until crisp-tender, 10 to 15 minutes.

Serves 4.

RUSTIC, WILTED SPINACH

Spinach never had it so good. Nor spinach lovers. This dish, accomplished in minutes in a hinged grill basket, is absolutely a knockout.

    10 ounces fresh spinach, stems removed
    1 tablespoon lemon juice
    2 tablespoons walnut oil
    Red wine vinegar
    ½ teaspoon freshly grated nutmeg
    Salt and freshly ground pepper

1 · Wash the spinach leaves; pat dry with paper towels. Place the leaves over the bottom of a lightly oiled hinged grill basket. Close the basket. Sprinkle each side with 1½ teaspoons lemon juice.

Brush each side with 1 tablespoon walnut oil. Then sprinkle each side with ¼ teaspoon vinegar and ¼ teaspoon nutmeg.

2 · Grill, in the basket, over hot or high, direct heat until slightly wilted, about 3 minutes per side. Transfer to a serving bowl and sprinkle with vinegar to taste. Add salt and pepper to taste.

Serves 4.

HERBED CHERRY TOMATOES

I usually cook the following herbed, roasted cherry tomatoes in a hinged grill basket, but careful chefs can do the same on skewers alone.

  1 pint cherry tomatoes, stems removed
  ¼ cup unsalted butter, softened
  1 tablespoon chopped chives
  1 tablespoon chopped fresh parsley
  1 tablespoon chopped fresh basil
  1 teaspoon chopped fresh oregano or marjoram
  Salt and freshly ground pepper

1 · Place the tomatoes on a plate and gently rub with the softened butter. Sprinkle the herbs, and salt and pepper to taste, over the tomatoes, turning the tomatoes to coat all sides lightly with herbs. Place in a hinged grill basket.

2 · Grill, in the basket, over hot or high, direct heat until skins begin to blister and turn crisp, about 2 minutes per side.

Serves 4 to 6.

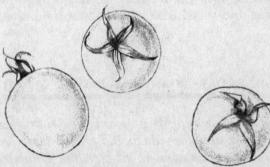

**HIGH HEAT!
NO MEAT!**

Vegetarians usually get the short end of the stick (make that a skewer) at the grill. But no longer. A wondrous vitamin-filled (due to the abbreviated cooking time) meal can be composed with no sweat for any green lover at your table.

While everyone else chomps sirloin, stir up a lettuce pancake, kabob some okra, enclose a handful of asparagus in a grill basket, or simply smear barbecue sauce on potatoes or corn and let the fire do the rest.

TOMATOES STUFFED WITH MONTEREY JACK CHEESE

For the following melted-cheese-stuffed tomato recipe, use not only Monterey Jack but any cheese that pleases you most—even the pepper- or caraway-seasoned varieties.

> 4 medium, firm tomatoes
> ½ cup grated, or finely diced, Monterey Jack cheese
> Freshly ground pepper

1 · Cut the tops of the tomatoes with a sharp knife. Turn the tomatoes upside down and gently squeeze out the seeds. Fill each tomato with 2 tablespoons cheese, tucking the cheese into the now empty seed chambers. Sprinkle with pepper.

2 · Cover-cook with vents open over hot or high heat until the tomatoes soften and the cheese melts, about 5 minutes.

Serves 4.

CHARCOAL-ROASTED WINTER SQUASH

Winter squash (which happily appears year round at supermarkets) makes a great summer side dish. I prefer acorn squash not so much for its flavor as its convenient size, but Hubbard will work just as felicitously with long-cooked roasts. (See note.)

2 acorn squash
Vegetable oil
4 teaspoons unsalted butter, softened
1 teaspoon honey

1 · Rub the squash with oil. Place directly in the hot coals (ember cooking). Cover-cook with vents open until the squash is tender, about 45 minutes.

2 · To serve, cut the squash in half lengthwise and scoop out the seeds with a spoon. Combine the butter and honey and brush over each half.

Serves 4.

Note: Since it is impossible to ember-cook on lava rocks, gas grill users should halve and seed the squash before cooking. Then brush the cut surfaces with melted butter. Cover-cook, flesh down, over medium-hot heat until lightly browned, about 10 minutes. Turn the squash over and brush with the butter-honey mixture. Cover-cook until tender, about 40 minutes longer.

GARLIC-ZAPPED ZUCCHINI

Zucchini sliced lengthwise and sloshed with all the wonderful Italian standby seasonings (garlic, olive oil, and basil) makes a wonderful American dish.

4 to 5 small zucchini, cut lengthwise into ¼-inch-thick slices
4 cloves garlic, crushed
½ cup olive oil
¼ cup chopped basil
Salt and freshly ground pepper

1 · Place the zucchini in a large shallow glass or ceramic dish.

2 · Mash the garlic in a small bowl. Add 2 tablespoons olive oil and mash until smooth. Whisk in the remaining oil, the basil, and salt and pepper to taste. Pour over the zucchini. Let stand 30 minutes.

3 · Grill over hot or high, direct heat until just tender, about 5 minutes per side.

Serves 4.

NATHALIE DUPREE'S CHARCOAL BROILED VEGETABLES

My good friend Nathalie Dupree, one of the best cooks (and cooking teachers) in the United States, came up with the following version of a totally American ratatouille.

2 small (not baby) eggplants
Salt
1 large yellow onion
Olive oil
1 large green bell pepper
1 large red bell pepper
¼ pound large white mushrooms, stems removed
¼ teaspoon chopped fresh rosemary
Vegetable oil
2 medium, firm ripe tomatoes, halved
2 medium zucchini, cut lengthwise into ¼-inch-thick slices
1 clove garlic, minced
Salt and freshly ground pepper
2 tablespoons chopped fresh basil
½ teaspoon chopped fresh thyme

1 · Halve the eggplants lengthwise. With a sharp knife, cut crosshatched slashes, about ½ inch apart, in the top of each half. Sprinkle with salt and place, flesh side down, in a colander for 30 minutes. Rinse and pat dry with paper towels.

2 · Preheat the grill.

3 · Make an onion "flower" by peeling the onion but leaving the root intact. Cut ¼-inch vertical slices from stem to root, not cutting through the root end. Turn the onion at a right angle (90 degrees) and repeat the process. The onion will form a chrysanthemum design when placed on its root end. Do not worry if you lose a few tiny pieces. Brush lightly with olive oil. Set aside.

4 · Brush both peppers with olive oil. Set aside.

5 · Brush the mushrooms with ¼ cup olive oil (the mushrooms will soak up much of the oil) and sprinkle with rosemary. Set aside.

6 · If using presoaked wood chips or chunks (chips for gas), sprinkle them over the hot coals or lava rocks. Brush the grid lightly with vegetable oil.

7 · Place the onion, root end up, over medium heat (the edge of the grid). Cover-cook with vents open 55 to 60 minutes. Do not turn the onion over or it will fall apart. When cooked, remove carefully with tongs and let rest *root end* up.

8 · Meanwhile, brush the eggplants with olive oil. Place, flesh down, over medium heat on the edges of the grid. Cover-cook with vents open, turning once after 20 minutes, for 40 minutes.

9 · At the same time, place the peppers in the center of the grid and cover-cook over hot or high heat, turning frequently until well charred, about 25 minutes. Carefully wrap the charred peppers in paper towels and in a plastic bag. Cool.

10 · Place the tomatoes cut side down on the grill. Cover-cook with vents open over medium-hot heat, turning once, for 14 minutes.

11 · Brush the zucchini with olive oil. Cover-cook with vents open over medium-hot heat, turning once after 5 minutes, for 10 minutes.

12 · Place the mushrooms on the grid and cover-cook with vents open over medium-hot heat, turning once after 5 minutes, for 10- minutes.

13 · Cut the eggplants into 1-inch strips. Scrape the seeds and skin from the peppers and cut into ½-inch-wide strips. Cut the tomatoes into ½-inch-wide strips. Cut the zucchini into 1-inch pieces. Cut the mushrooms into ½-inch strips.

14 · To assemble the dish: Place the peppers and mushrooms on the bottom of a shallow serving dish. Sprinkle with 1 tablespoon olive oil. Next, lay on the tomatoes and sprinkle with garlic, and salt and pepper to taste. Place the eggplant on top and sprinkle with basil and thyme, and, finally, add the zucchini and drizzle with 2 more tablespoons olive oil. Lightly toss the vegetable mixture and place the onion "flower" root side down, in the center. Gently force the "petals" apart with a fork. After presenting at the table, cut the onion into 4 to 6 pieces.

Serves 4 to 6.

Chapter 14

Rotisserie Cooking

SPIT ROASTING IS the very oldest method of cooking known to man. Why early explorers to this country were surprised to find Native Americans grilling fish on what they called *barbacoa* (or racks) is anyone's guess. Either this style of fire and smoke cookery had become obsolete in Europe, or perhaps the "civilized" Europeans were just taken aback by the sophistication of the so-called "wild savages" they found at the grill.

Food authority Raymond Sokolov declares the tradition of spit roasting can be traced back to at least the Trojan wars. And, several centuries later, records show that Hungarian villagers celebrated important weddings by "spitting an entire 2,000 pound ox stuffed with a calf stuffed with a lamb stuffed with a capon stuffed with a quail." How long this mammoth enterprise took to roast is a matter of sheer conjecture.

Modern power-driven rotisseries are actually based on an original clockwork device designed by a surprising name to the world of gastronomy, Leonardo da Vinci. The chief advantage to da Vinci's method of rotisserie cooking, or spit roasting, is that meat cooks evenly on all sides over (or next to) a medium-hot fire. Frequent basting is required to help seal the meat so its natural juices remain intact. But the taste is well worth the exercise. These days it is somewhat au courant to baste a rotisserie roast with a tied-together bundle of fresh herbs—such as rosemary or thyme—rather than your ordinary nylon brush, or a rag mop for that matter!

A rotisserie is the ideal outdoor oven for lovers of roasts with parchment-crisp exteriors. Some rotisseries even come with basket attachments meant for tumble-cooking smaller cuts of meat or vegetables, but roasting is the primary concern here.

Needless to say, if your unit is electric, secure an outdoor outlet nearby. Running extension cords from a random kitchen window is foolhardy and presents a mild hazard for the cook. (If you must, elect heavy-duty wiring.)

To mount a roast properly on a spit rod, look for uniformly shaped meats to ensure even roasting. Usually, the rotisserie outfit is equipped with two holding forks. Slip one onto the rod and insert the rod through the middle of the meat. Take care that the meat is centered on the rod. Push the prongs of the fork into the meat. Slip the second fork onto the rod and push its prongs into the other side of the meat. Now with palms open, gently roll the spit rod back and forth in your hands. If it rolls smoothly, the meat is secure and well balanced. If the roll is awkward or the meat slides, reinsert the prongs of the forks at right angles to each other to give a firmer grasp.

Rotisserie cooking requires the use of medium-hot, indirect heat. Though methods vary slightly from grill to grill, the coals, ideally, should be banked to one side of the drip pan under the meat, rather than around it. On some models, the drip pan must be placed slightly forward of the roast's outer edge to catch the juices as the spit turns. Whatever your particular style of rotisserie grill, be sure to read the manufacturer's instructions before using.

If your rotisserie is attached to a charcoal grill, be aware that more coals will probably have to be added during the spit-roasting process. The easiest way to accomplish this is to have about 15 coals preheating at the edge of the fire bed. Simply move them in as needed.

I go easy with wood flavorings at the rotisserie as a little smoke goes a long way. A few wood chunks or a small handful of presoaked chips is usually sufficient.

The basic techniques involved in preparing meats and poultry for the rotisserie are outlined in the recipes that follow. However, recipes detailed in Chapter 13, "Grilling and Covered Cooking," may easily be adapted for use on a rotisserie. A general timing and cooking chart for rotisserie cooking follows.

ROTISSERIE CHART ⚕

TYPE OF ROAST·	TIMING AND SUGGESTIONS*·
BEEF	
Roast (bone in)	Rub meat with bruised garlic and dry seasonings. Center on spit and roast, basting every 10 minutes. *Rare:* 14 minutes per pound (internal temp.: 125°); *medium:* 16 minutes per pound (internal temp.: 135°); *well:* 18 minutes per pound (internal temp.: 170°).
Roast (boned, rolled, and tied)	Rub meat as above or marinate briefly before rolling and tying. Center on spit and roast, basting every 10 minutes. *Rare:* 14 to 16 minutes per pound internal temp.: 125°); *medium:* 16 to 18 minutes per pound (internal temp.: 135°); *well:* 20 minutes per pound (internal temp.: 170°).
POULTRY	
Chicken (3 to 4 pounds)	Oil and truss chicken. Center on spit and roast, basting occasionally, until juices run yellow, about 1½ hours (internal temp.: 180°). Stop basting during last 20 minutes of roasting.
Rock Cornish Hens (1 to 1½ pounds)	Oil and truss hens. Center on spit and roast, basting occasionally, until juices run yellow, about 50 to 60 minutes (internal temp.: 180°).
Game Hens (squab, quail)	Oil and truss hens. Center on spit and roast, basting frequently, until juices run yellow, about 40 minutes.
Duckling (4 to 5 pounds)	Remove excess fat and prick fatty deposits in skin. Center on spit and roast, basting often with ice water, until juices run yellow, about 2 hours (internal temp.: 170°).
Goose (7 to 10 pounds)	Remove excess fat and prick fatty deposits in skin. Center on spit and roast, basting often with ice water and white wine, until juices run yellow, about 2½ to 3½ hours.
Turkey (8 to 10 pounds)	Oil and truss turkey. Center on spit and roast, basting occasionally, until juices run yellow, about 3 to 3½ hours.

PORK

ROAST (bone in)
Marinate pork. Center on spit and roast, basting frequently, until juices run yellow, about 22 minutes per pound (internal temp.: 170°).

ROAST (boned, rolled, and tied)
Marinate pork. Center on spit and roast, basting occasionally, until juices run yellow, about 25 to 27 minutes per pound (internal temp.: 170°).

SPARERIBS
Marinate ribs in one whole section. Center on spit accordion fashion and roast 20 minutes. Continue to roast, basting every 10 minutes, until juices run yellow, 35 to 40 minutes more.

LAMB

ROAST (bone in)
Marinate lamb. Center on spit and roast, basting occasionally. *Rare:* 10 to 12 minutes per pound (internal temp.: 135°); *medium:* 14 minutes per pound (internal temp.: 150°).

ROAST (boned, rolled, and tied)
Marinate lamb. Center on spit and roast, basting occasionally. *Rare:* 15 minutes per pound (internal temp.: 135°); *medium:* 18 minutes per pound (internal temp.: 150°).

VEAL

ROAST (boned, rolled, and tied)
Bard the veal and truss. Center on spit and roast until juices run yellow, about 25 minutes per pound (internal temp.: 155° to 160°).

* Times may vary depending on outdoor temperature and velocity of wind.

CHILI RUBBED PRIME RIB

A Southerner's version of Texas beef, this recipe combines the best of both regional tastes: hot peppers (ground) plus bacon drippings. The meat need not be basted. Lovers of well-to-medium beef may skewer the meat on the spit parallel to the bones for a crustier surface. Medium-rare-to-rare aficionados are advised to skewer the roast from side to side to avoid any well-done pieces.

    3 tablespoons bacon drippings
    1 clove garlic, crushed
    2 teaspoons chili powder
    ¼ teaspoon cayenne pepper
    ½ teaspoon tomato paste
    1 2-rib, prime beef rib roast (about 5½ pounds)

1 · Combine the bacon drippings, garlic, chili powder, cayenne pepper, and tomato paste in a bowl. Mix well and coat the beef with this mixture. Let stand 2 hours.

2 · Preheat the grill.

3 · Secure the meat on the spit rod.

4 · If using presoaked wood chips or chunks (chips for gas), or other flavorings, sprinkle over the hot coals or lava rocks.

5 · Attach the spit rod to the grill's rotisserie, with the beef over a drip pan, and rotisserie-cook about 1 hour and 10 to 15 minutes for rare (internal temperature: 125 degrees); about 1 hour and 25 minutes for medium-rare (internal temperature: 135 degrees). Let stand 15 minutes before serving.

Serves 4.

LEMON ROASTED ROCK CORNISH GAME HENS

Game hens, like all poultry, should be trussed before being secured to the spit rod. When rotisserie-cooking 2 birds at a time, line them up head to tail. If you require 3 or more hens, spit them boldly through their sides, turning every other hen in the opposite di-

rection (head to tail, and tail to head, etc.) and pushing them close together so they do not flop.

> 2 Cornish hens
> 2 large cloves garlic, bruised
> 1 lemon, sliced
> 4 3-inch sprigs fresh tarragon
> ¼ cup unsalted butter, melted
>   Juice of 1 lemon
> 1 teaspoon chopped fresh tarragon

1 · Preheat the grill.

2 · Rub each Cornish hen, inside and out, with a bruised garlic clove. In each hen, place the garlic, ½ sliced lemon, and 2 tarragon sprigs. Sew and truss. Secure on the spit rod.

3 · Combine the butter, lemon juice, and chopped tarragon in a bowl.

4 · If using presoaked wood chips or chunks (chips for gas), or other flavorings, sprinkle over the hot coals or lava rocks.

5 · Attach the spit rod to the grill's rotisserie, with the hens over a drip pan, and rotisserie-cook, basting every 10 minutes with the butter mixture, until the juices run yellow when pricked with a fork, about 50 minutes (internal temperature: 180 degrees). Let stand 10 minutes before serving.

Serves 2 to 4.

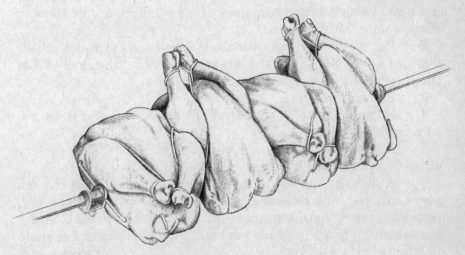

SPIT ROASTED "CHOOK"
WITH AUSTRALIAN JACKAROO SAUCE

Chook is Aussie slang for chicken. And Australian Jackaroo Sauce is the baste they generally sluice it with down under. A bottle of this spicy (but tomatoless) marinade was given to me on a recent trip to Sydney. What follows is my own American translation devised after reading the ingredients on the label.

    2 cloves garlic
    1 small shallot
    2 tablespoons lemon juice
    2 tablespoons cider vinegar
 1½ teaspoons chopped fresh parsley
    ¾ teaspoon chopped fresh oregano
    ½ teaspoon chopped fresh thyme
 2½ teaspoons Hungarian sweet paprika
    1 tablespoon unprocessed bran
    2 teaspoons lightly toasted wheat germ
    ½ teaspoon salt
    1 teaspoon sugar
    ½ cup vegetable oil
      Dash of hot pepper sauce
    1 chicken, about 3 pounds

1 · Combine all ingredients, starting with garlic, through the hot pepper sauce, in the container of a food processor or blender. Process until fairly smooth.

2 · Pat the chicken dry with paper towels and place, breast side down, in a deep bowl. Pour the jackaroo sauce over the chicken. Let stand covered 1 hour.

3 · Preheat the grill.

4 · Remove the chicken; reserve the sauce. Sew and truss. Secure on the spit rod.

5 · If using presoaked wood chips or chunks (chips for gas), or other flavorings, sprinkle them over the hot coals or lava rocks.

6 · Attach the spit rod to the grill's rotisserie, with the chicken over a drip pan, and rotisserie-cook, basting every 15 minutes with remaining sauce, until the juices run yellow when pricked with a fork, about 1½ hours (internal temperature: 180 degrees). Let stand 10 minutes before serving. *Serves 2 to 4.*

ANNA TERESA CALLEN'S FENNEL CHICKEN ON THE SPIT

Anna Teresa Callen's recipes are as poetic and richly Italianate as her distinctive and lyrical voice. Her original recipe called for ½ pound prosciutto, but I have reduced it slightly to ⅓ pound as most American-style prosciutto is oversalted. If you have access to the real thing, increase the amount to your taste.

1 chicken, about 3 pounds
1 tablespoon olive oil
⅓ pound thinly sliced prosciutto
3 cloves garlic
4 leaves fresh sage, or ½ teaspoon dried
¼ teaspoon fennel seeds
  Freshly ground pepper

1 · Pat the chicken dry with paper towels. Rub with olive oil. Let stand uncovered for 3 hours, or overnight in the refrigerator. Remove from the refrigerator 40 minutes before stuffing.

2 · Preheat the grill.

3 · Reserve 4 of the prosciutto slices. Place the remaining slices with 1 clove garlic, the sage, and fennel seeds in the container of a food processor. Process only until chopped. Fill the cavity of the chicken with this mixture. Insert 1 clove garlic into the neck cavity. Bruise the remaining clove garlic and rub over the chicken. Sprinkle with pepper. Cover the chicken with the remaining prosciutto slices. Secure and truss chicken with kitchen twine. Secure on the spit rod.

4 · If using presoaked wood chips or chunks (chips for gas), or other flavorings, sprinkle them over the hot coals or lava rocks.

5 · Attach the spit rod to the grill's rotisserie, with the chicken over a drip pan, and rotisserie-cook until the juices run yellow when pricked with a fork, about 1½ hours (internal temperature: 180 degrees). Let stand 10 minutes before serving, then cut into pieces with poultry shears.

Serves 4.

BARBECUE-MAYONNAISE ROASTED CAPON

A large capon or chicken (or a small turkey) will remain incredibly succulent and moist if it is coated prior to the fire in a dense layer of barbecue-flavored mayonnaise. I generally use All-American BBQ Sauce because I always have batches in the fridge, but any good commercial sauce will do. The notion of laving mayonnaise on fire-roasted foods, incidentally, was inspired by my neighbors, Craig Claiborne and Pierre Franey.

1 capon or chicken (or small turkey), about 7 pounds
1 clove garlic, bruised
2 small onions
2 large sprigs parsley
3 sprigs fresh summer savory
1 large sprig thyme
1 cup mayonnaise
5 tablespoons All-American BBQ Sauce (see page 299) or any
   good commercial barbecue sauce

1 · Preheat the grill

2 · Rub the capon or chicken with garlic. Place the onions, parsley, savory, and thyme in the cavity. Sew and truss. Secure on the spit rod.

3 · Combine the mayonnaise and barbecue sauce in a small bowl. Mix well. Spread ½ cup over the capon or chicken.

4 · If using presoaked wood chips or chunks (chips for gas), or other flavorings, sprinkle them over the hot coals or lava rocks.

5 · Attach the spit rod to the grill's rotisserie, with the capon or chicken over a drip pan, and rotisserie-cook, basting with remaining mayonnaise mixture every 30 minutes, until juices run yellow when pricked with a fork, about 2 hours (internal temperature: 180 degrees). Let stand 10 minutes before serving.

Serves 6.

APPLE-CIDER MARINATED DUCK

Basting a roast duck on a rotisserie with icy cold liquid allows it to become as crisp as Venetian glass without drying out the meat. Marinating a duck in cider prior to the fire gives it unparalleled flavor. Charcoal-grill owners should add water to the drip pan to prevent the grease from splattering and catching fire.

    1 duckling, about 4 pounds, trimmed of excess fat
1½ cups apple cider
    1 tart apple, peeled, cored, and cut into chunks
    1 onion, roughly chopped
   ¾ cup water, chilled
   ¾ cup wine, chilled

1 · Prick the skin of the duck all over. Place in a deep bowl and pour the cider over the top. Let stand, turning once, 2 hours.

2 · Preheat the grill.

3 · Remove the duck from the cider; pat dry. Place the apple and onion in the cavity. Sew and truss. Secure on the spit rod. Prick all over with a fork.

4 · If using wood chips or chunks (chips for gas), or other flavorings, sprinkle them over the hot coals or lava rocks.

5 · Attach the spit rod to the grill's rotisserie, with the duck over a drip pan, and rotisserie-cook 15 minutes.

6 · Meanwhile, combine the water and wine. Prick the duck again and baste with marinade. (Keep the water-wine mixture in the freezer between bastings.) Continue to rotisserie-cook, pricking and basting every 15 minutes, until juices run clear when pricked with a fork, about 1 hour and 45 minutes longer.

Serves 2.

PORCHETTA CASALINGA

Another Anna Teresa Callen specialty. This pork loin is actually wrapped in skin prior to spit roasting. The meat stays irresistibly tender, while the covering crackles to a golden shell to be served on the side. Most supermarket meat departments receive their pork preskinned, so special-order the skin in advance.

    1 boneless pork loin, about 4 pounds
       Pork skin to cover
       Salt and freshly ground pepper
  ¼ cup dry white wine
    1 large clove garlic, minced
  ½ teaspoon chopped fresh rosemary leaves
    3 bay leaves

1 · Place the boneless loin on the pork skin, and, using a sharp heavy knife, cut a piece that will cover the bottom and lower half of the loin. Cut another piece to match. Then cut 2 pieces for the ends of the pork. Again with a sharp knife, make holes in the center of each end piece for the spit rod.

2 · Rub the loin with salt and pepper. Rub with wine 1 tablespoon at a time. Sprinkle with garlic and rosemary.

3 · Place the pork on one long piece of skin (skin side out). Place the bay leaves across the top of the roast. Cover with remaining skin. Tie in place at 2-inch intervals. (Not too close together as the string is difficult to remove later.) Place the end pieces on the pork and tie in place. Refrigerate covered overnight.

4 · Remove the pork from the refrigerator and secure on the spit rod.

5 · Preheat the grill.

6 · If using wood chips or chunks (chips for gas), or other flavorings, sprinkle them over the hot coals or lava rocks.

7 · Attach the spit rod to the grill's rotisserie, with the pork over a drip pan, and rotisserie-cook until juices run yellow when pricked with a fork, about 1 hour and 40 minutes (internal temperature: 170 degrees).

8 · Remove the pork from the spit. Place on a cutting board. Using a sharp knife cut away the strings. Slowly lift up the skin at the edges, carefully loosening any loin meat that sticks. Roughly

chop or break up the pork skin. Place in a warm oven to dry out. Pass along with the pork.

Serves 8.

RASPBERRY BRUSHED SPARERIBS

I resisted roasting spareribs on a rotisserie for years, clearly on the basis of the strong taste of most commercial take-out ribs. If you, like me, have that built-in prejudice, try the following method. These raspberry-tinged ribs are incredibly brittle and moist at one and the same time. And the technique is easily mastered. Simply pretend you are basting a hemline when you insert the spit rod.

> 1 section meaty pork spareribs, about 4 pounds
>   Juice of 2 lemons
> 1 jar (12 ounces) raspberry preserves
> 3 tablespoons vinegar
> ½ cup chili sauce
> 1 teaspoon Dijon mustard

1 · Remove the membrane from the back of the ribs. Using a sharp knife, scrape all fat from the ribs, but take care not to pierce the flesh. Sprinkle with lemon juice. Let stand 40 minutes.

2 · Preheat the grill.

3 · Meanwhile, strain the raspberry preserves through a sieve into a medium saucepan. Pour the vinegar through the sieve to loosen the seeds. Discard the seeds. Add the chili sauce and mustard to the saucepan. Heat to boiling. Reduce the heat and boil gently for 2 minutes. Remove from the heat.

4 · Thread the ribs on the spit rod by forcing the tip of the rod in and out of the ribs at every 2 bone sections. Secure with the forks. Brush with the raspberry sauce.

5 · If using presoaked wood chips or chunks (chips for gas), or other flavorings, sprinkle them over the hot coals or lava rocks.

6 · Attach the spit rod to the grill's rotisserie, with the ribs over a drip pan, and rotisserie-cook 20 minutes. Baste with sauce and continue to rotisserie-cook, basting every 10 minutes, until crisp, about 35 minutes. Serve remaining marinade, reheated, on the side.

Serves 4.

SPITTED DIJON LAMB

This fairly classic rendering of a Dijonnaise roast leg is excellent on the rotisserie. When inserting the spit rod, aim it dead center at the large end of the roast and push it through so it comes out next to the bone at the small end.

1 leg of lamb, about 4 pounds
1 clove garlic, cut into slivers
½ cup Dijon mustard
2 tablespoons soy sauce
1 clove garlic, crushed
2 teaspoons chopped fresh rosemary
½ teaspoon ground ginger
2 tablespoons olive oil

1 · Prick about 30 holes with an ice pick in the top of the lamb. Insert slivers of garlic into every hole. Combine the remaining ingredients in a bowl and use it to coat the lamb. Let stand 2 hours.

2 · Preheat the grill.

3 · Secure the lamb on the spit rod, smoothing out the mustard sauce if necessary.

4 · If using wood chips or chunks (chips for gas), or other flavorings, sprinkle them over the hot coals or lava rocks.

5 · Attach the spit rod to the grill's rotisserie, with the lamb over a drip pan, and rotisserie-cook about 40 minutes for rare (internal temperature: 135 degrees), about 50 minutes for medium-rare (internal temperature: 150 degrees). Let stand 15 minutes before serving.

Serves 6.

BARDED VEAL ROAST

Barding a veal roast (wrapping it in a layer of fat) and spit-roasting it is the only way I ever cook that delicate cut outdoors. The fragile meat is just too lean to risk drying out by other methods, particularly as the price of veal is so astronomical. My own method of cookery that follows is loosely adapted from Outdoor Cooking *by the editors of Time-Life Books (Time-Life Books, 1983).*

     1 boneless veal roast, about 4 pounds; rolled, barded, tied
     3 tablespoons lemon juice
     ¼ cup olive oil
     ½ cup chopped fresh parsley
     3 tablespoons chopped fresh coriander
        Salt and freshly ground pepper

1 · Have your butcher bone the veal, roll, and bard it. Rub lemon juice over the veal. Rub in the olive oil. Sprinkle the veal with parsley, coriander, and salt and pepper to taste. Let stand 1 hour.

2 · Preheat the grill.

3 · Secure the veal on the spit rod.

4 · If using wood chips or chunks (chips for gas), or other flavorings, sprinkle them over the hot coals or lava rocks.

5 · Attach the spit rod to the grill's rotisserie, with the veal over a drip pan, and rotisserie-cook until the juices run clear when pricked with a fork, about 1 hour and 30 to 40 minutes (internal temperature: 165 degrees). Let stand 10 minutes before serving.

Serves 6 to 8.

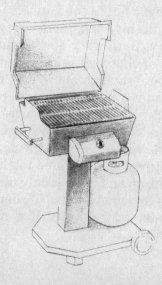

Chapter 15

Smoker Cooking

COOKING OUTDOORS ON a smoker is the closest a home cook can come to duplicating the taste and texture of real old-time barbecue as it is known in the South and Southwest. And while it may take hours before certain foods are adjudged ready for consumption (that is to say, at the proper "fall-apart-on-the-fork" stage), the entire process is really very simple to perform, greatly rewarding, and downright fun in the bargain.

As noted elsewhere in this book, there are two kinds of smokers: water (or wet) and dry. Both work on the same principle. A heat element (gas, electric, or charcoal) is located at the bottom of a cylindrical grill. The food rests high above on a grid.

The water smoker adds a pan (between the heat source and the food) that, when filled with liquid, introduces extra moisture into the cooking process—allowing one to cook even large cuts of meat for long periods of time without drying them out excessively.

Dry smoking, despite its name, is not a totally moisture-free process either; this cooking technique uses only the normal humidity in the air—plus smoke—to achieve foods of slightly dehydrated texture and intense woodsy taste. Indeed it is the presoaked or dry

268

wood chips added to the heat source in both cases that actually establish flavor.

The amazing thing about smokers is that a little fuel goes a long way. Because of this appliance's unique design, a mere 15 coals will last the hour and a half needed to produce smoker-cooked chicken breasts or seafood. And a fire pan filled with double the amount of charcoal, for long-cooked meats like brisket, will last several hours at least before any extra coals are needed to replenish the heat source.

Learning to control a smoker's internal temperature is vital. Keeping the air vents open increases the temperature; closing them, cools it down. Gas and electric smokers are less problematic, as the heat source is regulated manually. However, proper use of the vents is still imperative to control the air flow.

When using a water smoker, the pan will need to be refilled after approximately 4 hours of cooking time. When the pan sizzles and the internal temperature rises, you'll know it's time. Try not to look at the pan too often (or the food either for that matter), for every peek decreases the heat and increases the overall cooking time.

The actual degree of smokiness desired is controlled by the amount of wood (presoaked or dry, depending on the model) that is added to the heat source. I find a few chunks, or a handful of chips, are usually enough for my taste. But go heavier if you wish.

Foods for the smoker may be prepped exactly the same way as foods for the grill or covered cooker. That is, either marinated or rubbed prior to placement on the smoker's grid. However, they may also be cured. Curing, either by use of dry ingredients or brine, not only adds flavor but improves color as well. Salt, of course, is the basis of any cure. A dry cure of salt and sugar is figured on a ratio of 3 parts salt to 1 part sugar. On the other hand, with brines, the ratio of salt to water is much reduced: it may be as low as 1 part salt to 12 parts water. A good rule of thumb to observe is the old-fashioned precept: if an egg floats in the brine, there is enough salt content.

It should be pointed out that despite the use of a cure, smoker cooking is literally what the name implies. Food that is *smoked and cooked* over low, low heat (usually between 200 degrees and 225 degrees) until the internal temperature indicates it is ready to eat. Home-smoked foods do not have the resilient texture commonly associated with commercially smoked products, but they are wonderfully succulent! More to the point, they have an extended shelf life (1 to 2 weeks) in the refrigerator.

Be forewarned that boneless meats, such as brisket of beef and shoulder of pork, will undergo considerable shrinkage during smoker cookery. It is important to ask your butcher for untrimmed cuts. A heavy layering of fat on the meat holds shrinkage to a minimum. Merely cut off the fat before serving.

The recipes included in this chapter offer an eclectic overview of what is possible with smoker cooking. Since timings and methods vary with different models, become familiar with the ins and outs of yours. Follow the manufacturer's instructions. Then have fun! A very general timing chart for smoker cooking follows.

SMOKER CHART

TYPE OF FOOD ·	TEMPERA-TURE RANGE ·	HOURS FOR SMOKING* ·
BEEF		
BRISKET AND CHUCK ROASTS (about 4 pounds)	190° to 225°	**6 to 7 hours** (or until meat can be "pulled")
BONELESS, ROLLED ROASTS (3 to 4 pounds)	200° to 225°	**3 to 4 hours** (125° for rare, 135° for medium-rare)
POULTRY		
CHICKEN BREASTS (halved)	165° to 180°	**1½ hours** (or until firm to the touch)
ROAST CHICKEN (about 3 pounds)	200° to 225°	**4 to 5 hours** (or 180°)
TURKEY (12 pounds)	200° to 225°	**6½ to 8 hours** (or 180°)
DUCKLING (about 5 pounds)	200° to 225°	**5 to 6 hours** (or 170°)
PORK		
TENDERLOIN (about 3/4 pound)	170° to 180°	**3 to 4 hours** (or 170°)
SHOULDER OR BUTT (5 to 6 pounds)	200° to 225°	**7 to 8 hours** (or until meat can be "pulled")
VEAL		
BREAST (5 pounds)	200° to 225°	**6 to 7 hours** (or until meat pulls from the bones)
FISH		
WHOLE (1 to 5 pounds)	150° to 170°	**1 to 3 hours** (or until firm to the touch)
FILETS	150° to 170°	**1½ to 2 hours** (or until fish flakes)
STEAKS	150° to 170°	**2 to 3 hours** (or until fish flakes)
SHELLFISH		
SHRIMP AND LOBSTER	130° to 150°	**1 to 2 hours** (or until firm to the touch)

* Times will vary depending on outdoor temperature and velocity of wind. Times will also vary from model to model. All times are based on the use of a charcoal smoker. Gas and electric models cook much quicker; even as much as half the time.

FANCY COUNTY FAIR SMOKED BRISKET

Brisket is the hands-down, blue-ribbon ingredient for barbecue beef, particularly when the meat is marinated in a tangy vinegar marinade and topped with a dark rich barbecue glaze, slightly on the sweet side. A word to the wise: Do not skimp on the marination time. Serve with Dinah's Barbecue Sauce (see page 306), warmed through, just before serving.

1 untrimmed beef brisket, about 4 pounds
1 cup red wine vinegar
1 cup water
1 onion, sliced
2 cloves garlic, minced
8 whole cloves
6 sprigs fresh parsley
2 bay leaves
2 ribs celery with leaves, chopped
2 crushed juniper berries
1 teaspoon chopped fresh thyme, or ½ teaspoon dried
1 teaspoon chopped fresh rosemary, or ½ teaspoon dried
1 teaspoon chopped fresh basil, or ½ teaspoon dried
1 tablespoon brown sugar

1 · Place the brisket in a large glass or ceramic dish. Combine all the ingredients from the vinegar through brown sugar in a bowl. Pour over the meat. Refrigerate covered 30 to 48 hours. Remove from refrigerator 2 hours before smoker-cooking.

2 · Preheat a water smoker. (Charcoal smokers will require a full pan of briquets.)

3 · Add presoaked wood chips or chunks to the heat source. Put the water pan in place and add the marinade from the meat. Add water to fill the pan. Place the brisket on the highest food grid. Cover and smoker-cook, keeping the temperature between 190 degrees and 225 degrees, until meat is tender enough to cut with a fork, about 6 to 7 hours. (Add more preheated coals to the fire pan and more liquid to the water pan as required.) Serve sliced or "pulled" (shredded) with warm barbecue sauce.

Serves 4 to 6.

MY MOTHER'S BARBECUED CHUCK ROAST

My mother's unique barbecued pot roast is a longtime tradition at our family dinners. Here it has been converted to the smoker, with equally felicitous results. Though pure Coloradan by nature, the technique of foil-wrapping the meat to keep it from turning crusty is a Texan dispensation.

2 large onions, thickly sliced
1 chuck roast, 3¼ inches thick (about 3½ pounds)
8 ounces tomato sauce
2 tablespoons brown sugar
¼ teaspoon Hungarian sweet paprika
¼ teaspoon dry mustard
¼ cup lemon juice
¼ cup ketchup
¼ cup distilled white vinegar
1 tablespoon Worcestershire sauce

1 · Preheat a water smoker. (Charcoal smokers will require a full pan of briquets.)

2 · Add presoaked wood chips or chunks to the heat source. Put the water pan in place and add the onions to the pan. Add water to fill the pan. Place the chuck roast on the highest food grid. Cover and smoker-cook, keeping the temperature between 190 degrees and 225 degrees, 3 hours.

3 · Meanwhile, combine the remaining ingredients in a medium saucepan. Heat to boiling; reduce heat. Simmer 20 minutes.

4 · After 3 hours, remove meat from the cooker and replace the cover. Refill the water pan (and add additional preheated coals). Place the meat on a large piece of heavy-duty aluminum foil. Pour ½ cup barbecue sauce over the top. Seal the foil on all sides and return the package to the smoker. Continue to smoker-cook until meat is tender enough to cut with a fork, about 3 hours longer. Serve sliced or "pulled" (shredded), with the remaining barbecue sauce (reheated) on the side.

Serves 6.

CURED AND SMOKED CHICKEN BREASTS

The following recipe for smoked chicken breast employs a dry cure, rather than any marination. Moreover, the breasts are done in a dry smoker without water. Cooked over low, low heat, the warm air provides more than enough moisture to keep the meat succulent. Try apple wood as flavoring.

> 6 tablespoons kosher salt
> 2 tablespoons brown sugar
> 2 teaspoons five-spice powder (available in the gourmet department of most supermarkets)
> 2 teaspoons Hungarian hot paprika
> 2 cloves garlic, crushed
> 2 large chicken breasts, halved

1 · Combine the salt, brown sugar, five-spice powder, paprika, and garlic in a bowl. Mix well. Rub this mixture into the chicken breasts. Refrigerate covered overnight. Remove from refrigerator 1 hour before smoker-cooking.

2 · Lightly rinse the cure off the chicken breasts. Pat dry with paper towels. Place on a rack and allow to air-dry 1 hour.

3 · Preheat a *dry* smoker. (Charcoal smokers will require about 20 coals.)

4 · Add presoaked (or dry) wood chips to the heat source. Place the chicken breasts on the highest food grid. Cover and smoker-cook, keeping the temperature between 165 degrees and 180 degrees, until the breasts are firm to the touch and cooked through, about 1½ hours. Serve warm in individual pieces, or cold, sliced.

Serves 4 to 6.

HICKORY- AND GARLIC-SCENTED TURKEY

Turkey roasted in a water smoker is not only incredibly moist, but endowed with a rosy hue besides. Hickory gives the bird character, and garlic, added to the water pan, confers exceptional flavor.

    1 fresh (or frozen and thawed) 12-pound turkey
    1 onion, peeled
    2 carrots, peeled
    4 sprigs fresh parsley
    3 fresh sage leaves
    4 strips bacon
    1 whole head garlic, unpeeled, but separated

1 · Preheat a water smoker. (Charcoal smokers will require a full pan of briquets.)

2 · Meanwhile, pat the turkey dry inside and out and stuff the cavity with the onion, carrots, parsley, and sage. Sew and truss. Place the bacon strips over the breast.

3 · Add presoaked hickory wood chips or chunks to the heat source. Put the water pan in place. Add the garlic cloves. Add water to fill the pan. Place the turkey on the lower food grid. Cover and smoker-cook, keeping the temperature between 200 degrees and 225 degrees, until the juices run yellow when pricked with a fork, 6½ to 7½ hours (internal temperature: 180 degrees). (Add more preheated coals to the fire pan and more liquid to the water pan as required.) Let the turkey rest 15 minutes before carving.

Serves 8.

Carolina's Tenderloin of Pork

The best thing about tenderloin of pork is that it takes only half the time to smoker-cook as a larger, rolled roast. This version, with its mustardy basting sauce, is a specialty of the redoubtable Carolina restaurant in New York City.

    2 pork tenderloins, about ¾ pound each
    2 teaspoons Hungarian sweet paprika
    ½ teaspoon salt
    ¼ teaspoon freshly ground pepper
    ½ cup Dijon mustard
    3 tablespoons red wine vinegar
    3 tablespoons unsalted butter, melted

1 · Pat the tenderloins dry with paper towels. Combine the paprika, salt, and pepper in a bowl. Rub this mixture into the meat.

2 · Preheat a water smoker. (Charcoal smokers will require a full pan of briquets.)

3 · Meanwhile, combine the mustard, vinegar, and butter in a small saucepan. Heat to boiling; remove from heat.

4 · Add presoaked wood chips or chunks to the heat source. Put the water pan in place and add water to fill the pan. Brush the tenderloins with the mustard mixture and place on the highest food grid. Cover and smoker-cook, keeping the temperature in the 180-degree range, basting twice more during cooking, until the juices run clear when pricked with a fork, 3 to 4 hours (internal temperature: 170 degrees). Serve hot or cold, thinly sliced.

Serves 4 to 6.

Southern-Style Barbecued Pork

Barbecued pork is one of the prides of the South. But nobody down there seems to agree on the proper way to cook or serve it. The marinated pork that follows is authentic enough for even North Carolinians' appetites, but citizens of that state cannot concur on

*whether it should be served sliced, chunked, or "pulled" (shred-
ded). Hickory is their wood of choice, but maple and oak are
equally acceptable.*

    2 teaspoons salt
    1 tablespoon Hungarian sweet paprika
    2 tablespoons sugar
    ½ teaspoon cayenne pepper
    ½ teaspoon dry mustard
    1 teaspoon freshly ground pepper
    ⅔ cup water
    ¼ cup Worcestershire sauce
    ⅔ cup red wine vinegar
    ½ cup unsalted butter, cut into bits
    1 fresh pork shoulder, or butt, about 6 pounds
    2 cans (12 ounces each) beer

1 · Combine the dry ingredients in a medium saucepan. Stir in
the water. Heat to boiling; remove from heat. Stir in the Worcestershire sauce, vinegar, and butter. Stir to dissolve the butter. Place
the pork in a bowl and pour on 1 cup of the mixture. Let stand covered 2 hours, turning the pork occasionally.

2 · Preheat a water smoker. (Charcoal smokers will require a
full pan of briquets.)

3 · Add presoaked wood chips or chunks to the heat source. Put
the water pan in place and add the beer. Add water to fill the pan.
Place the shoulder or butt on the highest food grid. Cover and
smoker-cook, keeping the temperature between 200 and 225 degrees, 4 hours.

4 · After 3 hours, remove the meat from the cooker and replace
the cover. Refill the water pan (and add additional preheated
coals). Place the meat on a large sheet of aluminum foil. Pour ¾ cup
of the marinade over the meat. Seal the foil on all sides and return
the package to the smoker. Continue to smoker-cook until the meat
is tender enough to cut with a fork, 2½ to 3 hours longer. Serve
sliced or "pulled" (shredded) with the remaining sauce (reheated)
on the side, or with a sweet barbecue sauce of your choice.

Serves 6 to 8.

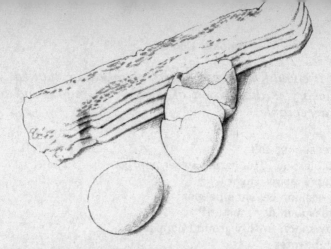

KAREN HARAM'S SMOKED BACON AND EGGS

Karen Haram is a dear friend who also happens to be a talented food writer for the San Antonio Express-News. *Her wildly improbable recipe for a smoked bacon and egg brunch dish made in a smoker requires the use of any 10-cup metal pan or Pyrex dish that fits on the grid. I wrap foil around the bottom of mine to keep it reasonably clean, but this recipe is so good, one might reserve a pan just for its use alone. Karen does. To vary the recipe, ham may be substituted for the bacon; sautéed green peppers or chile peppers may also be added.*

    1 pound bacon
    1 white onion, finely chopped
    2 to 3 cloves garlic, minced
      Unsalted butter
    4 cups croutons, fried in butter until crisp
    1 ¾ cups freshly grated Parmesan cheese
    8 eggs
    2 cups milk
    1 cup light cream or half-and-half
    1 teaspoon Dijon mustard
      Salt and freshly ground pepper
      Hungarian hot paprika

   1 · Sauté the bacon in a large heavy skillet until crisp. Drain on paper towels. Crumble and reserve.

   2 · Preheat a *dry* smoker. (Charcoal smokers will require 15 to 20 coals.)

   3 · Discard all but 3 tablespoons of bacon drippings from the skillet. Add the onion; cook over medium-low heat 1 minute. Add

the garlic; continue to cook, stirring occasionally, until soft but not brown, about 5 minutes.

4 · Rub a 2-inch-deep, 10-cup metal pan or Pyrex dish well with butter. Place the croutons over the bottom of the pan. Sprinkle the onion and garlic over the croutons. Spoon all but ¼ cup of cheese over the onions.

5 · Lightly beat the eggs in a large bowl. Add the milk, light cream or half-and-half, mustard, and salt and pepper to taste. Beat until mixed. Pour over the cheese. Sprinkle the eggs with the remaining ¼ cup cheese, the bacon, and paprika.

6 · Add presoaked (or dry) wood chips to the heat source. Place the pan on the highest food grid. Cover and smoker-cook, keeping the temperature between 150 degrees and 170 degrees, until the eggs are almost set, about 1½ hours. (I prefer the eggs to be slightly runny at the center.)

Serves 6 to 8.

BREAST OF VEAL SCANDINAVIAN STYLE

Breast of veal (unboned) is one of those difficult cuts of meat one never quite knows what to do with. Now you do! Smoker-cook it slowly, while basting with a mixture of coffee, cream, and brandy—an adaptation of an old Swedish roasting method.

1 breast of veal, unboned, about 5 pounds
1 clove garlic, bruised
   Salt and freshly ground pepper
1 cup coffee
¼ cup brandy
¼ cup heavy cream

1 · Preheat a water smoker. (Charcoal smokers will require a full pan of briquets.)

2 · Meanwhile, rub the veal with garlic and salt and pepper to taste. Combine the coffee, brandy, and cream in a bowl.

3 · Add presoaked wood chips or chunks to the heat source. Put the water pan in place and add water to fill the pan. Place the veal on the highest food grid and brush with the coffee-cream mixture. Cover and smoker-cook, keeping the temperature between 200 de-

grees and 225 degrees, and basting every hour, until the meat is tender enough to cut with a fork, about 6 hours. (Add more preheated coals to the fire pan and more liquid to the water pan as required.) Serve cut into individual ribs, or into slices.

Serves 4.

HONEY-CURED, SMOKED SALMON

Salmon cooked on a smoker does not have the texture of commercial smoked salmon or lox. For one thing, it is moister and less difficult to slice, and is possessed of sweeter flavor for another—both the result of brining the fish in honey and rum. Alderwood does any salmon proud.

> 1 quart water
> ½ cup salt
> ¾ cup honey
> ¼ cup golden rum
> ¼ cup lemon juice
> 10 cloves
> 10 peppercorns
> 10 allspice berries
> 1 bay leaf
> 1 large salmon filet, about 1¾ pounds
> Capers and lemon slices for garnish

1 · Combine all the ingredients from the water through the bay leaf in a large glass or ceramic dish deep enough to hold the salmon. Add the salmon, skin side up, to the brine and let stand 2 hours.

2 · Rinse the salmon with fresh water and pat dry. Place on a rack and allow to air-dry 1 hour.

3 · Preheat a *dry* smoker. (Charcoal smokers will require about 20 coals.)

4 · Add presoaked (or dry) wood chips to the heat source. Place the salmon, skin side down, on the highest food grid. Cover and smoker-cook, keeping the temperature between 150 degrees and 170 degrees, until the salmon is firm, about 1½ hours. Serve warm, or well chilled with capers and lemon slices.

Serves 4 to 6.

BASIL-BUTTERED, CURED AND SMOKED SHRIMP

Smoked shrimp make the very best hors d'oeuvre imaginable, particularly hot off the smoker. Like salmon, shrimp is smoker-cooked over very, very low heat, and, in this case, basted with a basil butter that has just a mite of Old Bay seasoning in it for good measure. Smoke shrimp over cherry wood, and you're in business.

3 cups water
1 clove garlic, minced
1 shallot, chopped
  Juice of 1 lemon
⅓ cup brown sugar
1 pound medium shrimp, shelled and deveined
¼ cup unsalted butter, melted
1 clove garlic, crushed
2 teaspoons finely chopped fresh basil
1 tablespoon lemon juice
1 teaspoon Old Bay seasoning (available in most supermarkets)

1 · Combine the water, minced garlic, shallot, juice of 1 lemon, and brown sugar in a deep bowl. Add the shrimp. Let stand 45 minutes. Rinse the shrimp with fresh water. Pat dry and place on a rack. Allow to air-dry 2 hours.

2 · Preheat a *dry* smoker. (Charcoal smokers will require about 15 to 20 coals.)

3 · Combine the butter, garlic, basil, 1 tablespoon lemon juice, and Old Bay seasoning in a bowl. Reserve.

4 · Add presoaked (or dry) wood chips to the heat source. Place two grids, at right angles to each other, at the highest grid setting. (This will prevent the shrimp from falling through.) Cover and smoker-cook 10 minutes. Baste with the basil-butter mixture. Cover and continue to smoker-cook, keeping the temperature between 130 degrees and 150 degrees, and basting every 10 minutes, until the shrimp are firm, 1 to 1½ hours. Serve warm as an hors d'oeuvre or an appetizer.

Serves 4 to 6.

Chapter 16

Before and After the Grill

Rubs, Marinades and Bastes,
Barbecue Sauces, and
Adjunctive Toppings

SAUCE FOR THE barbecue (as well as barbecue sauce itself) invokes a different image for different folks. Ages before sweet formulas became synonymous with the Deep South, a BBQ sauce was virtually nothing more than a fast rub (of salt, pepper, and spices) or a marinade (composed essentially of vinegar). The last named topping, liberally, and literally, applied to the slow-roasted meat with a clean dish mop, and any residual used for soppin' at the table afterward.

Vinegar marinades are particularly germane to the Gullah country of the Carolinas, where to this day, purists decry any alternative embellishment. However, in many parts of Texas, where a "meat rub" takes the place of basting sauce, the only soppin' adjunct likely to be served is thickened Tabasco.

In most of rural America today, the vast majority of homemade barbecue sauces are tomato-based, devised of commercial ketchup, chili sauce, or canned tomatoes—sometimes all three. Even so, it is the extra flavorings added to these sauces that make them geographically unique, just as it is the extra touches (toppings and adjunctive sauces) that give foods from the grill their especial savor and cachet to sophisticated chefs.

What follows is a collection of some of the very best rubs, marinades, bastes, barbecue sauces, and toppings representative these days of the American outdoor cooking style.

RUBS

All the rubs listed below may be made in advance and applied an hour or so before the dish hits the fire. It is important to note, however, that a longer stay always brings out a stronger flavor.

CHILI-BACON RUB

For beef and poultry.

> 3 tablespoons bacon drippings
> 1 clove garlic, crushed
> ½ teaspoon tomato paste
> 2 teaspoons chili powder
> ¼ teaspoon cayenne pepper

Combine all ingredients in a bowl. Mash until smooth.

Makes about ¼ cup.

GARLIC-ANCHOVY RUB

For beef, poultry, pork, lamb, and fish.

> 1 clove garlic, crushed
> 1 teaspoon anchovy paste
> 2 teaspoons olive oil
> ¼ teaspoon freshly ground pepper

Combine all ingredients in a bowl. Mash until smooth.

Makes about 1½ tablespoons.

NEW MEXICO CHILE SALVE

For beef, poultry, and pork.

> 3 tablespoons mild ground chiles, or chili powder
> 1 teaspoon Hungarian hot paprika
>   Pinch of coriander
> 2 or 3 tablespoons vegetable oil

Combine all ingredients in a bowl. Mash until smooth.

Makes about ⅓ cup.

GREEN CHILE TREATMENT

For beef, poultry, pork, and lamb.

> 1 can (4 ounces) mild or hot green chiles
> 2 teaspoons mild ground chiles or chili powder
> 3 tablespoons vegetable oil

Combine all ingredients in a food processor. Process until smooth.

Makes about ⅓ cup.

MARY NELL RECK'S GALVESTON RUB

For poultry and pork.

> 6 cloves garlic, crushed
> 1 tablespoon cayenne pepper
> 2 tablespoons paprika
> 1 tablespoon lemon juice

Combine all ingredients in a bowl. Mash until smooth.

Makes about ⅓ cup.

SESAME, MUSTARD RUB

For beef, poultry, pork, lamb, and fish.

- 1 clove garlic, crushed
- 1 teaspoon mustard seeds
- ½ treaspoon finely slivered lime peel
- 2 teaspoons lime juice
- 2 tablespoons sesame oil

Combine all ingredients in a bowl. Mash until fairly smooth.

Makes about 3½ tablespoons.

RED DEVIL RUB

For beef, poultry, pork, and fish.

- ¼ cup country-style Dijon mustard (with seeds)
- 2 teaspoons olive oil
- ¼ cup finely slivered fresh basil leaves
- ½ teaspoon freshly ground pepper
- ¼ to ½ teaspoon cayenne pepper

Combine all ingredients in a bowl. Mix thoroughly.

Makes about ½ cup.

HOTTED HONEY RUB

For poultry and pork.

- ¼ cup prepared horseradish
- 1 teaspoon Hungarian hot paprika
- 2 teaspoons soy sauce
- 2 teaspoons honey

Combine all ingredients in a bowl. Mash until smooth.

Makes about ⅓ cup.

OLD MOLASSES COVER

For poultry and pork.

- 2½ tablespoons Dijon mustard
- ¼ cup chili sauce
- 4 teaspoons molasses

Combine all ingredients in a bowl. Mix thoroughly.

Makes about ½ cup.

ROSEMARY AND ALLSPICE RUB

For beef, poultry, pork, and lamb.

- 1 large clove garlic, crushed
- 10 allspice berries, crushed
- ½ teaspoon finely chopped rosemary leaves
- 2 tablespoons olive oil

Combine all ingredients in a bowl. Mash until smooth.

Makes about ¼ cup.

SOUTH TEXAS CHUCK-WAGON RUB

For beef.

- 1 clove garlic, crushed
- 1 teaspoon seasoned pepper
- 1 teaspoon ground dried mild chiles
- ¼ teaspoon cayenne pepper
- 1 teaspoon seasoned salt

Combine all ingredients in a bowl. Mash until smooth.

Makes about 2 tablespoons.

MARINADES AND BASTES

A marinade is any combination of spices and herbs mixed with some acidic liquid (like vinegar, soy sauce, wine, or citrus juice) used to flavor and/or tenderize foods. A standard rule of thumb for marinating times: up to 30 minutes for delicate fish filets and vegetables; up to 1 hour for generous-cut fish steaks, chops, and chicken; and an overnight stint (in the refrigerator) for large portions of meat and less-than-tender cuts of beefsteak. Leftover marinades should be used as subsequent bastes, which may also be nothing more than a brushing of melted butter or oil.

RED WINE AND PEPPER MARINADE

For beef, poultry, pork, and lamb.

- 1 small clove garlic, crushed
- 1 teaspoon vegetable oil
- ¼ cup red wine
- 1 teaspoon allspice berries, crushed
- 2 teaspoons black peppercorns, crushed

Combine all ingredients in a bowl.

Makes about ⅓ cup.

EDIE ACSELL'S MARINADE

For beef, poultry, pork, fish, and vegetables.

- 3 cloves garlic, minced
- ½ cup safflower oil
- ½ cup tomato juice
- ½ cup soy sauce (I use Kikkoman)
- ½ cup brown sugar
- ½ teaspoon freshly ground pepper

Combine all ingredients in a bowl.

Makes about 2 cups.

SPICY VINEGAR MARINADE

For large cuts of beef, poultry, pork, and lamb.

1 cup red wine vinegar
1 cup water
1 onion, sliced
2 cloves garlic, minced
8 cloves
6 sprigs parsley
2 bay leaves
2 ribs celery with leaves, chopped
2 juniper berries, crushed
1 teaspoon chopped fresh thyme, or ½ teaspoon dried
1 teaspoon chopped fresh rosemary, or ½ teaspoon dried
1 teaspoon chopped fresh basil, or ½ teaspoon dried
1 tablespoon brown sugar

Combine all ingredients in a bowl.

Makes about 3½ cups.

PAT FUSCO'S GEORGIAN MOPPIN' SAUCE

For poultry and pork.

1 teaspoon salt
1 tablespoon Hungarian sweet paprika
¼ teaspoon cayenne pepper
¼ teaspoon dry mustard
½ teaspoon freshly ground pepper
⅓ cup water
2 tablespoons Worcestershire sauce
⅓ cup red wine vinegar
¼ cup unsalted butter, cut into bits

In a medium saucepan, combine the dry ingredients with the water. Heat to boiling; remove from heat. Add the Worcestershire sauce and vinegar. Stir in the butter.

Makes about 1¼ cups.

Vinaigrette Marinade

For beef, poultry, pork, fish, shellfish, and vegetables.

   1 small clove garlic, crushed
   ¼ teaspoon coarse salt
   ½ teaspoon Dijon mustard
   2 teaspoons lemon juice
   ¼ cup olive oil
   1 teaspoon red wine vinegar
   ¼ teaspoon freshly ground pepper

Mash the garlic and the salt together in a small bowl with the back of a spoon. Stir in the mustard and lemon juice. Whisk in the olive oil, vinegar, and pepper.

Makes about ⅓ cup.

Hummus Marinade

For poultry, lamb, and fish.

   4 large cloves garlic
   4 tablespoons white sesame seeds
   6 tablespoons olive oil
   1 cup canned chick-peas
     Juice of 1 large lemon
   1 tablespoon chopped fresh parsley
   ¼ teaspoon salt
   1 teaspoon dark sesame oil

In the container of a food processor or blender, place the garlic cloves, sesame seeds, and 2 tablespoons olive oil. Process until smooth. Add the chick-peas, lemon juice, parsley, and salt. Process once more. Slowly add the remaining 4 tablespoons olive oil and the sesame oil.

Makes about 2 cups.

KOREAN SESAME AND GINGER MARINADE

For beef, lamb, and pork.

- 4 large cloves garlic, crushed
- 2 teaspoons grated fresh ginger root
- 2 tablespoons sugar
- 2 tablespoons peanut oil
- 2 scallions, chopped
- ½ teaspoon crushed, dried hot red peppers
- 2 tablespoons toasted white sesame seeds
- 6 tablespoons soy sauce

Combine all ingredients in a bowl.

Makes about 1¼ cups.

ROSE LEVY BERANBAUM'S TANDOORI MARINADE

For poultry, lamb, and seafood.

- 2 tablespoons lemon juice
- 2 tablespoons lime juice
- 2 teaspoons salt
- ½ cup plain yoghurt
- 2 medium cloves garlic, quartered
- 1 teaspoon minced ginger root
- ½ teaspoon cumin seeds
- ½ teaspoon ground coriander
- ¼ teaspoon turmeric
- ½ teaspoon cayenne pepper
- ¼ teaspoon freshly ground pepper
- ⅛ teaspoon ground cinnamon
- Pinch of ground cloves

Sprinkle the food to be marinated with lemon and lime juice. Combine the remaining ingredients in the container of a food processor. Process until smooth.

Makes about ¾ cup.

BLOODY MARY MARINADE

For poultry, pork, and fish.

¾ cup V-8 juice
¼ cup vodka
1 teaspoon prepared horseradish
1 teaspoon lemon juice
½ teaspoon soy sauce
   Dash of hot pepper sauce

Combine all ingredients in a bowl.

Makes about 1 cup.

ARGENTINIAN CHIMICHURRI-STYLE MARINADE

For beef and poultry.

½   cup vegetable oil
½   cup malt vinegar
¼   cup water
2   tablespoons chopped fresh parsley
3   large cloves garlic, minced
1   teaspoon cayenne pepper
1   teaspoon salt
1½ teaspoons chopped fresh oregano leaves
½   teaspoon freshly ground pepper

Combine all ingredients in a glass jar with a tight-fitting lid. Let stand at room temperature for 24 hours.

Makes about 1⅓ cups.

THAI-STYLE MARINADE

For poultry and pork.

- Peel of 1 lemon
- Peel of 1 orange
- ½ cup soy sauce
- ½ cup oyster sauce
- ½ teaspoon chopped ginger root
- 2 cloves garlic
- 1 tablespoon chopped fresh cilantro (Chinese parsley)
- ¼ teaspoon freshly ground pepper
- 1 small bay leaf
- 2 tablespoons honey

Combine all ingredients in a bowl.

Makes about 1¼ cups.

ORANGE/HONEY MARINADE

For poultry, pork, and seafood.

- ½ cup orange juice
- 4 teaspoons honey
- 4 teaspoons vinegar
- ½ teaspoon finely slivered orange peel

Combine all ingredients in a bowl.

Makes about ⅔ cup.

CHINESE RED MARINADE

For pork.

    1 clove garlic, crushed
    ½ teaspoon freshly ground pepper
    ½ teaspoon finely grated ginger root
    4 teaspoons soy sauce
    4 teaspoons honey
    4 teaspoons dry sherry
    ½ teaspoon five-spice powder (available in the gourmet department of most supermarkets)
    4 teaspoons chili sauce

Combine all ingredients in a bowl.

Makes about ¾ cup.

TANGY VIETNAMESE-STYLE MARINADE

For poultry, pork, and seafood.

    2 cloves garlic, crushed
    3 shallots, minced
    ¼ cup peanut oil
    3 tablespoons *nuoc mam* sauce (available in most Oriental groceries; to make see page 85)
    2 tablespoons sugar
    ¼ teaspoon bouillon powder
    ¼ teaspoon freshly ground pepper

Combine all ingredients in a bowl.

Makes about ¾ cup.

SPICY SOUTHWESTERN MARINADE

For beef, poultry, pork, and lamb.

- 1 cup Bloody Mary mix
  Juice of ½ lemon
- 1 tablespoon prepared horseradish
- 1 tablespoon Dijon mustard
- 2 tablespoons finely chopped mild canned green chiles
- ½ teaspoon freshly ground pepper

Combine all ingredients in a bowl.

Makes about 1⅓ cups.

ASIAN BLACK BEAN MARINADE

For poultry, pork, and lamb.

- 2 tablespoons black bean sauce (available in the gourmet department of most supermarkets)
- ½ teaspoon dry mustard
- 2 tablespoons dry sherry
- 2 tablespoons soy sauce
- 1 tablespoon sesame oil

Combine all ingredients in a bowl.

Makes about ½ cup.

HINT-OF-GINGER MARINADE

For poultry, pork, and fish.

> ¾ cup soy sauce
> ¼ cup dry sherry
> 1 small carrot, peeled, minced
> 1 clove garlic, minced
> 1 tablespoon minced sweet red pepper
> 1½ teaspoons minced ginger root
> 2 small scallions, finely chopped
> 1 teaspoon grated lemon peel

Combine all ingredients in a bowl.

Makes about 1¼ cups.

LEMON BASTING SAUCE

For poultry, pork, lamb, fish, and shellfish.

> ¼ cup lemon juice
> ½ cup olive oil
> 1 small clove garlic, minced
> Pinch of dried oregano, crushed
> ½ teaspoon finely grated lemon peel
> Salt and freshly ground pepper to taste

Combine all ingredients in a bowl.

Makes about ¾ cup.

CAFE BEAUJOLAIS'S FINE FISH MARINADE

For poultry, pork, lamb, and fish.

    ½ cup dry white wine
    ½ cup soy sauce
    ¼ cup water
    2 tablespoons light brown sugar
    1 small white onion, minced
    1 small clove garlic, crushed
    ⅛ teaspoon hot pepper sauce
    ¼ teaspoon freshly ground pepper

Combine all ingredients in a bowl.

Makes about 1½ cups.

THE COACH HOUSE WINE MARINADE

For poultry, fish, and shellfish.

    1 cup dry white wine
    3 large shallots, minced
    2 large cloves garlic, minced
    2 tablespoons olive oil
    2 tablespoons lemon juice
    1½ tablespoons Dijon mustard
    10 peppercorns, crushed

Combine all ingredients in a bowl.

Makes about 1½ cups.

NORTH CAROLINA MOPPIN' SAUCE

For poultry and pork.

1½ cups cider vinegar
1 tablespoon dry mustard
2 teaspoons cayenne pepper
1 tablespoon Worcestershire sauce
1 tablespoon vegetable oil

Combine all ingredients in a medium saucepan. Slowly heat to just *below* the boiling point. Let cool 2 hours.

Makes about 1½ cups.

AUSTRALIAN JACKAROO SAUCE

For poultry, pork, and lamb.

2 cloves garlic
1 small shallot
2 tablespoons lemon juice
2 tablespoons cider vinegar
1½ teaspoons chopped fresh parsley
¾ teaspoon chopped fresh oregano
½ teaspoon chopped fresh thyme
2½ teaspoons Hungarian sweet paprika
1 tablespoon unprocessed bran
2 teaspoons lightly toasted wheat germ
½ teaspoon salt
1 teaspoon sugar
½ cup vegetable oil
Dash of hot pepper sauce

Combine all ingredients in the container of a food processor or blender. Process until fairly smooth.

Makes about 1 cup.

BARBECUE MAYONNAISE MARINADE

For poultry and pork.

1 cup mayonnaise
5 tablespoons barbecue sauce (see pages 298–307)

Whisk the ingredients together in a bowl.

Makes about 1¼ cups.

BARBECUE SAUCES

No one is quite sure where the notion for *barbecue sauce* came from. Some credit it to the early Spanish settlers who splashed sherry and roasted peppers on their meat. Others insist the Native Americans of the Southwest (along with their Mexican neighbors) were concocting sauces of tomato pulp, herbs, and grated fresh horseradish long before the first Europeans set foot on our shores. Reputedly served with smoked meat and fish, this condiment sounds remarkably like present-day cocktail sauce. More pertinently, most barbecuers for years have always used what is most readily at hand locally.

Southern-based Coca-Cola, for instance, adds zip to a famous Georgian recipe and Coors beer gives unusual savor to a Coloradan favorite. Maple syrup is often found in barbecue sauces of the Northeast while molasses (normally associated with shoofly pie) seasons the senses—and the saucepans—of the Pennsylvania Dutch. The apricot- and pineapple-tinged marinades of Northern California are without a doubt inheritances from the large Asian population, just as the fiery chile flavorings of the Southwest are bequests of the Mexicans.

Since barbecue sauces are by nature basically free-form, the ingredient proportions as noted in the following recipes need not be exact, but can be increased or decreased to accommodate individual tastes.

CANNED SMOKE

Some barbecue fanatics, with an excessive taste for smoke, insist on the addition of an ingredient known as "liquid smoke" to flavor their sauces. It is rumored that Thomas Jonathan Jackson (otherwise known as "Stonewall") came up with the formula for this woodsy seasoning. While overseeing the preparation of barbecued pork for his troops, Jackson discovered that the tar of burned wood could easily be dissolved in water—creating a liquid with a strong smoky taste. It took awhile for Jackson's conceit to catch fire, however.

It wasn't until 1895 in Ulysses, Nebraska, that "liquid smoke" was first commercially produced. With the advance of modern technology, tars and resins have been "scientifically" removed, thus gaining liquid smoke the classification of "a natural food product" by the U.S. Department of Agriculture.

I never use "liquid smoke" in sauces, as it can overpower the natural smoky quality of foods hot off the grill.

ALL-AMERICAN BBQ SAUCE

For beef, poultry, pork, seafood, and vegetables.

    1 tablespoon unsalted butter
    1 onion, finely chopped
    ¾ cup ketchup
    3 tablespoons Worcestershire sauce
    2 tablespoons A-1 steak sauce
    1 tablespoon cider vinegar
    3 tablespoons brown sugar
    ¼ cup water
      Dash of hot pepper sauce

Melt the butter in a medium saucepan over medium-low heat. Add the onion; cook 5 minutes. Do not brown. Stir in the remaining ingredients. Heat to boiling; reduce heat. Simmer uncovered 20 minutes.

Makes about 1 cup.

TEXAS SOPPIN' SAUCE

For beef, poultry, and pork.

> 2 cloves garlic, roughly cut
> 1 small dried, hot red pepper
> ½ teaspoon chopped fresh cilantro (Chinese parsley) or ¼
>   teaspoon dried
> ¼ teaspoon ground cumin
> ½ teaspoon anise seeds
> ½ teaspoon salt
> 2 tablespoons brown sugar
> 1 tablespoon Worcestershire sauce
> 1 cup cider vinegar
> 2 cups ketchup
>   Hot pepper sauce

Combine all ingredients through vinegar in the container of a blender or a food processor. Process until smooth. Transfer mixture to a medium saucepan and add the ketchup. Heat to boiling; reduce heat. Simmer uncovered 30 minutes. Add hot pepper sauce to taste.

Makes about 3 cups.

SKITCH HENDERSON'S TULSA TOPPIN'

For beef, poultry, and pork.

> 2 tablespoons unsalted butter
> 1 large onion, finely chopped
> 1 clove garlic, minced
> 1 can (16 ounces) tomato sauce
> 1 cup cider vinegar
> 1 cup V-8 juice
> ½ cup prune juice
>   Finely slivered peel from ½ lemon
>   Juice of 1 lemon
> 1 bay leaf
> 6 juniper berries, crushed
> ½ teaspoon cayenne pepper
> 2 tablespoons brown sugar

Melt the butter in a medium saucepan over medium-low heat. Add the onion; cook 1 minute. Add the garlc; cook 2 minutes. Add the remaining ingredients. Heat to boiling; reduce heat. Simmer uncovered until thickened, about 30 minutes. Remove bay leaf before using.

Makes about 6 cups.

NATHALIE DUPREE'S COCA-COLA BARBECUE SAUCE

For poultry and chicken.

    2 tablespoons unsalted butter
    1 onion, finely chopped
    2 cloves garlic, minced
    1 bay leaf, crumbled
    2 cups ketchup
    6 ounces Coca-Cola
    1 tablespoon Worcestershire sauce
    1 teaspoon Dijon mustard
    2 teaspoons wine vinegar
      Salt and freshly ground pepper

Melt the butter in a medium saucepan over medium-low heat. Add the onion; cook 1 minute. Add the garlic; cook 4 minutes longer. Do not brown. Stir in the remaining ingredients. Heat to boiling; reduce heat. Simmer uncovered, stirring occasionally, 1 hour.

Makes about 1½ cups.

OHIO VALLEY SOOTHING SYRUP

For poultry and pork.

> 2 tablespoons unsalted butter
> 1 tablespoon dry mustard
> ½ cup maple syrup
> 1 cup chili sauce
> ½ cup ketchup
> ½ cup cider vinegar
> 1 teaspoon celery seeds, crushed
> 1 teaspoon cayenne pepper
> ½ teaspoon salt

Combine all ingredients in a medium saucepan. Heat to boiling; reduce heat. Simmer uncovered 20 minutes.

Makes about 2 cups.

JOHNNY REB SAUCE

For beef, poultry, and pork.

> 2 tablespoons unsalted butter
> 1 medium onion, finely chopped
> 1 cup diced celery
> 1 cup tomato sauce
> 1 teaspoon Dijon mustard
> 1 tablespoon brown sugar
> 1 tablespoon lemon juice
> 1 tablespoon cider vinegar
> ¼ cup water
> 1 tablespoon chili powder
> ½ teaspoon cayenne pepper
> Pinch of ground cloves
> ½ teaspoon salt
> ⅛ teaspoon freshly ground pepper

Melt the butter in a medium saucepan over medium-low heat. Add the onion. Cook 5 minutes. Stir in the remaining ingredients. Heat to boiling; reduce heat. Simmer uncovered 30 minutes.

Makes about 2 cups.

LBJ BBQ Sauce

For beef, poultry, and pork.

½ cup ketchup
¼ cup cider vinegar
½ teaspoon brown sugar
½ teaspoon chili powder
¼ teaspoon salt
¾ cup water
1 large celery rib, roughly chopped
1 large bay leaf
1 clove garlic, roughly chopped
1 small white onion, roughly chopped
2 tablespoons Worcestershire sauce
1 teaspoon lemon juice
½ teaspoon Hungarian hot paprika
2 tablespoons unsalted butter

Combine all ingredients in a medium saucepan. Heat to boiling; reduce heat. Simmer uncovered 20 minutes. Strain.

Makes about 1¼ cups.

Georgia Peach Sauce

For poultry and pork.

1 medium onion, finely chopped
1 cup peach preserves
1 tablespoon ketchup
¼ cup brown sugar
1 teaspoon Hungarian sweet paprika
¼ cup cider vinegar
¼ cup Worcestershire sauce
1 teaspoon dry mustard
¼ teaspoon hot pepper sauce

Combine all ingredients in a medium saucepan. Heat to boiling; reduce heat. Simmer uncovered 10 minutes.

Makes about 2⅓ cups.

AMISH STICKIN' SAUCE

For poultry, pork, and sausage.

> 2 tablespoons unsalted butter
> 1 onion, finely chopped
> 2 cloves garlic, minced
>   Juice of 1 orange
> 1 tablespoon softened raisins
> 2 tablespoons cider vinegar
> 2 tablespoons vegetable oil
>   Grated rind of 1 orange
> 1 cup molasses
> 1 cup ketchup
> 2 teaspoons chili powder
>   Pinch of ground cloves
> 1 teaspoon Dijon mustard
> 1 teaspoon Worcestershire sauce
> 2 teaspoons crushed, dried hot red peppers
> ½ teaspoon salt

1 · Melt the butter in a medium saucepan over medium-low heat. Add the onion; cook 1 minute. Add the garlic; cook 4 minutes. Do not brown.

2 · Meanwhile, combine the orange juice with the raisins, vinegar, and oil in the container of a food processor or blender. Process until smooth. Add this mixture, along with the remaining ingredients, to the saucepan. Heat to boiling; reduce heat. Simmer uncovered 15 minutes.

Makes about 3 cups.

BERT GREENE'S FREETOWN BARBECUE SAUCE

For beef, poultry, and pork.

> 2 tablespoons vegetable oil
> 1 onion, finely chopped
> 1 clove garlic, minced
> 1½ teaspoons minced ginger root
> 1 can (8 ounces) plum tomatoes with juice, mashed
> ½ cup chili sauce
> 2 tablespoons dark brown sugar
> 3 tablespoons honey
> 3 tablespoons soy sauce
> 3 tablespoons dry sherry
> 2 teaspoons chili powder
> Pinch of cayenne pepper
> Pinch of dried oregano

Heat the oil in a medium saucepan over medium-low heat. Add the onion; cook 1 minute. Add the garlic and ginger; cook 4 minutes. Stir in the remaining ingredients. Heat to boiling; reduce heat. Simmer uncovered 30 minutes.

Makes about 2 cups.

RASPBERRY BRUSH

For pork, duckling, and game birds.

> 1 jar (12 ounces) raspberry preserves
> 3 tablespoons red wine vinegar
> ½ cup chili sauce
> 1 teaspoon Dijon mustard

Strain the preserves through a sieve into a medium saucepan. Pour the vinegar through the sieve to loosen the seeds. Discard seeds. Add the chili sauce and mustard to the saucepan. Heat to boiling; reduce heat. Simmer 2 minutes.

Makes about 2 cups.

SAN FRANCISCO SWEET 'N' SOUR SAUCE

For pork.

⅓ cup dried apricots
1½ cups water
1 shallot, minced
3 tablespoons vegetable oil
½ cup tarragon vinegar
¼ cup honey
½ teaspoon soy sauce
¼ cup ketchup
½ teaspoon dried oregano
½ teaspoon salt
¼ teaspoon freshly ground pepper

1 · Combine the apricots with water in a small saucepan. Heat to boiling; reduce heat. Simmer uncovered until tender, about 25 minutes. Cool slightly.

2 · Place the apricots with the liquid (about ½ cup) in the container of a food processor or blender. Process until smooth. Transfer to a medium saucepan; add remaining ingredients. Heat to boiling; remove from heat.

Makes about 1½ cups.

DINAH'S BARBECUE SAUCE

For beef, poultry, and pork.

1 tablespoon unsalted butter
1 medium onion, sliced
1 clove garlic, chopped
1 cup chili sauce
1½ cups dark corn syrup
½ teaspoon bouillon powder
2 tablespoons soy sauce

1 · Melt the butter in a heavy skillet over medium-high heat. Stir in the onion and garlic. Cook until the onion and garlic are well

burnished, about 10 minutes. Transfer to the container of a food processor or blender. Process until smooth.

2 · Transfer the processed mixture to a medium saucepan. Stir in the remaining ingredients. Heat to boiling; reduce heat. Simmer uncovered 30 minutes.

Makes about 2 cups.

ROCKY MOUNTAIN HIGH

For beef and pork.

2 tablespoons unsalted butter
1 medium onion, finely chopped
1 clove garlic, minced
1 can (12 ounces) beer
½ cup tomato juice
¼ cup Worcestershire sauce
¼ cup brown sugar
½ lemon, sliced
1 tablespoon Hungarian sweet paprika
2 tablespoons Dijon mustard
2 tablespoons mild ground chiles
1 teaspoon crushed, dried hot red peppers
   Pinch of marjoram
   Pinch of thyme
½ teaspoon salt
¼ teaspoon freshly ground pepper
1 tablespoon tomato paste

Melt the butter in a medium saucepan over medium-low heat. Add the onion; cook 1 minute. Add the garlic; cook 4 minutes. Stir in the remaining ingredients. Heat to boiling; reduce heat. Simmer uncovered 30 minutes. Remove lemon slices.

Makes about 1½ cups.

BOUGHTEN BARBECUE SAUCES

In addition to the made-from-scratch recipes, there are quite a few respectable barbecue sauces on the market today. Unfortunately, most of the best are available by mail order only. But, in my opinion, they are well worth the postage.

I judge a bottle of commercial basting brew by its delicate balances of sweet and sour, spice and smoke. But let your own palate be your guide.

Curley's: A very dark, unctuous sauce wonderful for pork, chicken, or ribs. Available from Curley's Famous Hickory Burger, Inc., Box 1584, Hutchinson, KS 67501.

K. C. Masterpiece (Prairie Village, Kansas): In many folks' minds, the ultimate barbecue sauce—thick, sludgy, with hints of molasses. Available from Vocational Services, c/o Masterpiece, 101 West 18 Street, North Kansas City, MO 64116.

Gates' Bar-B-Q Sauce: A highly flavorful sauce made with tomatoes, vinegar, and spices. Available from Gates and Sons Bar-B-Q, 4707 Paseo, Kansas City, MO 64110.

Maurice Bessinger's Piggie Park Barbecue Sauce: From the South, this famous sauce is tomatoless and heavy on the mustard and vinegar. Write to Piggie Park Enterprises, Box 847, West Columbia, SC 29169.

D. L. Jardine's Chuck Wagon Recipe Barbecue Sauce: Spicy, smoky, and on the thin side, this Texas-made sauce is perfect for moppin' and/or soppin'. Write to D. L. Jardine's Texas Foods, Box 18868, Austin, TX 78760.

Lexington Barbecue Sauce: From one of the most famous of North Carolina's many barbecue joints, this sauce is also on the thin side—peppery with a vinegar base. Available from Lexington Barbecue, 10 Highway 79-70S, Lexington, NC 27292.

Everett and Jones Barbeque Sauce: *New West* magazine called Everett and Jones the barbecue sauce against which all others must be judged. "The sauce defies the odds against such things with a successful mixture of heady fruit-sweetness and peppery clout." Enough said. Carried by Macy's and other Northern California stores, write for source information to Everett and Jones Barbeque, 2676 Fruitvale Avenue, Oakland, CA 94601.

Firehouse No. 1 Bar-B-Que Sauce: Carl English inherited the spicy secret for his sauce from his grandfather, who sold ribs from a pushcart in Kansas. The sauces range from one- to three-alarm in "hotness." Available in many specialty stores or from Firehouse No. 1, 501 Clement Street, San Francisco, CA 94118.

Wicker's Barbecue Cooking Sauce: A thin sauce with no sweeteners and no tomatoes, this vinegar-based concoction packs a wallop, but is not a barn burner. Write to Wicker, Inc., Box 126, Hornersville, MO 63855.

Johnny Harris Barbecue Sauce: A Georgia favorite. Not too thick, with a slight smoky flavor and mustard and vinegar added for tang. Available from Johnny Harris Barbecue Sauce Company, P.O. Box 3598, Savannah, GA 31404.

Santa Cruz Barbecue Sauce: A very spicy, slow-simmered sauce that reflects a Mexican heritage. Adds zip to pork, chicken, and beef. Write to Santa Cruz Chili & Spice Company, P.O. Box 177, Tumacacori, AZ 85640.

Touch of South: Touch of South barbecue sauce, smoky and thick, was launched to fill a void for homesick Southerners living in L.A. From Touch of South, 1173 Point View Street, Los Angeles, CA 90035.

Texas Barbeque Sauce: A thick, tomato-based sauce with hints of mustard and ginger, this sauce is packed in home-canning jars. Available in many specialty stores, or write for information to Cattlebaron Foods, Inc., P.O. Drawer 800037, Dallas, TX 75380.

Heinz Thick and Rich Barbecue Sauce: It stands to reason. Heinz makes an excellent thick, ketchup-based sauce that comes in six different flavors. Available in supermarkets everywhere, or write J. J. Heinz Co., Pittsburgh, PA 15212.

Sarah's Best!: A dark, thin tomato-based sauce redolent of spices and honey, this sauce can be purchased in many specialty stores or write Sarah's Best!, Railroad Avenue, South Fallsburg, NY 12779.

TOPPINGS AND ADJUNCTIVE SAUCES

A dab of butter and a sprinkling of salt and pepper are often the perfect topping for a grill-roasted steak or filet of fish. But it would be sheer sacrilege to serve barbecued chicken without an extra dollop of its sauce on the side. Some dishes, in fact, take on totally new dimensions when a contrasted flavoring is added at the last moment.

A few adjunctive toppings and sauces that I often use to enhance grilled or outdoor roasted foods follow. Most are used to complement and coalesce flavors; others, purposefully titillate the tastebuds.

RED PEPPER HOLLANDAISE

For steak, grilled chicken, grilled fish steaks, and vegetables.

    1 red bell pepper
    2 egg yolks
    2 tablespoons lemon juice
    ¼ teaspoon Dijon mustard
    6 tablespoons unsalted butter, frozen
    ¼ teaspoon hot pepper sauce
       Salt

1 · Roast the peppers over a gas flame, on the grill, or under a broiler until charred. Carefully wrap in paper towels; place in a bag. Let cool for 5 minutes. Rub off the skin with paper towels. Core, seed, and roughly chop. Place in the container of a food processor. Process until smooth.

2 · Beat the egg yolks with the lemon juice and mustard in the top of a double boiler. Place over simmering water and stir in the pureed pepper. Stir the mixture until it begins to thicken. Stir in the butter, 1 tablespoon at a time, until smooth and thick. Stir in the hot pepper sauce. Add salt to taste. Keep over warm water.

Makes about 1 cup.

BEURRE ROUGE
(*Red Butter Sauce*)

For grilled steak, chicken, or fish.

    ¼ cup red wine vinegar
    ¼ cup dry red wine
    4 teaspoons finely chopped shallots
    ½ cup cold unsalted butter, cut into bits
    1 tablespoon finely chopped chives
    1 teaspoon lemon juice
       Salt and freshly ground pepper
       Chopped fresh parsley

1 · Combine the vinegar, wine, and shallots in a small saucepan. Heat to boiling; boil until almost all the liquid has been evaporated. Remove from heat and immediately beat in 2 tablespoons chilled butter.

2 · Return the saucepan to low heat and stir in the remaining butter, by bits, until the sauce is the texture of thickened cream. Stir in the chives, lemon juice, and salt and pepper to taste. Transfer to a serving bowl. Sprinkle with parsley.

Makes about ⅔ cup.

HOT SPICY MINT SAUCE

For roast or grilled lamb.

    10 ounces mint jelly
    ½ teaspoon crushed, dried hot red peppers
    2 tablespoons red wine vinegar
    2 tablespoons chopped fresh mint

Place the jelly and peppers in a medium saucepan. Slowly heat to boiling; reduce heat. Gently simmer, stirring frequently, until jelly is smooth and peppers are slightly softened, about 5 minutes. Stir in the vinegar; cook 3 minutes longer. Stir in the mint; cook 1 minute. Serve warm.

Makes about 1¼ cups.

TOMATO BÉARNAISE

For any grilled meats.

1 large shallot, minced
½ teaspoon fresh tarragon
1 teaspoon chopped fresh parsley
¼ cup tarragon vinegar
¼ cup white wine
1 firm plum tomato, peeled, seeded, and minced (about
    3 tablespoons)
3 egg yolks
½ cup unsalted butter, frozen
    Salt and freshly ground pepper

1 · Combine the shallot, tarragon, parsley, vinegar, wine, and tomato in a small saucepan. Heat to boiling; boil until almost all the liquid has evaporated. Remove from heat.

2 · Beat the egg yolks in the top of a double boiler over hot water until smooth. Whisk in the tomato mixture. Whisk in the butter, 1 tablespoon at a time, until thickened. Add salt and pepper to taste. Keep over warm water.

Makes about 1 cup.

NASTURTIUM BUTTER

For grilled chicken, fish, and vegetables.

¼ cup unsalted butter, softened
1 small shallot, minced
⅛ teaspoon hot pepper sauce
½ cup nasturtium leaves, torn
    Salt

In a medium bowl, whisk the butter with the shallot, hot pepper sauce, and nasturtium leaves until well mixed. Whisk in salt to taste. Cover and refrigerate. Remove from refrigerator at least 30 minutes before serving.

Makes about ½ cup.

BERT GREENE'S GUACAMOLE SAUCE

For steak, pork chops, lamb chops.

> 2 ripe avocados
> Juice of 1 large or 2 small limes
> 2 tablespoons grated red onion
> 4 teaspoons olive oil
> 2 teaspoons finely minced fresh basil
> ½ teaspoon salt
> Freshly ground pepper

Slice the avocados in half lengthwise. Remove pits. Scoop the flesh of the avocados into a bowl. Sprinkle with lime juice. Mash the avocados with a fork until fairly smooth. Mix in the onion, oil, basil, salt, and pepper to taste. Refrigerate until ready to serve.

Serves 4 to 6.

SPINACH-HERB SAUCE

For grilled steak, grilled or roasted chicken, roast duck, and grilled fish.

> 5 ounces fresh spinach leaves, washed and dried
> 1 tablespoon chopped fresh basil
> 1 shallot, sliced
> ¼ teaspoon salt
> ½ cup walnut oil
> 2 tablespoons lemon juice
> 2 tablespoons wine vinegar
> Freshly ground pepper

Place the spinach, basil, and shallot in the container of a food processor. Process until smooth. Add the salt, oil, lemon juice, and vinegar. Process 1 minute longer. Add pepper to taste.

Makes about 1 cup.

RED PEPPER AND BASIL ZABAGLIONE SAUCE

For grilled chicken and fish.

1 fresh, small red Italian hot pepper (or jalapeño)
3 egg yolks
¼ cup white wine
¼ cup clarified butter, cooled
1 tablespoon finely minced basil
1 teaspoon finely minced chives
Salt and freshly ground pepper

1 · Roast the pepper over a gas flame, on the grill, or under a broiler until charred. Carefully wrap in a paper towel; place in a plastic bag to cool. Rub off the skin with paper towels. Seed, devein, and mince the pepper.

2 · Place the egg yolks and wine in a medium saucepan. Cook over medium-low heat, whisking constantly, until mixture begins to thicken. Remove from heat and place saucepan on a cool, dampened towel; continue to beat until mixture cools slightly. Whisk in the clarified butter, the minced hot pepper, basil, chives, and salt and pepper to taste.

Makes about ¾ cup.

PROCESSOR ROUILLE

For grilled chicken, duck breasts; turkey breasts, fish steaks, and grilled vegetables.

1 medium potato (about 5 ounces), peeled, chopped
½ cup chicken broth
1 small red bell pepper, seeded, roughly chopped
3 cloves garlic
3 jarred hot cherry peppers, well drained, stems removed
1 jar (2 ounces) pimientos, well drained
1 teaspoon chopped fresh basil leaves
¼ teaspoon chopped fresh thyme or a pinch of dried
¼ teaspoon red wine vinegar
Dash of hot pepper sauce
5 tablespoons olive oil (approximately)
Salt and freshly ground pepper

1 · Place the potato and chicken broth in a medium saucepan. Heat to boiling; reduce heat. Simmer until potato is barely tender. Add the red pepper. Cook 3 minutes longer. Drain, reserving broth. Return broth to saucepan and keep hot over low heat.

2 · Fit a processor with a steel blade. With motor running, drop the garlic through the feed tube. Add the cherry peppers, pimientos, potato, red pepper, basil, thyme, vinegar, and hot pepper sauce. Process until smooth.

3 · With motor running, slowly add the oil, 1 tablespoon at a time, until mixture thickens. Remove rouille from processor container and whisk in 2 to 3 tablespoons reserved chicken broth. Add salt and pepper to taste.

Makes about 1½ cups.

TOMATO SAUCE IN THE NICE STYLE

For grilled poultry, pork, grilled fish and shellfish.

        2 tablespoons unsalted butter
        1 tablespoon olive oil
        1 onion, finely chopped
        1 clove garlic, minced
     1½ teaspoons anchovy paste
        ½ cup clam broth
     1½ cups chopped seeded tomatoes
        1 cup tomato sauce
        ½ teaspoon chopped fresh oregano, or ¼ teaspoon dried
        ¼ teaspoon chopped fresh thyme, or a pinch of dried
        1 tablespoon chopped fresh basil
          Salt and freshly ground pepper

Heat the butter with the oil in a large saucepan over medium-low heat. Add the onion; cook 1 minute. Add the garlic; cook 2 minutes. Stir in the anchovy paste, clam broth, tomatoes, tomato sauce, and herbs. Heat to boiling; reduce heat. Simmer uncovered until tomatoes are soft, about 20 minutes. Add salt and pepper to taste.

Makes 2½ to 3 cups.

ROASTED PEPPER MAYONNAISE

For any grilled meat or fish.

    1 red bell pepper
    1 green bell pepper
    2 egg yolks
    1 tablespoon wine vinegar
      Juice of ½ lemon
    ½ teaspoon soy sauce
      Pinch of ground white pepper
    1½ teaspoons Dijon mustard
    1 cup vegetable oil
    ½ cup olive oil
      Dash of hot pepper sauce
    1 shallot, finely minced
    1 tablespoon boiling water

1 · Cook the peppers in boiling, salted water 2 minutes. Drain. Roast on a foil-lined baking sheet in a 350-degree oven for 50 minutes. Cool. (Or grill covered over direct heat until charred and soft, about 30 minutes. Carefully wrap the charred peppers in paper towels and place in a plastic bag. Cool.)

2 · Peel the peppers with a sharp knife. Remove seeds. Finely chop.

3 · Beat the egg yolks in a large bowl until light. Slowly beat in the vinegar, lemon juice, soy sauce, white pepper, and mustard. Beat in the oils, 1 tablespoon at a time, until thick. Add the hot pepper sauce, shallot, boiling water, and peppers. Chill.

Makes about 2½ cups.

OLIVE BUTTER

For grilled steaks, lamb, and fish steaks.

 1 small shallot, roughly chopped
 ¼ cup pitted black olives
 ¼ cup unsalted butter, softened
 ⅛ teaspoon cayenne pepper
 ⅛ teaspoon freshly ground pepper
 1 teaspoon chopped chives
 2½ teaspoons chopped fresh parsley

Combine the shallot and black olives in the container of a food processor. Process until smooth. Add the butter, cayenne, and freshly ground pepper. Process until smooth. Stir in the chives and 2 teaspoons parsley. Transfer to a serving bowl. Sprinkle with remaining parsley. Cover and refrigerate. Remove from refrigerator ½ hour before serving.

Makes about ½ cup.

TANGY SOUR CREAM SAUCE

For grilled chicken and lamb.

 ½ cup sour cream
 2 teaspoons country-style Dijon mustard (with seeds)
 2 teaspoons horseradish

Combine all ingredients in a bowl. Whisk until light. Refrigerate until serving.

Makes about ¾ cup.

COLD CUCUMBER SAUCE

For grilled chicken, Cornish hens, lamb, and fish.

> 1 medium cucumber, peeled, seeded, and finely chopped
> ½ teaspoon salt
> ½ teaspoon red wine vinegar
>   Pinch of sugar
> 8 ounces sour cream
> 1 teaspoon Dijon mustard
> 1 shallot, minced

1 · Place the cucumber in a colander. Sprinkle with salt, vinegar, and sugar. Let stand 30 minutes. Lightly rinse with cold water. Drain, pressing out excess liquid with the back of a spoon.

2 · Beat the sour cream with the mustard in a medium bowl until light. Beat in the shallot and cucumber. Chill until ready to serve.

Makes about 1⅓ cups.

RAITA SAUCE

For grilled chicken, pork, lamb, and fish.

> 4 small kirby or 2 regular cucumbers, peeled and finely
>   chopped
> ½ teaspoon salt
> ½ cup plain yoghurt
> 1½ teaspoons chopped fresh cilantro (Chinese parsley)
> ½ teaspoon finely chopped chives or scallion ends
>   Freshly ground pepper

1 · Place the cucumbers in a strainer. Sprinkle with salt. Let stand 15 minutes. Press lightly with the back of a spoon to drain.

2 · Place the cucumbers in a medium bowl. Add the yoghurt, cilantro, and chives or scallion ends. Mix well. Add pepper to taste. Refrigerate until ready to serve.

Makes about 1 cup.

BEERY MUSTARD SAUCE

For grilled chicken, pork, lamb, and sausages.

⅓ cup English dry mustard
⅓ cup tarragon vinegar
⅓ cup beer
3 eggs
6 tablespoons brown sugar
¼ cup unsalted butter
½ teaspoon salt
⅛ teaspoon freshly ground pepper
½ teaspoon chopped fresh tarragon, or a pinch of dried
    tarragon

1 · Place the mustard, vinegar, and beer in a small bowl. Do not stir. Cover and let stand in a cool place overnight.

2 · Place the mustard mixture in the top of a double boiler over hot water; whisk until smooth. Add the eggs, one at a time, whisking vigorously after each addition. Gradually whisk in the brown sugar until smooth. Beat in the butter, salt, and pepper; cook until thick, about 5 minutes. Do not overcook or eggs will curdle. Stir in the tarragon. Refrigerate for 24 hours before serving.

Makes about 1 pint.

A GLOSSARY OF TERMS FOR COOKING WITH FIRE AND SMOKE

Ash catcher: Metal container, located either inside or underneath the grill, to catch ashes from the burning coals.

Barbecue: Hot smoke cookery over low heat that requires long periods of cooking time.

Bastes: Any liquid or marinade that is used for brushing food during cooking.

Brazier: A grill used for charcoal broiling foods. An "open" brazier has a partial cover with rotisserie attachment.

Charcoal briquets: A pressed compound of hardwood and various fillers.

Charcoal, lump: Natural coals, left over from burning logs, that have been chopped up for home use.

Coal grate: A grid that holds the charcoal.

Coal pan: A pan that fits under the grate and doubles as ash catcher.

Covered cooking: Cooking with a kettle-type cooker that has a cover with vents and is similar to oven baking.

Direct heat: A process in which the food is grilled or cooked directly over hot coals or lava rocks.

Drip pan: An aluminum-foil pan that is placed under foods so they do not cook directly over hot coals or lava rocks.

Ember cooking: Cooking foods (corn, potatoes, onions, squash, etc.) by placing them in with the hot coals.

Fire bowl or box: The bottom portion of the grill.

Flare-up: When fat dripping onto hot coals or lava rocks catches fire.

Grid: The wire rack that the food is cooked on.

Grill: The whole cooking unit, whether charcoal, gas, or electric. Gas grills use either natural or LP (liquid petroleum) gas.

Grilling: Charcoal broiling foods over direct heat without the use of a cover.

Indirect heat: A process in which the food is cooked over a drip pan, and *not* directly over hot coals or lava rocks.

Lava rocks: Bits of volcanic lava heated by gas jets or an electric element that cook food in place of charcoal.

Marinades: Any combination of spices and herbs mixed with some acidic liquid (such as vinegar, soy sauce, wine, or citrus) used to flavor and/or tenderize foods.

Rotisserie cooking: Spit roasting on a grill. Rotisserie units can be electric or battery powered. Most grills with rotisserie attachments are covered or partially covered.

Rubs: A mixture of ingredients (often dry) that is rubbed into foods prior to cooking to intensify flavor.

Sauces: Generally, the barbecue sauces (sweet, tomato-based) that are served with cooked foods, but also adjunctive sauces that complement such foods.

Searing: The grilling of meats over high heat to brown the meat and seal in the juices.

Smoker cooking: The use of a dry smoker or water smoker that allows food to be cooked over very low heat, with hot smoke that flavors and cooks the food.

Vents: The openings in the fire bowl or cover that regulate airflow and control the interior temperature of the grill.

Water spritzer: A plastic container that squirts streams of water onto very hot coals that are causing flare-up.

SOURCE LIST

Most major department stores, hardware stores, and cookware shops carry all the utensils that you could ever want for your outdoor cooking cupboard. Most grill manufacturers offer a large selection as well.

Wood chips and lump charcoal, however, are not always easy to find (though there is a boom in the making), so an abbreviated source list follows:

Bosman Industries, Inc., P.O. Box 3726, Shreveport, LA 71103. Hickory that comes in sticks.

Coleman Patio Products, 250 North St. Francis Street, Wichita, KS 67202. Osage orange chunks, as well as hickory.

Complete Kitchen, 863 Post Road, Darien, CT 06820. Occasionally stocks hardwood coals from Connecticut. No mail orders.

Flying Foods International, 43-43 Ninth Street, Long Island City, NY 11101. Two-inch chunks of mesquite wood.

Laredo Industries, 1919 Pennsylvania Avenue, NW, Washington, D.C. 20006. Mesquite chunks.

Lazzari Fuel Company, P.O. Box 34051, San Francisco, CA 94034. Carries genuine mesquite charcoal.

Luhr Jensen & Sons, Inc., P.O. Box 297, Hood River, OR 97031. Alder, apple, cherry, and hickory chips.

Northcoast Valley Company, Box 1752, Santa Rosa, CA 95402. Packages Grapesmoke, cuttings from Cabernet, Merlot, and Zinfandel grapevines.

Turkey Hill Farms, RD 1, Box 163, Red Hook, NY 12571. Five varieties of chips: apple, cherry, hickory, mesquite, and a cob and maple combo.

Williams-Sonoma, P.O. Box 7456, San Francisco, CA 94120-7456. Wood chunks and chips, and, from time to time, dried fennel from Italy and dried herbs from France.

Index